Knowledge and Environ

American and Comparative Environmental Policy

Sheldon Kamieniecki and Michael E. Kraft, series editors

For a complete list of books in the series, please see the back of the book.

Knowledge and Environmental Policy
Re-Imagining the Boundaries of Science and Politics

William Ascher, Toddi Steelman, and Robert Healy

The MIT Press
Cambridge, Massachusetts
London, England

For information about special quantity discounts, please email special_sales @mitpress.mit.edu

This book was set in Sabon by Toppan Best-set Premedia Limited.
Printed and bound in the United States of America.

Library of Congress Cataloging-in-Publication Data

Ascher, William.
Knowledge and environmental policy : re-imagining the boundaries of science and politics / William Ascher, Toddi Steelman, and Robert Healy.
    p.   cm.—(American and comparative environmental policy)
Includes bibliographical references and index.
ISBN 978-0-262-01437-3 (hardcover : alk. paper)—ISBN 978-0-262-51437-8 (pbk. : alk. paper) 1. Environmental policy. 2. Science—Political aspects. 3. Science and state. I. Steelman, Toddi A. II. Healy, Robert G. III. Title.
GE170.A82   2010
363.7'0561—dc22

                                                                2009048450

10   9   8   7   6   5   4   3   2   1

With special thanks to those who educated us and helped us understand knowledge in its many forms. For Toddi Steelman, her parents, Lance and Emma Steelman; for Bob Healy, his many teachers and mentors, especially Leland S. Burns and Frank Mittelbach at UCLA; for William Ascher, his parents Meyer and Beckie Ascher and Professor Harold D. Lasswell.

Contents

Series Foreword

During the George W. Bush administration, White House policymakers on numerous occasions ignored or manipulated scientific data, and they were often criticized for doing so, particularly by environmentalists who were convinced that the science bolstered their own policy positions. The Bush administration often gave more weight to political beliefs and goals than the views of scientists, policy analysts, and other professionals, most notably in the case of climate change. In response to such decisions across a wide spectrum of issues, by 2004, more than 4,000 scientists, including 48 Nobel Prize winners and 127 members of the National Academy of Sciences, accused the White House of distorting and suppressing science to suit its political goals. The use of science in policymaking, rarely among the most visible issues, rose to some prominence during the 2008 presidential election, and President Barak Obama singled it out for special mention in his inaugural address in January 2009. "We will restore science to its rightful place," he said, leaving no doubt about his commitment to evidence-based public policy in general and specifically with regard to the environment, energy use, and climate change.

The history of public policy over the past four to five decades is replete with cases involving the abuse of science. The Bush administration was hardly the first to ignore inconvenient science, economics, public health studies, or national security analyses in support of its political agenda. Indeed, one of the best examples dates to the 1950s and 1960s when key legislators and corporate executives manipulated the generation and communication of scientific data related to tobacco and its health effects. Despite the definitive Surgeon General's report of 1964 on smoking and heath, the tobacco industry, backed by its supporters in Congress, argued that cigarettes were safe and possibly even beneficial to public health.

Eventually, independent research showed the opposite to be true. The public was only told years later that the tobacco industry actually had knowledge early on that cigarette smoking causes a number of significant health problems. As this example illustrates, members of Congress and other legislative bodies, much like the president, also face difficulties in incorporating science and other expert knowledge in policymaking.

How knowledge influences the policymaking process is one of the most fundamental questions in studies of public policy, but it is also much more complex than often appreciated. This is particularly true in environmental policy, where science is expected to play a strong role in setting broad policy goals as well as in development of the administrative rules and regulations that form the bedrock of contemporary government action. Yet the balance also could tilt too much the other way. The problem is not just that obstacles exist to the use of science in policymaking. Even policymakers who are open to the idea of using science fairly must confront the real challenges presented by the structure of the knowledge-policy relationship. Formal science has a clear role to play in environmental policy and many other areas, but decision making must also be open to other forms of knowledge.

In this book, William Ascher, Toddi Steelman, and Robert Healy seek to untangle the connections between knowledge, politics, and public policy. Their goal is to explore how knowledge processes, initially structured in an effort to separate politics from science, are in many ways highly dysfunctional and fail to contribute as they should to sound environmental policy. They set out to do this by dividing knowledge processes into three functions, generation, transmission, and use, and then systematically analyzing the effects of these functions on policy processes. As a result, they are better prepared than previous students of the subject to offer sensible recommendations for how the constraints on knowledge production, communication, and use can be overcome and environmental policymaking can be strengthened. A notable contribution of the book is its careful integration of literature on science, politics, and policy and its application to the challenge of understanding the role of knowledge in the environmental policy arena.

The authors do a masterful job in the introductory chapters of introducing the central concepts involved in the application of knowledge in environmental policymaking and in expertly laying out the central questions that should be asked. The succeeding chapters address those questions clearly and concisely, weaving in the pertinent literature and selected case studies to offer an integrated and informative assessment. Their discussion of how uncertainty and lack of knowledge can pose dilemmas for policymakers is particularly strong, and in the concluding chapter they are able to offer a plethora of insights and recommendations for the most appropriate and accurate use of knowledge in environmental policy.

The book illustrates well the goals of the MIT Press series in American and Comparative Environmental Policy. We encourage work that examines a broad range of environmental policy issues. We are particularly interested in volumes that incorporate interdisciplinary research and focus on the linkages between public policy and environmental problems and issues both within the United States and in cross-national settings. We welcome contributions that analyze the policy dimensions of relationships between humans and the environment from either a theoretical or empirical perspective. At a time when environmental policies are increasingly seen as controversial and new approaches are being implemented widely, we especially encourage studies that assess policy successes and failures, evaluate new institutional arrangements and policy tools, and clarify new directions for environmental politics and policy. The books in this series are written for a wide audience that includes academics, policymakers, environmental scientists and professionals, business and labor leaders, environmental activists, and students concerned with environmental issues. We hope they contribute to public understanding of environmental problems, issues, and policies of concern today and also suggest promising actions for the future.

Sheldon Kamieniecki, University of California, Santa Cruz
Michael Kraft, University of Wisconsin-Green Bay
American and Comparative Environmental Policy Series Editors

Preface

One of the most notable developments of the past half century or so has been the explosion of human knowledge. It has been accompanied by two parallel and closely related phenomena: a remarkable improvement in the technology used to communicate knowledge that has facilitated the diffusion of knowledge throughout society and significant improvements in the educational background of policymakers and others who participate in decision making. We have more, and better, knowledge; it is much more available to policymakers; and policymakers are far better able to understand it. Why, then, have we not seen a ratcheting up in the quality of policymaking? Moreover, in a knowledge-rich situation, one might expect a greater degree of consensus among various interests and the general public about what is the "right" thing to do. Yet, in so many areas of policymaking we see increasing conflict, rather than consensus.

This movement toward better policy and toward more consensus should be especially pronounced in the management of the environment. Fifty years ago, our knowledge of many environmental processes was rudimentary. Rachel Carson had pointed out the disastrous effect on wildlife of the pesticide DDT, but little was known about thousands of other organic chemicals that were widely dispersed in the environment. Air pollution was a visible problem in many American cities, but scientists were just starting to understand the role of automobiles in generating ozone and nitrogen oxides. Technologies to purify sewage and to remove sulfur from power-plant-stack gases were experimental and very expensive. The word *ecology* was understood only by scientists. When used by elected officials or by the public, scientists would chuckle about their misapprehension.

Now, although we know so much about the environment, our policies have not shown an equivalent improvement in effectiveness or efficiency. Many obvious problems are still unaddressed. The volume of legislative wrangling and environmental law suits also provides abundant evidence that increased knowledge does not lead to consensus. There must be a story here. Are the thousands of scientists who have been working on environmental problems producing the wrong kind of knowledge? Is there some structural failure in communicating knowledge from scientists to policymakers? If there is, does the defect arise from the scientists or from the policymakers?

Over the past decade, each of this book's authors, individually and together, has taught and written on these topics. For example, Healy has been interested in the role of "knowledge entrepreneurs" in trying to put certain issues on the policymaking agenda. This led, among other work, to an article on how "state of the environment" reports are used by both government agencies and private-sector actors. He has also been interested in how the Forest Service's Renewable Resource Planning Act (RPA) program generated massive amounts of new information, and the impact that has had on forest policy debates. Ascher served on the EPA Scientific Advisory Board Committee on Valuing the Protection of Ecological Systems and Services (the usual caveats hold that the opinions expressed in this book do not represent the views of any committee, advisory board, or agency); he was struck by the complexity and under-recognized influences of how environmental valuation and benefit-cost analyses are done and the impacts they have. This experience also revealed more about the role and limitations of public input into the environmental policy process, which he has explored in collaboration with Steelman. Her research has focused on the challenges of integrating science, policy, and decision making, often with a focus on the role of community involvement in policy processes. Methodologically, she explored how multiple methods of inquiry contribute to integrating knowledge.

About two years ago, we thought that the amount and scope of this work might warrant bringing together the above publications in a single volume. As we started to write an introduction to the collection, we kept coming up with new ideas on the knowledge-in-policymaking issue, many of which did not appear in our previously published articles. We also felt the need to express—and to analyze—the pervasive discontent of both knowledge generators (especially scientists and local citizen groups) and of knowledge users (legislators and bureaucrats) regarding how knowledge influences policy. How was it that we have much more environmental knowledge than was available to us a generation ago and still those generating the knowledge so often feel misunderstood or ignored, while the policymakers feel as though they are constantly confronted with mixed messages and lack the means for sorting good information from bad?

That question transformed this volume from a collection of published papers to an entirely new book. Here we try to carefully describe the knowledge-policy nexus, identify specific problem areas, and propose solutions. We give separate treatment to knowledge generation, knowledge transmission, and knowledge use and show how these functions are distinct yet subject to important feedback mechanisms. We note that some forms of knowledge tend to be privileged in policymaking, while other forms are likely to be discounted or ignored. One theme that runs through the entire book is the importance of "politics" (in the general sense of nonmarket competition among groups and individuals) throughout the knowledge-policy relationship. And we reach the conclusion—which will be surprising to some readers—that this is, in general, a good thing (though certain aspects should be controlled).

We owe a debt of gratitude to those who assisted us in the writing of this book. Several individuals helped us along the way. In 2007, Ascher and Steelman presented some of the basic ideas to participants at the Annual Policy Sciences Institute held in Claremont, California. The feedback from the audience was particularly helpful in shaping our ideas in those early stages. George Hess gave a thorough reading of our first chapter and provided important constructive feedback.

We hope this book will be of interest to those who make policy and to those who try to influence it. And we hope it will answer some questions and assuage some frustrations among the enormous number of environmental scientists who believe their work has policy implications, but who do not know how to make the right connections.

William Ascher, of Claremont, California
Toddi Steelman, Raleigh, North Carolina
Robert Healy, Durham, North Carolina

1

Knowledge in the Environmental Policy Process

Frustrations with Science and Policymaking

Nearly everyone concerned with making environmental policy believes that science should have a major role in it. Environmental policy typically deals either with the management of diverse natural systems or with the impact of pollution on the health of living organisms, especially humans. These questions seem clearly within the purview of a number of the physical, social, and biological sciences. Climatologists try to anticipate the nature and magnitude of global climate change; biologists and ecologists try to assess how these and other changes will affect plant and animal populations; toxicologists attempt to understand the potential consequences of the growing number of chemicals in the air and water; economists, political scientists, and psychologists seek to understand human responses to mandatory regulations and appeals to volunteerism. But neither the scientists who generate knowledge nor the policymakers who use it are satisfied with how science affects policy. Scientists are often disheartened with how their hard-won knowledge is misunderstood, distorted, or (perhaps worst of all) ignored. Legislators and administrators complain that scientists are not prepared to give them information that is truly useful in a timely manner. When scientists seek more funding to answer questions they believe will be policy relevant or that will further their research agendas, policymakers respond that they have not gotten good value for the enormous amounts already expended.[1]

The disjuncture between science and policy was particularly strong during the presidency of George W. Bush (2001–2009) when environmental science did not influence policy because political and ideological considerations were paramount. Patterns of abuse of environmental science were widespread within the U.S. Environmental Protection Agency (EPA)[2] and in other agencies that generate, transmit, and use science.[3] Violations included falsifying data and results; selectively editing documents; creating false uncertainty; tampering with scientific procedures; intimidating, censoring, and suppressing scientists; retaliating against whistle-blowers; delaying the release of scientific findings; disregarding legally mandated science; allowing conflicts of interest; and corrupting scientific advisory panels.[4] In addition to these operational-level challenges, the Bush administration made structural changes to how science and knowledge processes were governed—for example, centralizing decision making, homogenizing agency decision making, reducing transparency, and weakening enforcement and monitoring.[5]

The Barack Obama administration has been, at least to the time of writing (February 2010), not only willing to give science a fair hearing, but actively reliant on it to support important parts of its policy agenda. In his inaugural speech, the new president promised to "restore science to its rightful place," a clear dig at the aforementioned Bush administration practices. Many of the specific promises in the speech, including developing new energy technologies and addressing "the specter of a warming planet," implied a faith in the ability of science to guide policy. One of the new president's first acts, taken on March 20, 2009, was to issue an executive order providing that guidelines be established "to ensure that in this new administration we base our public policies on the soundest science, that we appoint scientific advisors based on their credentials and experience, not their politics or ideology."[6] The economic stimulus bill provided large increases in funding for scientific research, especially for the National Institutes of Health and the National Science Foundation. The president even appointed noted scientists to several policymaking posts, notably physicist Steven Chu as secretary of energy, energy expert John Holdren as presidential science advisor, and ecologist Jane Lubchenco as head of the National Oceanic and Atmospheric Administration.[7]

With the administration's access to such talent and obvious receptivity to science-based ideas, can we expect a new era of environmental and natural-resource policy in which scientific objectivity drives all parties toward consensus, policies are effective and efficient, and both scientists and policymakers are pleased with their policy dialog? We do not think this outcome likely. The problem of moving from scientific discovery to science-based policy is, as we demonstrate throughout this book, a systemic one and not merely a question of trust or goodwill.

We believe that a science-friendly administration will still find frustrations in the relation of science and the making of environmental policy and that scientists will continue to feel misunderstood and often ignored. Moreover, "formal science"—the sort of knowledge most people associate with highly trained and specialized scientists, legitimized by their credentials and reinforced by conventional scientific protocols—cannot convey the full range of knowledge that policymakers ought to take into account, including local knowledge, public sentiments, and policy preferences. Formal science is prone to filtering out information that does not meet its standards of rigor or replicability or that is not disseminated through "acceptable" pathways. An overreliance on the knowledge provided by formal science can lead to neglect of political considerations necessary to enact effective environmental policies. Integrating formal science with other important types of knowledge inevitably involves political interplay in a number of ways that we explore throughout this book.

The historical duel between the primacy of science or politics needs to be reframed. The problem is not that other scholars have ignored the dilemmas. The complexity of the tensions arising in the interactions of science, politics, and policymaking has been a growing preoccupation of studies of knowledge in the environmental policy process. This preoccupation is reflected in the broad-stroke assessments of the role of expertise across the whole range of policy issues[8], the treatments of environmental knowledge per se,[9] and works focusing on specific environmental issues such as endangered species conservation,[10] climate change,[11] and forestry.[12] They all recognize that there is no incontrovertible, unassailable ensemble of data and theory that must be accepted as the sum total of relevant and reliable knowledge. The selection and weighting of sources and forms of knowledge will always be controversial, and the use of one set of knowledge inputs rather than another will always further some agendas over others. Knowledge generated by scientific efforts and other processes will often be designed and used to promote particular goals. In this respect, scientific and other forms of knowledge are inevitably politicized.

We agree with Mark Brown[13] that the politicization of science requires a rethinking of how science and democratic practice interact and that it is important to examine how different institutions mediate different forms of expertise and representation. Yet we do not share his rosy view that politicized science—science that conveys values and therefore implicit political demands—is more of an opportunity for democracy than a threat. Such a characterization depends on the widely varying impacts that politicized science will have on the balance of values and objectives that can be effectively conveyed to policymakers. The primacy of science in some contexts may undercut the representation of other values as well as other forms of knowledge. We challenge the assumption that more and better science alone will lead to improved environmental decision making. Disproportionate neglect of either politics *or* science creates dysfunctions in how knowledge influences environmental decision making. Finding a more balanced marriage between science and politics can lead to better environmental decision making for the common good.

Thus, our intent in this book is simple, although the application is at times complex. Our goal is to explore how the knowledge processes, currently structured in a futile effort to separate politics from science, are dysfunctional in many respects. Building on this diagnosis, we provide recommendations for how these problems may be addressed. To make sense of the confusing complexity of knowledge processes, we divide knowledge processes into three functions—*generation, transmission, use*—and we explore the effects of these functions on the policy process itself. These functions overlap and feed into each other. We believe that this framework will allow the reader to make sense of the often confusing world where knowledge intersects with politics and policy.

The book's major contributions are to integrate existing and published literature on science, politics, and policy and to apply that literature to the role of knowledge in the environmental policymaking arena. We situate science and other forms of knowledge in the mainstream of policy analysis. Environmental policy—like other policy—is made through a multistage policy process. Formal science can and should influence this process pervasively, and there are certain key points at which science is particularly relevant.

Our approach involves setting out a "policy process" theory of policymaking and then identifying the specific places and ways in which science and other knowledge enter the process. It also involves looking at science and scientists through the lens of political economy—scientists are not godlike generators of pure knowledge but rather part of a process in which they interact with political actors and respond to institutional forces. This insight is admittedly not novel in itself. Scholars of the subfield of "science, technology, and society" have long been attuned to the social construction and cultural situation of science;[14] this book moves beyond that literature to situate science and other forms of knowledge in the mainstream of environmental policy analysis. Infusing these insights into the policy process is new.[15] Ann Keller (2009) examines scientists' efforts to serve as neutral advisors across the stages of agenda setting, legislation, and implementation, yet our focus on the processes of generation, transmission, and use of knowledge reveals the fundamental limits in the concept of neutrality, even if some scientists see themselves as striving to provide value-free advice. We believe this contribution is novel and will be of interest to a broad cross-section of readers.

This book is for scientists who would like to make their work more relevant to environmental policy as well as for policymakers who are convinced that their decisions should be informed by science, but who have too often found science (and scientists) insufficiently relevant to their needs. We hope the book will be of interest to academics and their students in the policy analysis and science policy field.

By wading into this world, we intentionally enter the debate about the social construction of science. In our view, science is thoroughly embedded in social and political practices. That said, we also believe that a real biophysical world exists in which science has an essential role. We are not antiscience relativists. Our intention here is to better integrate science about this biophysical world into the realm of policy, while acknowledging the social and political influences on that knowledge. We also aim to increase the legitimacy of other types of knowledge, such as local knowledge and public preferences, which are unjustifiably assumed to be tainted because of the social and political influences on their construction.

A Preview of Our Arguments

Science is a subset of "knowledge." Science encompasses our understandings of underlying ecosystem processes, how pollutants move through the environment, and how changes in environmental conditions affect people and other living organisms. Advances in scientific knowledge are usually incremental, but there have been major breakthroughs. In environmental science, one such important breakthrough was the discovery that DDT, considered a relatively safe pesticide after trials on humans, had disastrous effects on some birds' reproductive ability. Because of the well-deserved prestige of the methods of formal science, its input to debates over environmental policy has long been privileged. However, this role is now under considerable challenge. William Clark, Ronald Mitchell, and David Cash argue that "science no longer holds the 'numinous' legitimacy once accorded to religion and royalty. Instead, it must gain 'civil legitimacy' through freely negotiated agreement among affected parties as to what rules and procedures should govern its meaning and use."[16]

Moreover, other kinds of knowledge besides formal science are also crucial to making good policy. They include *local knowledge* that is typically provided through place-based experience or learned during policy implementation. For example, local knowledge can include the many things that indigenous people know about local conditions, such as rainfall patterns and their interaction with crop productivity. It can also include knowledge of the political hierarchy in a community—which is vital information when policy seeks to influence local behavior. Local knowledge is grounded in action, commitment, and involvement in a specific context, so it is harder to formalize and communicate.[17] Local knowledge can entail subjective insight, intuition, and hunches; it contributes to Michael Polanyi's observation that "we know more than we can tell."[18] The technical dimension of local knowledge can involve concrete know-how, crafts, and skills applied to specific trades or practices—something Claude Lévi-Strauss referred to as "the science of the concrete."[19] The cognitive aspect entails mental models, beliefs, perceptions, schema, and other hard-to-articulate viewpoints through which individuals perceive, make sense of, and define their world.

The final form of knowledge that we consider is *public preferences*: beliefs and priorities that provide insight into various individuals' or groups' support of or opposition to a given position or outcome and into the intensity of these positions. In short, it is knowledge that is revealed through political behavior. It includes information about who will support or oppose a given policy and how much energy they are likely to devote to participation in the policy process. It also includes knowledge about distributional consequences—a type of knowledge provided by interest groups. Public preferences provide relevant information on the satisfaction that stakeholders will derive from various policy outcomes. Although such preferences are not the end-all of considerations that policymakers must take into account, they cannot be ignored. Policymakers are particularly interested in the intensity of preferences. Who will write letters to the editor? Who will demonstrate? Who will bring a lawsuit? Who will contribute to a political campaign or cease to contribute to a campaign if a given decision is made? For bureaucrats, what supporter or opponent of a policy has influence with the bureaucrats' agency superiors or political overseers? We situate the kind of knowledge most people associate with scientists, along with local knowledge and public preferences, within the broader category of knowledge relevant to environmental decision making.

The contest between the knowledge generated through formal science and other sources of knowledge is especially important in shaping the debate about what knowledge is considered in decision making. In part, this is because the rules and protocols that guide the creation of formal science are relatively clear when compared to those for the variety of other types of knowledge that influence decision making. However, decision makers often do not know what to make of other forms of knowledge or what standards should be applied to deem them credible or legitimate. We do not mean to imply here that the formal scientific enterprise is superior; it has its own shortcomings.[20] In fact, some argue that science itself is in need of change or at least adaptation to the new problems we face as a society. Under this belief, the problem is not so much in the way science is used, but in the way science is practiced.[21]

In addition to broadening the scope of knowledge to include local knowledge and public preferences, we divide knowledge processes into four categories for systematic consideration: the *generation* of knowledge, the *transmission* of knowledge, the *use* of knowledge, and the *effects* of knowledge on the policy process itself. These four categories provide an organizational framework for the book. Specialists in the field of policy analysis will recognize them as close parallels to particular "functions of the policy process," a widely used model of how issues are raised, how policy alternatives are proposed and considered, and how a policy is selected and implemented.[22]

The Science-Politics Embrace

A main theme throughout the book is that knowledge generation, transmission, and use reflect not only a technical process that creates and compiles scientific, local, and preference-based information, but also a political process.[23] Politics, in this context, does not undermine "sound policy," as the common depiction of politics presumes ("We were making real progress toward a good policy until politics reared its ugly head"). Rather, politics is the process to establish the goals—preferably sound ones—to be pursued by policy. "Special-interest" or selfish politics does of course occur in many instances. Yet if politics is seen in its broad sense of interest-driven behavior expressed through various nonmarket institutions, we must conclude that politics is the essential process of "shaping and sharing of values" that usually gives rise to some level of conflict.[24] Healthy politics—including policy-relevant science, pertinent local information, constructive public involvement, and conflict resolution—can serve to clarify and secure the common interest in knowledge generation for environmental decision processes. Failure to recognize the explicit role that politics plays in knowledge generation, transmission, and use means that politics becomes embedded in implicit forms that distort the roles or functions that knowledge can play.

Contrary to what many observers might expect, new knowledge does not necessarily induce contending interest groups to converge toward a science-based agreement on what policy should be chosen. Rather, as Paul Sabatier argues, various interests selectively mine new knowledge, including scientific findings, for arguments that buttress their specific positions.[25]

Politics infuses all aspects related to the generation, transmission, and use of knowledge in environmental decision making. We counterintuitively question the wisdom and practicality of reinforcing the boundaries between science and politics. Maintaining a charade that draws clear boundaries only serves to discredit science, devalue other forms of knowledge that can be useful in environmental decision making, and drive politics into back rooms where its influence is opaque but ubiquitous. The frustrations in linking science and policymaking are real, but they cannot be remedied by creating harder, stronger boundaries between the scientific enterprise and politics.[26] Embracing politics and the many forms of knowledge that inform policymaking is the only realistic path to creating better environmental policy, both for the public good and for the restoration of confidence in science.

Rethinking Privileged Knowledge

A second theme of the book concerns the privileging of certain types of knowledge and the hidden "governing biases" that this privileging has on the policy process itself. These invisible governing biases, unlike the high-profile nature of the clashes between science and politics, are all the more serious because they are barely recognized by most people involved in the process. This privileging creates self-reinforcing properties that shape the very processes by which future knowledge is produced and applied. Interactive effects among the generation, transmission, and use of knowledge result in changes in the institutions that shape policymaking. For example, the demand for and availability of knowledge can change the skills required of actors if they are to be effective in influencing policy and the relative level of importance they have in policymaking. Important knowledge, even within science, sometimes receives insufficient standing because certain methods of analysis and certain types of scientists are privileged over others. This effect occurs through prejudices in research funding, the filtering of knowledge through such transmission vehicles as refereed scientific journals, selective information requirements of decision-assisting analytic techniques such as benefit-cost analysis, and other partialities in how science and knowledge processes are governed. Many economists and decision theorists would regard formal benefit-cost analysis to be of indisputable value.[27] Because this method of analysis is favored, it is elevated over other applications and knowledge within the decision-making process. A crucial implication is that knowledge dynamics influence the relative power and status of key participants in the policymaking process and the arenas where decisions are made.

We identify several traps that people fall into where some knowledge forms are privileged over others:

Credibility Seeking: The tendency for scientists and lay people to generate, transmit, or use knowledge that *appears* to be more rigorous or valid than other types of knowledge, which often leads to the neglect of other valuable knowledge. Apparent rigor is typically associated with explicit, overtly systematic, controlled, and often quantitative approaches. Knowledge generated through approaches that do not meet these criteria, however, may capture considerations that the apparently rigorous methods cannot. This point is very often missed.

Assumption Drag: The propensity to accept automatically the assumptions embedded in previously generated, transmitted, or used knowledge without questioning their validity. Erroneous assumptions often persist even after their validity has been contradicted by data. The "founder effect" of iconic status of groundbreaking knowledge that remains in currency long after its obsolescence is one form of assumption drag.

Certainty Prejudice: A preference for knowledge that can be proven with certitude or directly observed over knowledge that is subjected to even small amounts of uncertainty, even in cases where it might be prudent to take action before complete certainty is known.

Legal Biases: Situations where administrative laws, legislation, or precedent prohibit taking some forms of knowledge into account, while favoring other forms of knowledge. Such situations include those in which judicial admissibility doctrines favor some forms of knowledge over others as evidence in court.

Status Hierarchies: The tendency to defer to knowledge provided by individuals who appear to be better credentialed and more senior, hail from a perceived "better" institution, or meet a preconceived notion of what an expert on the topic should look like. This deference reduces the chances that important practical and context-specific knowledge will be applied to formulate solutions.

Knowledge in the Functions of the Environmental Policy Process

Knowledge is often considered an "input" into environmental policy-making, but this description does not do justice to the multiple roles that knowledge plays. It can inform the problem; clarify goals and objectives; identify and evaluate alternatives; support courses of action; prescribe rules, guidelines, or actions for management; determine which rules ought to be applied; and evaluate progress. Knowledge spans the bio-physical data and science relevant to the behavior of ecosystems as well as the impacts on human health, ecosystem health, and natural resources. It also encompasses the understanding of social, political, and economic aspects of human behavior as either drivers of or responses to environmental conditions and changes.

To appreciate the full range of roles that knowledge can play, it is useful to elaborate on how knowledge figures into the various functions of the environmental policy process. Figure 1.1 displays the flow of activity from the generation of knowledge to its application to decision routines that establish environmental regulations, resource-management doctrines, and environmental and conservation practices.

For the purposes of formulating and enacting policies that affect the environment—for better or for worse—we need to focus on *relevant* knowledge. Although people may disagree about the relevance of information because of the goals and theories that they hold, we can certainly identify the broad range of knowledge that is needed for policymaking.

Not all knowledge generated by various sources is channeled into policy considerations because each bit of knowledge has to pass through filters of acceptability before it is widely used. Yet the canons of scientific acceptability do not typically reflect an orderly, consensual process of selecting the correct and rejecting the suspect. Instead, the process usually reflects clashes among different schools of thought, different disciplines, and subdisciplines as well as debates over the accuracy of measurement approaches. Therefore, the concept of "accepted environmental knowledge" relevant to the choice of environmental policies does not refer to a universal consensus, but rather to the knowledge accepted and employed by those in authority to participate in the multistage process of making environmental policy decisions. As a consequence, *who* decides on *what* knowledge is of crucial importance. As long as the knowledge falls within the bounds established by the admissibility of particular types of information dictated, in some cases by the governing laws, some individuals matter more than others when it comes to determining what kind of knowledge is acceptable.

The activity flow starts with the *generation of* knowledge, sometimes by formal science, sometimes by local entities (e.g., local environmental organizations, individuals with special knowledge). This knowledge includes not just factual knowledge, but also knowledge

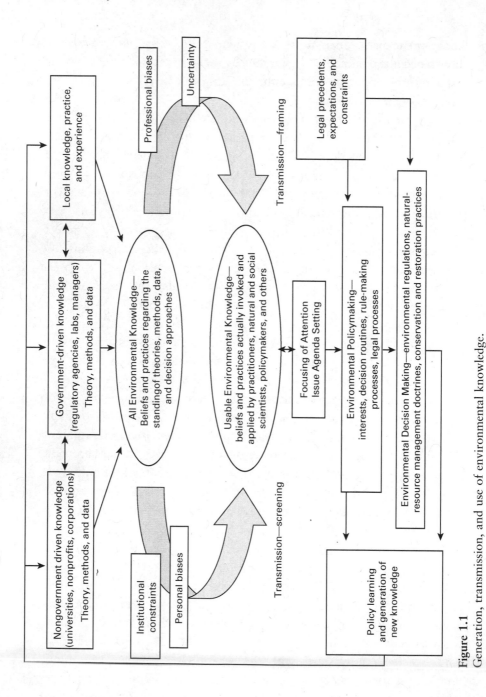

Figure 1.1
Generation, transmission, and use of environmental knowledge.

about preferences. Then the knowledge is *transmitted*. This transmission reflects stakeholders' interests and the issues that dominate their focus of attention. The media and interest groups play important roles in terms of focusing public and political attention and setting the agenda for both the selection and implementation of policies.[28] Consider, for instance, the role of Al Gore's film *An Inconvenient Truth* in advancing the climate-change agenda in the United States or the use of the polar bear by environmental groups as the symbol to catalyze support for addressing climate change.

Policies are then *selected* and *implemented*. We have observed that policy selection is strongly influenced by policymakers' beliefs (which are influenced by the knowledge transmitted to them) as to whether the problem before them presents risks.

Before a public policy or rule can be applied, its appropriateness must be assessed through both scientific and formal regulatory and legal procedures. For the scientific assessment, the primary challenge is that knowledge largely consists of "all things being equal" propositions that must be applied to real-world contexts in which all things are rarely equal. Uncertainty often arises even when theory is strong because the relative strength of various effects may be unknown even if the dynamics of each effect are well known.[29]

For the formal procedures, each element of the environmental protection regime can be enacted only after its legal status is resolved. In the United States and many other countries, environmental regulations are subjected to intensive litigation in which the admissibility of knowledge is centrally at issue. Battles over admissibility are essentially battles over what forms of knowledge will be allowed to have standing. What is to be considered "junk science" as opposed to solid science? Why do U.S. courts so often reject the findings of animal experiments and thereby conclude that threats to human health are insufficiently conclusive? The question of what constitutes adequate accuracy of information, certainty of theory, and rigor of analytic routines has no simple answer.

The less obvious aspect of environmental policymaking is the use of particular decision routines, whether at the decision makers' discretion or required by legal or administrative mandates. These routines can include explicit benefit-cost analysis (full comparison of benefits and costs, expressed in a common metric—typically in monetary terms), cost-effectiveness analysis (the choice of the least costly option for accomplishing a given set of objectives), compensation formulas required by law, enforcement of specified rights, responses to stakeholders' preferences, and implementation of negotiated settlements. The relevance of knowledge to the choice and subsequent standing of decision routines is that the appropriateness of particular routines and of the inputs for using them also has to be filtered according to relevant scientific standards. These routines and inputs are often subject to scientific dispute. For example, explicit benefit-cost analysis and cost-effectiveness analysis require estimates of the value of the respective benefits and costs. The various valuation techniques have strengths and weaknesses as well as supporters and detractors. In addition, court battles often loom in the disputes over which routines are required and what methodologies are sufficiently rigorous to be admissible in legal proceedings. Even the *anticipation* of legal battles can determine the choice of decision routine and supporting methods as government analysts and managers try to avoid lengthy and costly legal challenges.

Finally, *implementation*—the outputs from environmental policymaking and decision making—contributes to policy learning and the generation of new knowledge. This knowledge may or may not be picked up by the many participants in the process to inform the next iteration in the generation of environmental knowledge.

The Criteria for Assessing the Generation, Transmission, and Use of Environmental Knowledge

Several criteria are relevant when considering whether knowledge is adequate for environmental decision making. The health of knowledge processes cannot be assessed without clarifying the characteristics of sound processes that are more likely to yield environmental policies that serve the common interest. We suggest that appropriate criteria include comprehensiveness, dependability, selectivity, timeliness, relevance, openness, efficiency, and creativity, as detailed in table 1.1. We are not arguing that a particular unit of knowledge must meet all these criteria, but rather that the processes of generation, transmission, and use serve

Table 1.1
Relevant Criteria for Evaluating Knowledge Generation, Transmission, and Use

Criteria	Definition
Comprehensiveness	completeness of the knowledge available; a suitable level of inclusiveness for a given context
Dependability	factual reliability of knowledge generated, transmitted, and used by individuals with recognized competence, including technical proficiency and subject matter–based or place-based expertise
Selectivity	appropriately targeted boundaries for gathzering information and doing analysis
Timeliness	the need for knowledge to be up to date and available to decision makers
Relevance	the need to stay focused on the given problem
Openness	transparent knowledge generation, transmission, and use processes
Efficiency	reasonableness in the expenditure of resources in relation to the knowledge generated, transmitted, and used
Creativity	imagination utilized in the generation, transmission, and use of ideas

the common interest best when they enhance the ensemble of knowledge according to these criteria.

The knowledge generated, transmitted, and used should be *comprehensive* and *dependable*. Comprehensiveness refers to the completeness of the available knowledge as appropriate for a given context. Dependability refers to the factual reliability of information. Knowledge should be generated from persons who have competence in their given areas of expertise.[30] This expertise can extend to technology, subject matter, or contextual place-based knowledge. The peer-review process used in the biological, physical, and the social sciences is an attempt to ensure dependability in the transmission and use of scientific research findings—a necessary precaution when scientific knowledge is being generated by hundreds of thousands of researchers at tens of thousands of institutions scattered across the globe. The dependability of knowledge is more easily ascertained when events, trends, and conditions have been studied for some time.

Yet because we live in a world bounded by time and resource constraints, knowledge also must be *selective*.[31] Selectivity does not contradict, as it might seem to at first glance, the criterion of comprehensiveness. Selectivity refers to appropriately targeted boundaries for gathering, transmitting, and using information and analysis; following a broad scanning of potentially relevant considerations, the imperative of efficiency in situations of constrained resources calls for concentrating on those considerations and dynamics that warrant attention and action. *Timeliness* denotes the need for knowledge to be up to date and available to decision makers; we shall see that the problem of obsolete or delayed information is chronic. *Relevance* suggests the need to stay focused on the given problem; doing so is complicated by the fact that different actors often use different problem definitions. *Openness* concerns the idea that knowledge generation, transmission, and use should occur in transparent ways that outsiders can understand and evaluate. Esoteric analysis is difficult for participants in the policy process to digest. *Efficiency* in knowledge generation, transmission, and use refers to a reasonable expenditure of resources relative to the knowledge gained for the effort. *Creativity* calls for thinking outside the box when generating, transmitting, and using knowledge—looking for insights and alternatives that might otherwise not be considered.

Criticisms of particular efforts in knowledge generation, transmission, and use focus on violations of one or more of these criteria. Yet because there are multiple criteria, they often must be traded off with each other. Problems arise when the criteria are not met or when some criteria matter more than others to some participants in the decision-making process. For instance, comprehensiveness may need to be traded off with selectivity or timeliness to meet the demands of deadline-driven decision making. This trade-off is often what is meant by the term *best available science*. Scientific findings that are more accurate might be available in the future, but decision makers often need to work with what is available in the present. Making these trade-offs poses difficulties for those who seek to generate, transmit, and use knowledge. It is impossible to satisfy all criteria simultaneously, and decisions about which criteria are most important will be determined contextually given the decision-making situation.

The Specific Problems in Knowledge Generation, Transmission, and Use

Why is knowledge *generation* difficult and how might we be able to understand better some of the dysfunction in the knowledge-generation process? It is not possible to cover all of the problems in this book, so in chapter 2 we focus on a subset of problems that we identified as particularly noteworthy. These problems include (1) diversification of knowledge generation; (2) complexity and uncertainty; (3) biases in knowledge generation; and (4) challenges with public input.

In recent decades, the sources of knowledge generation have expanded and diversified greatly.[32] Universities and government agencies have been joined by a host of nonprofit entities, from foundations to trade associations to "think tanks." Greater plurality in knowledge generation has created difficulty in how to assess or evaluate the quality of knowledge that is transmitted and used in environmental decision-making processes.[33] Without clear standards, guidelines, or principles, it is difficult to determine what constitutes comprehensive, dependable, selective, relevant, or efficient knowledge generation.

Knowledge used in environmental decision making is complex and uncertain, and the complexity of natural and socioeconomic systems feeds into the uncertainty associated with knowledge generation.[34] Complexity likewise means that the multiple institutions, agencies, and organizations that generate knowledge are fragmented, making it difficult to coordinate existing knowledge.[35] The consequence of interactions between complexity and uncertainty is that attaining comprehensiveness in knowledge is impossible.

Several biases are evident in the way knowledge is generated. Excitement over breakthroughs in knowledge generation fails to emphasize the prejudices that accompany these techniques. For instance, despite the impressive advances in technical methods for gauging the public's preferences by assessing people's "willingness to pay" for environmental improvements, these methods are unavoidably incomplete in the range of considerations that they can convey.[36] The prevailing techniques, whether based on inferences from economic behavior or stated preferences, will privilege certain considerations over others.[37] Moreover, in knowledge generation the typical preference for generalized knowledge over more contextual knowledge often has the accompanying consequence of discounting local knowledge and public input. The outcome from these biases is that knowledge generation often fails to be comprehensive, dependable, relevant, or open.

Finally, the public can contribute useful information to the decision-making process, and we have many modalities for soliciting input from the public. However, this increase in knowledge has not made decision-making easier.[38] Moreover, there is confusion over the purpose and intent for which knowledge from the public is solicited.[39] These public input challenges mean that knowledge generated is not comprehensive, dependable, relevant, or open.

In chapter 3, we cover four problems related to the *transmission* of knowledge. A multitude of channels transmit knowledge, ranging from the popular to the highly technical. Even the generation of knowledge serves to transmit the prior studies on which the new studies are based, as do the decision-aiding analyses that precede policy decisions. This chapter identifies some fundamental problems related to the *transmission* of knowledge, including: (1) the persistence of the privileged position of science; (2) the diversification of knowledge-transmission vehicles; (3) uncertainty as a problem in knowledge transmission; and (4) biased focusing of attention through knowledge transmission.

Formal science has occupied a favored position in the hierarchy of knowledge that is transmitted in environmental policymaking. Modes of transmission that endow knowledge with high standing may not be the modes that convey the most important or the most balanced knowledge. As a consequence, the prestige of certain channels may devalue or divert attention from other types of knowledge that cannot qualify for dissemination through these channels. Because formal science is but one category within the broader construct of knowledge, when it is used as the primary filter for transmission, it is overly selective in bounding the knowledge that is used in policymaking. As we explore in depth, local farmers in the Klamath River basin were denied a voice in predicting the consequences of water management during drought periods, and the U.S. Fish and Wildlife Service's (FWS) expert "biological opinions" led to catastrophic economic and social outcomes. The censoring of non-quantifiable information also led the U.S. EPA to undervalue the benefits of stricter water regulations. The British government ignored local sheep herders' concerns about the Chernobyl disaster's impact on their flocks, which led to the loss of entire herds. U.S. nuclear policy has taken many missteps by dismissing public anxieties over nuclear risks as scientifically naive, even though the important political fact has been the anxieties themselves. In short, the culture, institutions, and rules that shape the transmission of knowledge always run the risk of filtering out knowledge that may enlighten policymakers regarding considerations that ought to be taken into account. Such filtering has the consequence of limiting comprehensiveness, jeopardizing dependability, and inappropriately bounding selectivity for knowledge transmitted in policymaking.

Since the 1980s, we have witnessed enormous diversification in the vehicles through which knowledge can be transmitted. The rise of personal computers, the Internet, and Web-based tools such as blogs, wikis, Twitter, Facebook, MySpace, and other social-networking sites, as well as numerous software applications that allow knowledge to be processed, analyzed, and communicated have transformed how knowledge moves.[40] For example, today it is possible to mobilize people around the country with a single email or tweet. Long reports and detailed maps can be posted on sites or distributed as email attachments. Videos, including short clips captured by cell phones, can be posted on YouTube. A variety of inexpensive technologies makes it possible for lectures, radio and television programs, and even entire academic courses to be available for public download. The diversification in knowledge transmission has made it difficult to ascertain what constitutes dependable knowledge or how to be appropriately selective regarding transmission sources.

Scientists' treatment of uncertainty colors how knowledge will be screened and framed for purposes of policymaking. Administrative, legal, and professional biases lead to risk-averse behavior, limiting the type of knowledge transmitted and used in environmental decision making.[41] This limitation results in knowledge that is not comprehensive, dependable, or selective.

Focusing attention in knowledge-transmission processes means that not all knowledge generated makes it into environmental policymaking. Available knowledge can focus attention on only a subset of the huge range of environmentally relevant issues. Policy entrepreneurs have been particularly important in environmental policy debates, some working on behalf of environmental causes or environmental organizations, some working for industries or antiregulatory groups. We believe that an important subset of the policy entrepreneur is the "knowledge entrepreneur." This individual or organization attempts to influence the entire policy process, from setting the agenda to defining policy alternatives to selecting and implementing final policy by controlling the flow of policy-relevant knowledge. The more technical (and technocratic) modern policymaking has become, the greater has been the space for knowledge entrepreneurs to exert influence. The knowledge transmitted is accordingly not comprehensive, may not be dependable, and is sometimes unsuitably selective.

The *use* of environmental knowledge—that is, the application of environmental knowledge to policy decisions—relies on knowledge generated and interpreted in a political context. This relationship raises important questions about how individuals and organizations use knowledge. Knowledge can be used not only as an aid to analysis, but also as a promotional strategy. Legitimate uncertainty can be manipulated to discredit science or justify inaction. Institutional interests can suppress, oversimplify, and distort scientific information. Many alternatives for dealing with environmental protection and resource management are vulnerable to inappropriate, interest-driven simplification.

In the second part of chapter 3, we investigate specific problems related to the use of knowledge. We cover seven aspects of how knowledge is used in the environmental decision-making process: (1) mandatory uses of knowledge; (2) privileging of knowledge used; (3) uncertainty in using knowledge; (4) coping with inadequate knowledge; (5) the role of knowledge in defining objectives and considering alternatives; (6) the role of knowledge in addressing implementation, evaluation, and termination challenges; and (7) the relationship between power dynamics and knowledge use.

In some situations, specific types of knowledge are mandated to be used in policymaking. These legal requirements limit what knowledge can or cannot be used. Formal science and quantitative approaches occupy privileged positions when knowledge is used in environmental decision making. Policymakers seek credibility and typically believe they gain it when leveraging science and quantitative data. Uncertainty and inadequate knowledge are invoked when policymakers wish to delay decision making. Once an issue becomes prominent on the policy agenda, legislative bodies and executive agencies usually have only a short time to select among alternative policies. Information used by policymakers may be less than timely, which will lead them either to make poor decisions or to grant broad post facto discretion to administrative agencies. Uncertainty also influences strategic decisions regarding how policy prescriptions are treated. These dynamics result in trade-offs between comprehensiveness of the knowledge available and the timeliness and efficiency of decisions to be made.

Knowledge is also used and new knowledge is often generated even as policies are implemented. However, implementers are generally not the knowledge generators or transmitters and have generalist backgrounds that make it difficult for them to understand the limitations and nuances of technical knowledge. In fact, different individuals or entities involved in invoking and applying policies may look at the available knowledge from different perspectives, depending on their mandates and goals. The need for monitoring—or collecting knowledge to see if the policy is working—is often overlooked, which then lessens the chance that knowledge acquisition can influence the termination of a poorly performing policy or refine the performance of an existing policy. At a minimum, lack of good feedback mechanisms can lead to great inefficiency and delay in policy change through policy learning. Finally, the proliferation of knowledge means that we have seen an increase in knowledge professionals. Skills, access, and capacity for using knowledge have clear distributional consequences for who gets to use knowledge and for what purposes.

The Impacts and Feedbacks of Knowledge on the Policy Process

Knowledge is not simply an input into the policy process; it also changes in many different ways the governing processes associated with it, from the institutions of decision making to the principles that these institutions employ in environmental policy and management. The availability of knowledge induces the use of decision routines geared to using such knowledge, whether these routines are the most appropriate for realizing the common interest or not. In chapter 4, we detail two primary policy-making dimensions affected by knowledge. They include the arenas where decision making takes place and the status and relative balance of power possessed by participants in policymaking.

Knowledge can also shift the *arena* where policymaking takes place. Consider how the politics of environmental policy are played out in the controversies over acceptable scientific methods. In the case of the U.S. Office of Management and Budget (OMB), the office requires quantitative information for decision making on environmental regulation, a requirement that privileges easily quantifiable and monetizable impacts over other aspects of environmental policy effects. It also creates an opportunity for the OMB to become a gatekeeper on all environmental regulatory decisions, thereby shifting policymaking from the legislative to the administrative branch. Thus, the rise of some analytic routines result in the privileging of this knowledge, the skill sets to use the knowledge, and the institutions that become home for the participants and the strategies employed. Participants in the policy process then try to place issues strategically so they can take advantage of the favorable dispensation the issues may receive in a given venue. In this way, knowledge creates the opportunity for participants to shop for the best arena where their issue will be treated most sympathetically.

The relative *balance of power and standing* accorded to participants in environmental decision making can hinge on the knowledge deemed relevant for those processes. The nature of knowledge and the prevailing standards for "acceptable" knowledge shape the relative power of political and bureaucratic institutions that are generating and applying this knowledge. For example, the demands for and availability of knowledge can change the skills required of actors if they are to be effective in influencing policy.[42] The relative standing of different forms of knowledge and of different approaches to environmental policy analysis similarly shape the relative influence of the actors involved in the policy process. Insofar as quantitative environmental data are considered essential, the experts generating these data will be more influential, and the activists making moral appeals to "rights" are likely to be marginalized. The same questions are relevant for assessing the appropriate roles for so-called local or indigenous knowledge. Insofar as local knowledge is respected, local people's perspectives will have more weight. By the same token, the increasing prominence of expert valuation has led to subtle but important shifts in how public preferences are incorporated into environmental decision making. Rivalries among professionals with different expertise result in the positioning of some knowledge as more worthy or valuable than others.

In chapter 5, we detail the numerous feedbacks that exist among the generation, transmission, and use of knowledge and the ultimate effects that these feedbacks have on policymaking. Four patterns are evident in these feedbacks. First, the generation, transmission, and use of knowledge reinforce one another by elevating the standing of knowledge that is created and demanded. Second, different laws, regulations, and policies draw on or invoke different types of knowledge, which in turn reflect different normative principles. Third, strategic behavior by participants in the policy process leads to modifications to or contestations of any knowledge that impinges on their interests or positions. Fourth, science and advocacy intersect with differing objectives, which requires new forms of mediation.

In chapter 6, we breathe life into the more theoretical concepts elaborated on in chapters 2–5. We detail three cases—the conflict over water allocation in the Klamath basin, the controversy over regulating Bisphenol A, and the obstacles to establishing a robust regulation for concentrated animal-feeding operations—and explain how the various problems with knowledge in the environmental decision-making process are present in each case. The three cases are typical in the sense that they illustrate some of the challenges and opportunities that arise when considering knowledge in environmental decision making. We believe that these cases and their more applied lessons will ground the reader in a common perspective and make more concrete some of the abstract points raised earlier.

Improving the Role of Knowledge in the Environmental Policy Process

Many of the prevailing assumptions about knowledge are unrealistic or misguided, given the role that knowledge actually plays in contemporary environmental decision making. We need a more realistic appraisal of the limits and capacity of knowledge in environmental decision making so that knowledge generation, transmission, and use can better serve the common good. The goal in the final chapter is to reimagine the role for knowledge generation, transmission, and use by taking into account twenty-first-century realities.

In chapter 7, this reimagining leads to recommendations to improve the role of knowledge in environmental decision making. Much of the book is devoted to explaining how the relation of knowledge to policy works and to showing where it is strongest and most constructive as well as where it is weakest and most dysfunctional. Some of our recommendations have long been discussed but not implemented. Some are entirely novel. In this chapter, we also point to some of the factors that have inhibited the implementation of these alternatives.

The overarching thrusts of our recommendations are to:

Provide a greater role for collaboration between scientists and nonscientists in the generation, transmission, and use of "knowledge hybrids." Each form of knowledge has its advantages and disadvantages. Some forms of knowledge meld science, local knowledge, and public preferences. These knowledge hybrids capitalize on the strengths of each knowledge type while compensating for its vulnerabilities.

Engage in "guerrilla tactics" to reveal the uncertainties inherent in science and to combat the sometimes exaggerated privileging of conventional science. Guerrilla tactics require greater transparency regarding the assumptions, incompleteness, and legitimate disagreements of formal science, without exaggerating the extent of disagreement that naturally arises when scientists focus their input into the policy process on issues that are still controversial.

Enhance discipline in knowledge processes. Resisting the individual, professional, and institutional biases against some forms of knowledge and exerting greater tolerance for knowledge generated through other paradigms will create a more equal playing field for all relevant knowledge to enter into environmental decision making.

Revise the standards by which we evaluate knowledge. More realistic expectations for dependability and comprehensiveness in light of the timeliness and relevance needed for policymakers will create a less hostile arena for scientists and others to participate in environmental decision making.

Institutionalize knowledge hybrids throughout knowledge processes. Incentives, culture, and structures can be aligned to support consistently the generation, transmission, and use of knowledge hybrids as appropriate for a given context.

Promote adaptive management and governance.   Systematic feedbacks in decision processes can be created to embrace uncertainty and to integrate learning among science, local knowledge, and public preferences.

Defend the integrity of science.   The management and governance of science can be reformed to protect scientists and the institution of science.

Enrich all knowledge processes through greater funding.   Additional funding, as opposed to the reallocation of existing funding, is needed to enhance local knowledge and public-preference knowledge in light of current emphasis on science. Likewise, a balanced emphasis across generation, transmission, and use is desirable.

2

The Generation of Policy-Relevant
Environmental Knowledge

The generation of knowledge entails gathering, interpreting, theorizing, modeling, endorsing, and synthesizing information and insights. One—but not the only—purpose of knowledge generation is to make theory and data available as inputs to the decision-making process. It also includes developing analytical techniques such as monitoring and measuring approaches and evaluative assessment technologies. Many practices and methods exist to generate knowledge, including casual observation, fieldwork, interviews, content analysis, social surveys, qualitative and quantitative models, and public-involvement methodologies.

Knowledge is created by individuals who are embedded in organizations and institutions that play important roles in how knowledge is transformed and legitimized.[1] Knowledge generation was historically the domain of universities and governments. However, it has been diversified remarkably in recent years.[2] New actors, such as nonprofit organizations and for-profit companies, have joined vigorously in the process. The diversification of knowledge generation has profound implications for our expectations for knowledge, who produces it, and how it is used. The locus of the generation of knowledge is important because it has implications for the perceived legitimacy of knowledge among groups of knowledge producers, transmitters, and consumers.

Knowledge generated through "science" connotes the application of specific protocols, values, and norms. Science has been shaped by institutional belief in peer review and other methodological practices that seek to ensure the reliability and validity of findings. These cognitive and social norms shape what counts as significant problems, who is credentialed to practice science, and what constitutes sound science. This type of formal, explicit, protocol-driven science can be organized into distinct paradigms that not only provide thematic foci for research, but also create boundaries for moving knowledge in these fields forward.[3] Once created, scientific knowledge is most commonly diffused back to disciplinary peer communities rather than to the public. This type of knowledge has historically been generated and assessed at universities by academics within disciplinary communities and at research laboratories in government and industry.

Other types of knowledge are created and shared within broader, transdisciplinary social and economic contexts and thus are more difficult to label than "science."[4] Practitioners carry out local and public-preference knowledge creation often in the context of a specific problem or application. This knowledge generation is difficult to separate from the sociocultural practices in which it is embedded. The implication is that there is no one "objective" truth, but rather multiple truths derived from personal experience that must be reconciled through discourse, interaction, and negotiation.[5] Local and public-preference knowledge draws on theory, empirics, and established disciplinary understanding as held by practitioners. However, it may not advance disciplinary knowledge or understanding as long as the discipline requires evaluation of general applicability and testing that is rigorous according to the canons of formal scientific practice. Results from these other types of knowledge are transmitted primarily back to those who participate in the application for which the problem was relevant. Quality is judged by whether the problem was solved or the application was successful.

There is a complicated and less clear-cut association of knowledge types with the specific institutions, organizations, and entities that generate and use knowledge. A variety of actors generates knowledge in the environmental decision-making arena. This relationship is important because different types of institutions shape different beliefs about how knowledge should be generated.[6] Universities may create a culture and expectation for generating formal science, whereas community groups, industry, and nonprofit organizations may place greater emphasis on local and public-preference knowledge generation. But these characterizations break down quickly, and universal generalizations do not hold.

Challenges in Knowledge Generation

Given these characteristics of knowledge generation, when and why does it present problems? Two themes run throughout this chapter. First, rarely is the generation of knowledge for environmental decision making a systematic process. Knowledge is generated by numerous, often uncoordinated people and institutions, only some of whom will be actors in a given decision-making process. We sometimes have too little knowledge or sometimes suffer from information overload, and the generation of knowledge is not usually well timed to serve the needs of policymaking. Second, knowledge generation is a political process because it occurs within a social context that is ultimately affected by the value systems of institutions, professions, and individuals. The politicization of knowledge has some positive aspects, in particular the encouragement of local and public-preference knowledge, but it also presents serious challenges to supporting good policy decisions.

Why is knowledge generation difficult, and how might we begin to understand better some of the dysfunction in the knowledge-generation process? We detail several categories of problems, which is helpful in understanding how we can engage in more enlightened knowledge generation as well as in realizing more clearly the trade-offs involved in how knowledge is generated. These categories of problems include: (1) diversification in knowledge generation; (2) complexity and uncertainty; (3) biases in knowledge generation; and (4) the challenge of public input.

Diversification of Knowledge Generation

The pool of participants who generate knowledge for environmental decision making expanded enormously in the post–World War II era. This diversification has created uncertainty in what constitutes dependable or valid knowledge for consideration in environmental decision-making processes. In addition to the dependability criterion, the diversification of knowledge generation has stirred up conflict with the comprehensiveness, selectivity, relevance, and efficiency criteria. For example, with so many people and institutions creating knowledge, it became and continues to be difficult to know what constitutes appropriate boundaries for comprehensiveness or how to reconcile comprehensiveness with selectivity, relevance, and efficiency.

The diversification of the sites of knowledge generation, from the historical base in universities and governments to a much broader set of institutions, has given more scope to other forms of knowledge creation. Local knowledge, often generated in the context of a specific problem or application, may be funded or even created by stakeholder groups in the course of identifying and promoting their particular interests. Unorganized actors, such as individuals who write comments in reaction to draft national-forest plans or maintain Web sites critiquing genetically engineered organisms, are less likely to be associated with formal knowledge-generating institutions. Local and preference-based knowledge generation is undertaken by a variety of participants in for-profit business, nonprofit organizations, and government agencies.

Universities are increasingly under pressure to make themselves more "relevant" to pressing social problems, so academicians have also participated more actively in these alternative forms of knowledge generation. The justification for the enormous funding and status of universities is based in part on the expectation that they will generate knowledge. The range of university specializations that can contribute to the creation of knowledge for environmental decision making is striking—including social science, engineering, biophysical sciences, veterinary science, medical science, epidemiology, law, and others. The post–World War II explosion in the number of U.S. university graduates transformed jobs that previously were held by nongraduates.[7] Greater opportunities for university education of engineers, scientists, and nontechnical graduates led to the democratization of higher education in terms of access to the highest credentials, but they also created a gap between these highly credentialed professional scientists and the lay public.

The growth in education parallels in part the diversification of research. Whereas research had been an elite activity prior to World War II, postwar research branched out to include a broader array of participants, including the business community, venture capitalists, patent lawyers, production engineers, research engineers, and scientists both inside and outside university settings. [8] As research moved toward greater applications, it was difficult to keep it confined to university departments or academic settings. New institutional arrangements led to links between government, industry, universities, and private companies.

Governments have historically played a dominant role in certain aspects of knowledge generation. Government agencies both fund an enormous amount of research and conduct it in government laboratories. Roughly twenty thousand U.S. federal scientists and engineers are classified as researchers[9]; more than thirty-two thousand federally employed scientists and engineers are in the "life sciences";[10] and the federal government devotes roughly $30 billion annually to fund scientific research in colleges and universities,[11] with considerable control over the foci and nature of this research. For most environmental indicators, whether they concern the use of land or the generation of pollutants, governments are the sole data source. Federal, state, and local governments also sponsor and conduct research, create reports, and facilitate meetings where knowledge creation takes place. Federal agencies as diverse as the Department of Defense, the Department of Energy, the EPA, the Department of Interior, the National Institutes of Health, the National Science Foundation, the Centers for Disease Control and Prevention, and the Department of Agriculture sponsor active research and development (R&D) programs that total billions of dollars annually. In a typical year in the middle of the first decade of the 2000s, the U.S. federal government budgeted roughly $2.0 billion for R&D on natural resources and the environment, a comparable amount for agriculture, and $1.6 billion for R&D on energy, with nearly $8 billion earmarked for "general science and basic research."[12] State and local governments similarly participate in research, independently or in conjunction with universities. State-level departments of transportation, wildlife, agriculture, environment, and natural resources, among others, often seek knowledge about various environmental phenomena that impact their programs or their constituencies. Local governments including soil- and water-conservation districts, planning departments, and city councils solicit the help of researchers and others to compile information about problems they face. Many local governments have environmental advisory committees that include local experts, including scientists. Study commissions abound, set up by federal, state, and local governments. Finally, international governmental organizations sponsor research through the United Nations, the World Bank, the European Union, the

International Union for the Conservation of Nature, and the Organization for Economic Cooperation and Development, to name just a few.

Nonprofit organizations' employment and funding of environmental scientists is another significant development. Although some institutions devoted to conducting research about various public-policy issues emerged early in the 1900s (e.g., the Carnegie Endowment for International Peace in 1910, the Brookings Institution in 1916, the Twentieth Century Fund in 1919), the rise of nonprofit "think tanks" really began with the RAND Corporation in 1945, financed largely through federal research contracts. Both Brookings and RAND work broadly on public-policy issues, including environmental topics, and the number of nonprofit organizations devoted exclusively to environmental issues began to grow after midcentury. Part of the mission of these institutions was to harness science, research, and other knowledge to assist in environmental protection. Other institutions emerged to focus predominantly on conservation and environmental protection. Perhaps the most successful in influencing environmental policy through research is the Washington-based think tank Resources for the Future, founded as a follow-up to the widely publicized 1952 report of the President's Commission on Materials Policy (otherwise known as the Paley Commission). The World Resources Institute, also based in Washington, has also been quite influential through its research on international environmental and conservation issues.

Some of these organizations try to maintain their credibility for objective research by eschewing advocacy, but others were established to take on advocacy roles and to generate knowledge not only to inform them, but to push a policy agenda. For instance, The Nature Conservancy, founded in 1951, works in all fifty states and more than thirty countries to protect biodiversity through collaborative, science-based planning. It has played a very important role in conducting Natural Heritage Inventories in which states or counties identify species or ecosystems of special importance and assess levels of threat. The Environmental Defense Fund (now called Environmental Defense), founded in 1967, generates and synthesizes science, economics, and law to address environmental problems. The Natural Resources Defense Council, established in 1970, integrates science and law to safeguard the earth's resources. The U.S. Public Interest Research Group was founded in 1972 to use research, advocacy, and organization to protect consumers. Environmental protection has been a large part of their action agenda and has spawned state-level research groups in forty-seven states and Washington, D.C. Numerous other advocacy-based groups—including the National Wildlife Federation, World Wildlife Fund, Conservation International, the Wilderness Society, and the Sierra Club, among many others—create and promote environmental knowledge.

The prevalence of these national groups should not obscure the importance of state-level and local groups that also participate in knowledge generation. For instance, local watershed groups, community forestry groups, and environmental justice organizations often participate in the consolidation and creation of knowledge to move their concerns onto more public agendas.

For-profit companies also engage in knowledge creation through their own research, participating in industry groups that sponsor or oversee laboratories and collaborations with governmental and nongovernmental entities. For example, the Electric Power Research Institute has become a major source of information for the electric utility industry, including work on environmental topics such as water use and greenhouse gas emissions. Over time, private firms have played a larger role in funding knowledge generation. In 1960, private firms in the United States supplied 42 percent of all expenditures for R&D, in comparison to 58 percent that came from the federal government. By 2006, industrially financed R&D constituted 65 percent of the total, with federal funding providing 23 percent.[13] Of course, much of the private-sector research is devoted to product development and process improvement.

The generation of knowledge by this multiplicity of actors is influenced by the actors and research funders' own value perspectives.[14] It is not unusual for generators of knowledge to analyze information, consolidate facts, or carry out original research to bolster policy positions they have already adopted or are thinking of adopting. For example, the Conservation Foundation, a Washington-based environmental think tank, did some of the earliest work on effects of trade liberalization on the environment and came to the conclusion that companies rarely moved overseas to avoid environmental regulation.[15] Along with other research, including work by academics, this work helped persuade several environmental groups to support the North American Free Trade

Agreement. Similarly, in the 1970s the National Forest Products Association sponsored work on future timber supply and demand in the United States and found that there was insufficient wood to meet future demand. This finding helped support policies that gave tax breaks for reforestation. The Wilderness Society analyzed the economics of national-forest timber sales and found a preponderance of below-cost sales, which led them to advocate for a reduced timber cut on the national forests.

Why is it that well-trained, reputable scientists generate knowledge that closely mirrors the views of their employers or funders? Are knowledge generators being corrupted by external political forces, or are they simply slaves to available funding? Scholars have pointed to the importance of compatibility in institutional, professional, and personal values.[16] In other words, knowledge generators gravitate to organizations with mutual underlying values in order to research questions consistent with their personal intellectual interests. These values can include such fundamental aspects as how high a standard of proof is necessary for accepting an environmental hazard. Thus, the scientists who are comfortable only with a high standard of proof gravitate to business and some government agencies, whereas those who accept risk at a fairly low standard of proof gravitate to environmental organizations or other, more environmental-oriented agencies.

Having said this, we must also point out that without funding and institutional support, "compatible" scientists will not be able to work on their preferred lines of research. Funding organizations such as the National Science Foundation, the National Institutes of Health, the EPA, and foundations can often shape the research agenda and thus the direction of knowledge generation. These organizations can not only set agendas for research, but influence the expression of the professional and personal values within the knowledge-generating community. Both the knowledge-generation agenda and the problem definitions held by funders and environmental knowledge generators in turn influence policymakers and stakeholders' corresponding agendas and problem definitions (and vice versa). For example, the Pew Foundation has had an important influence on research on climate change and ocean management. And Exxon Mobil has encouraged researchers who take a skeptical position on the anthropogenic contribution to global warming. As scientists, practitioners, and analysts focus on particular issues, their communications with one another and with broader audiences are also likely to influence policymakers' focus of attention.

Another implication of the wider variety of institutions and actors generating knowledge for different purposes and operating under different constraints is that boundaries blur as "hybrid science" is created. This plurality of production results in uncertainty in how to evaluate knowledge. Multiple standards apply and must be traded off against each other. The implication is that there must be give and take as different value sets are shaped and shared within an inherently political process.

Complexity and Uncertainty

Knowledge from the scientific process is generated with great care and effort, but it is nonetheless uncertain and complex. The growth and resulting complexity of knowledge contribute to both the fragmentation of knowledge and the increased difficulty of coordination among institutions involved in environmental protection. The complexity of natural and socioeconomic systems feeds into the uncertainty associated with knowledge. Scientific uncertainty can stem from data limitations, weak theory, or random variation.

We have argued that the intersection of complexity and uncertainty means that fully satisfying the comprehensiveness criterion for knowledge generation is impossible. One might assume that experts—disciplined by the scrutiny of other experts, the need to maintain reputation and credibility, and the internalized norm of conducting and reporting research as objectively as possible—should be able to provide a check in the system for determining when knowledge is sufficiently comprehensive. However, these factors do not play as great a role as one might expect because the complexity of environmental systems means that complete analysis is impossible. Given the impossibility of comprehensiveness, selectivity is unavoidable, giving space for different predispositions to color the analysis in ways that cannot be fully identified or criticized. Therefore, this complexity becomes not only a major challenge for knowledge, but also a crucial factor in understanding why scientific disagreements defy resolution and how values influence the environmental policy process.

Complexity Complexity can be defined as the multiplicity of inter-connected relationships and levels.[17] It poses a paradox for knowledge generation. On the one hand, assessing complexity promises to deliver a more sophisticated understanding of environmental phenomena. On the other hand, complexity makes it difficult to satisfy the comprehensive-ness criterion. How do we know we are sufficiently comprehensive when there is so much to be known about a topic? In other words, how can we apply the selectivity and efficiency criteria appropriately?

Complexity in environmental knowledge generation comes from two sources. First, knowledge is generated by a variety of disciplines and specialists. Hydrologists, geologists, silviculturists, economists, biologists, soil scientists, geneticists, sociologists, spatial technology experts, historians, and policy-oriented contextual specialists, among others, contribute to a collective understanding of environmental problems. The complexity of ecosystems and the knowledge required to understand these systems are enormous, which makes knowledge integration more difficult.[18] Consider, for instance, the considerable amount of scientific information needed to understand climate change. Ecosystems and social systems are nested, from the microscopic to the global level, in such complicated ways that understanding the interactions has prompted the development of remarkably complex models. Ocean currents, atmospheric reflectance, and vegetation growth, among other topics, are relevant. However, few if any scientists have the complete knowledge or ability to integrate these dynamics into accurate models that replicate the complexity of the whole system. Assessing the validity of the complex models is often beyond the capacity of individual or even groups of scientists, let alone nonscientists. Taking into account the complexity of environmental problems is appropriate, but it may also require an inordinate amount of knowledge and analytic processing. As a consequence, an additional level of uncertainty arises from the inevitably imperfect integration of different types and levels of knowledge. Environmental scientists thus face the very awkward dilemma that they cannot credibly vouch for these models' validity. However, the environmental policy process requires policymakers and the public to form judgments about these scientists' credibility.

Second, environmental knowledge generation is complex because the current institutional infrastructure for generating knowledge is fragmented, which increases the difficulty of coordination among institutions involved in environmental protection. On the U.S. federal level, diverse programs and agencies that oversee knowledge generation have evolved from uncoordinated statutory mandates, resulting in a patchwork of knowledge-generation entities. Institutional complexity results from a matrix of shared and overlapping responsibilities among intra- and interorganizational structures of resource-management agencies,[19] which can make coordination among various levels of government more complicated.

Consider, for instance, the fragmentation in knowledge generation related to "green" building and development practices. Engineers, hydrologists, architects, planners, building material and equipment suppliers, horticulturalists, builders, wildlife biologists, home buyers, and others create or analyze knowledge relevant to green building practices. Architects, engineers, energy agencies, and equipment manufacturers generate knowledge about energy use. Wildlife agencies generate knowledge about how building practices can minimize impact on terrestrial and aquatic habitats. Forestry agencies generate knowledge on how to preserve tree canopies and green infrastructure. At the same time, water-quality agencies create information about how to prevent storm water runoff, minimize sedimentation in waterways, and establish buffers to lessen erosion. The experts span the public, private, nonprofit, and research sectors.

This diffuse knowledge generation makes utilizing the knowledge difficult for end users who seek to acquire it. Redundancies within agencies or programs also make knowledge consolidation and integration a challenge. Wildlife, trees, and water interact, but the fragmentation of agency and organization structures makes it difficult to gauge the comprehensiveness of existing knowledge.

When environmental knowledge is disorganized or fragmented, existing information is not efficiently integrated to play the most constructive role in the decision-making process. Analytic resources are wasted, and knowledge is not efficiently deployed by those who would make better policies if they were exposed to it. For example, the U.S. Green Building Council, developer of the now famous Leadership in Energy and Environmental Design (LEED) standard for commercial buildings, has found that there is also a demand for LEED standards for homes and neighborhoods. Enormous expertise on both of these topics already existed among architects and planners, respectively, but until the U.S. Green Building Council established its certification program, the needed centralization and standardization was lacking.

Legislation and legal frameworks reinforce the fragmentation of information generation and narrowly constrain the ability to think more comprehensively about some environmental problems. The U.S. Endangered Species Act (ESA) of 1973 is a case in point. The ESA narrows data collection to focus only on the listed species and their habitat—to the exclusion of other relevant information. This focus can be an impediment to adopting policies that would protect tracts of land that might contain not only the target species, but a number of others, listed and unlisted.

In contrast, other laws are so comprehensive that the generation and collection of information becomes unmanageable. These criticisms have been leveled at the National Environmental Policy Act (NEPA) of 1969 and the data-collection requirements for environmental impact statements and environmental assessments.[20] To evaluate the impacts of a proposed federal action, an agency must collect data—in environmental impact statements and in the environmental assessment process—about all the proposed alternatives under consideration as well as the cumulative impacts. Given the proposed project and scope of action, some of these data-collection efforts are enormous.

In addition to these rather mundane reasons why complexity is difficult to address, the very nature of formal science is itself also an obstacle to information generation. Formal science has been very successful in addressing "problems of simplicity" (systems that can be modeled through the interaction of pairs of variables affecting very small numbers of units). It has prevailed over analytic challenges marked by "disorganized complexity" (many units or variables that are not organized in interdependent ways) through statistical approaches that capture general tendencies. Formal science is far less well equipped, however, to address deeply complex problems, characterized by impacts of substantial numbers of interactive variables.[21] A host of environmental problems is subject to organized complexity as multiple biological, geophysical, chemical, economic, and sociopolitical variables interact with one another in influencing large numbers of individual plants, animals, humans, and institutions. Ronald Brunner and Garry Brewer elegantly demonstrate that even complete understanding of the relationships among pairs of variables in complex systems often does not permit the prediction of outcomes unless parameters are precisely known[22]. Thus, uncertainty about the details of the context undermines the predictive power even of totally correct theory.

Coping with Uncertainty Scientific uncertainty is often invoked as the justification for knowledge generation in environmental decision making. The line of reasoning is as follows. Science is a set of verifiable facts and theories about reality. If we know more about this verifiable reality, then we can take action to resolve an environmental controversy. In essence, if we can reduce the scientific uncertainty, then the course of action will become clearer. As a consequence of this framing, the "[r]eduction of uncertainty is a central, perhaps the central goal of scientific research carried out in the context of environmental controversies."[23] Policymakers and scientists often find common cause in the doctrine of "scientific management"—the cluster of outlooks and practices that emphasize the reduction of scientific uncertainty, research that focuses on general, aggregated results, and theory that seeks general laws about the relationships in human and natural systems.[24] The driver of the grand designs by which scientific management structures its decision making is the scientific and technical knowledge analyzed and presented by experts.

Scholars and practitioners differ with regard to different types of uncertainty. Type I uncertainty represents random or stochastic variability in the outcome of a repeatable experiment.[25] This type of uncertainty is associated with playing a slot machine or flipping a coin. It can be quantified by gathering information, but it cannot be reduced. Every time you flip the coin, you will have a 50 percent probability of getting heads, and you cannot change the uncertainty by knowing more about the coin or the conditions under which it is tossed.[26]

Type II uncertainty is due to ignorance or incomplete knowledge that affects our ability to understand a given phenomenon.[27] We may lack information or sound theory or both. Type II uncertainty provides the primary framing for understanding how scientific information fits into knowledge generation for environmental decision making. If we know more, then we can reduce Type II uncertainty. There are many examples of where the reduction of Type II uncertainty has played a positive role in environmental decision making. One early example—a classic in environmental health—was the discovery in the mid–nineteenth century that wells polluted by sewage, not atmospheric transmission, was the cause of cholera epidemics.[28] Another was the discovery by A. J. Haagen-Smit in the late 1950s that the "smog" plaguing Los Angeles was directly related to the action of sunlight on automobile emissions. Until these discoveries, policies were ineffective or even counterproductive. A more recent example is the knowledge behind the Montreal Protocol on Substances That Deplete the Ozone Layer (1989), which mandated the phasing out of chlorofluorocarbons (CFCs) because they depleted ozone high in the atmosphere. In this case, science provided both clarification and the impetus for decisive political action.

A particularly important subtype of Type II uncertainty is "parametric" uncertainty. Simply put, even if the relationships among relevant variables are well understood, the relative weight (or parameter) of each effect may be uncertain. Thus, for the climatologist who is trying to predict global climate change, the challenge is that global warming can be caused by the well-understood greenhouse effect, global cooling can be triggered by greater density of reflective matter in the atmosphere (the albedo effect, the extreme version being "nuclear winter"), and other variations in Earth's temperature can be caused by variations in the sun's radiation. The question is what magnitude each effect will have. It took many years before global environmental assessments crystallized a scientific consensus that human activity was causing significant global warming.[29] By the same token, for the social scientist trying to understand conservation efforts, two effects on public behavior can be expected from the fact that the Kyoto Protocol to reduce greenhouse gas emissions was ratified by some countries, but not by others. On the one hand, the ratification will impress upon some residents and firms of ratifying countries that global climate change is so serious that they must take individual actions to conserve energy beyond the limitations imposed by the protocol. On the other hand, the failure on the part of the United States and other countries to accept these limitations will provoke some residents of ratifying countries to reject as unfair any steps they must take to curb their expanding energy consumption. Both of these dynamics are perfectly reasonable; that is, we would expect some individuals to behave according to the first pattern, others according to the second. Yet the projection of energy consumption is still unclear because of uncertainty as to what weight to give to each pattern. Although science can reduce Type II uncertainty, it typically cannot accurately gauge the remaining Type I uncertainty. Alexander Shlyakhter reports that experts who are projecting population growth, energy use, and other broad trends underestimate the range of their confidence intervals by factors of two to ten times, depending on the nature of the trends being forecast. This underestimation is understandable, given that one's assessment of uncertainty has to be based on what one knows, not on what is beyond one's ken. Shlyakhter uses the insightful expression "unsuspected uncertainty."[30]

Although scientific uncertainty can often be reduced, the pace of scientific findings do not necessarily coincide with decision-making demands for timeliness. For instance, the 1980 National Acid Precipitation Assessment Program (NAPAP) was devised as a policy-oriented research exercise to generate knowledge sufficient to achieve scientific consensus on the causes and effects of acidic deposition. Although NAPAP science reduced uncertainty related to some acid-deposition processes, the final report was not completed until 1991, after the passage of the Clean Air Act Amendments of 1990, which dealt aggressively with emission of acid-precursor sulfur compounds. The justification for the research was to provide data, analyses, and assessment to inform the debate on reauthorization of the Clean Air Act, but a combination of missed deadlines and legislative impatience resulted in the legislation's being passed before the NAPAP final reports could be issued.[31] The NAPAP Oversight Review Board conceded that "science is an on-going process that does not fit neatly into a policy-driven timetable and may be antithetical to it" and emphasized that although science can "inform" decision-making processes, it is not a substitute for those processes.[32] The scientists involved clearly reduced uncertainty about some aspects of acid deposition, but making the science available for timely decision making was a greater challenge.

What seemed to be certain yesterday might conversely be recognized as less certain today or in the future due to advances in understanding. This kind of fluctuation from confidence to ignorance and back again seems to have characterized research in the broad field of environmental determinants of cancer, where scientists have alternately emphasized the role of particular chemical compounds and each individual's genetic makeup. Because the type of uncertainty can change over time, we can talk about uncertainty only in the present tense. Consequently, there is debate in academic communities over what constitutes inherent randomness versus what is simply unknown or unexamined about the system under study.[33] Some philosophers of science believe there is only one type of uncertainty, that which stems from lack of knowledge (Type II),[34] and thus do not make a distinction between the different types of uncertainty (Type I and Type II). However, the distinction is important in guiding the generation of knowledge helpful for decision making. Should research focus more on gathering data to propel existing theory, developing better theory, or bringing relationships into theoretical models to try to understand what were previously defined as random shocks?

Adding to uncertainty is the fact that environmental systems undergo continual flux, rendering old relationships no longer valid. For example, the relationship between humidity and forest fire risk changes with the density of diseased trees in the forest. Thus, a model may be fully correct in explaining outcomes to date but still fail to predict future trends and the impact of policy interventions insofar as conditions and understanding have changed. Gilberto Gallopín and his colleagues argue that because complex systems exhibit irreducible uncertainty, knowledge obtained through insight and understanding is not synonymous with the capacity for prediction, and awareness of risk may not necessarily lead to the capacity to intervene in order to reduce or control risk.[35] These insights suggest that a different approach to science is needed, including a more reflexive attitude about risk and how societal choices are framed. In short, formal science has been overly optimistic about the prospects of predictability and control.[36]

One implication of the limitations of predictive science is that policy measures based on even the best-validated and most credible scientific knowledge may fail. Environmental decision making needs to be nimble in reacting to failures, and knowledge of how to cope with uncertainty becomes as important as the reductionist knowledge of the laboratory or the simulation model. For example, strategies for responding to the still-unknown magnitude of global climate change—diversifying crops, hardening storm-prone sites, and inducing people to move from highly vulnerable areas—will not come out of formal science alone, although the scientific effort is an essential part of the generation of relevant knowledge to develop effective responses.

Another implication is that the assessment of risk levels itself has an inherent element of uncertainty. The brilliance of probability theory has been to reflect stochastic (i.e., random) variability. Yet probability estimates cannot fully address the uncertainty regarding whether the understanding that generated the probability estimates is itself in error. This factor explains, in part, why experts are consistently overly optimistic about the accuracy of their own predictions.[37] In a world where climate change, bioengineered life forms, and long-lasting radioactive and toxic wastes have permanent perturbation potential, we need to take this overconfidence into account. As Gallopín and his coauthors put it, "absence of proof of danger is not the same as the proof of the absence of danger."[38]

Decisions must proceed even in light of uncertainty, which has implications for how we deal with the comprehensiveness criterion. If something is unknowable in terms of current means of knowing (Type I), then it is certainly excludable for comprehensiveness purposes. If something is knowable but not yet known (Type II), then research can enhance comprehensiveness. What knowledge generators believe is important to know is not objectively determined, but rather culturally defined based on the participants involved in the process and their views about complexity. Thus, our collective understanding of uncertainty provides the boundaries for what can and cannot be considered comprehensive in the generation of knowledge for environmental decision making.

Complexity with Uncertainty   Greater comprehensiveness in knowledge generation may exacerbate problems in environmental decision making when additional knowledge reveals complexity in natural and social systems. Two conditions illustrate how more scientific information can aggravate rather than alleviate problems in environmental decision making. The first condition occurs when more information reveals unknown complexities in natural systems.

Uncertainty is inevitable in complex natural and social systems, in part due to the dynamics of coevolving systems that involve both humans and nature. Managed resources change as a result of human intervention, which means that surprises are inevitable and new uncertainties will emerge.[39] In addition, ecological thinking has changed in the past three decades to recognize that nature is seldom linear and that ecosystem processes are filled with uncertainty.[40] A generation ago, ecologists believed ecosystems tended toward a single, knowable "climax."[41] Current thinking, in contrast, emphasizes random events (fire, disease) and the subsequent "path dependency" that sets the ecosystem onto a path that differs from what would have occurred under other possible conditions or events. In these situations, as more scientific information is made available, the meaning of that information may be unclear, leading to ambiguity in the interpretation of the new information. Data consequently do not always contribute to improving estimates of probability and may even increase the perception or recognition of uncertainty. As Fikret Berkes, Johan Colding, and Carl Folke suggest, there is a fundamental difference between the view that quantitative prediction is difficult and data intensive and the view that nature is not in equilibrium and inherently unpredictable. Therefore, no analysis is immune from attack for lack of comprehensiveness.[42]

As complexity increases, our confidence in what we know can become less certain. In the NAPAP example, scientists focused on acid deposition as the main causal agent but found that dieback and decline of forests were a function of more complex, multistage processes that involved the interaction of multiple variables.[43] No firm causal link was found between acid rain and forest death or decline. One scientist commented that they were "trying to track down what may be a relatively small increment of stress, superimposed on a complex set of natural stresses. That background of stresses may vary from stand to stand and even from tree to tree."[44] Because the impact of acid deposition on forests was considered more complex at the end of study than at the beginning, the findings were perceived as of little use for decision-making purposes.[45]

Another example illustrating how more information may reveal added complexity is the case of the Yucca Mountain Radioactive Waste Site in Nevada. Even after twenty years of research on the rates of water flow through rock at the Yucca Mountain Site, recognized uncertainties have only increased.[46] Beginning in the 1980s, hydrologists estimated rates of water flow to be between 4.0 and 10.0 millimeters per year. Further research over the next twelve years reduced these estimates to 0.1 to 1.0 millimeter per year. This final range was sufficient for the U.S. Department of Energy to meet the standards set by the EPA to proceed with the construction of the site. At that time, knowledge about water-flow rates had achieved the "status of conventional wisdom."[47] To confirm this conventional wisdom, the Department of Energy drilled a tunnel to test whether the moisture in rocks at the actual level of the proposed repository was consistent with the estimates. The rocks told a different story. The tests indicated that the percolation of water was ten times faster than estimated in the previous studies. Estimates were then revised to state that probable water flow rates were between 1.0 and 30.0 millimeters per year. However, repeat studies have yielded inconsistent results.[48] In this case, the generation of new scientific information about the conditions at Yucca Mountain resulted in more uncertainty rather than less.

The recognition of complexity in human/environment interactions and the accompanying uncertainty make it challenging to think about what constitutes sufficient comprehensiveness in knowledge generation to move forward in a timely manner in a decision-making process. There are numerous examples of decisions made in the face of increasingly recognized complexity and uncertainty. As mentioned earlier, the NAPAP study failed to produce a final report in time to inform the Clean Air Act Amendments of 1990, despite more than a decade of research by hundreds of scientists at a cost of $630 million dollars.[49] The studies attempting to link acid deposition to forest damage were in any case inconclusive. And yet, even in the presence of uncertainty, President George H. W. Bush made a decision, working in conjunction with the Senate majority leader George Mitchell (D-MI), to support and pass new clean-air legislation and to address the problem of acid deposition. Despite the remaining and increased uncertainty in the Yucca Mountain example, President George W. Bush likewise made the decision to sign a resolution in 2002 that allowed the Department of Energy to apply for a license to construct the nuclear waste repository at the site. As Daniel Sarewitz puts it, "Uncertainty about facts need not be an impediment to political resolution of heated controversy."[50] We can reject the idea that scientific uncertainty must be resolved before actions should be taken because no amount of data or theory will be able to eliminate all uncertainty.

The second condition under which knowledge generation as an input will exacerbate problems in environmental decision making holds when additional scientific information highlights differences between competing bodies of knowledge and expands the realm of what is known and unknown. Although one definition of uncertainty is the lack of scientific understanding or incomplete knowledge, another is the lack of coherence among competing understandings.[51] The generation of different types of knowledge can thus fuel, rather than slake, environmental controversies. Consider that plant geneticists and molecular biologists view the debate over genetically engineered organisms (GEOs) through very different disciplinary lenses than those utilized by ecologists or population biologists. Plant geneticists and molecular biologists tend to value the benefits from GEOs, such as better resistance to environmental stresses, greater agricultural productivity, lower input of fertilizers and pesticides, and crops that can remediate soils and watersheds.[52] Ecologists and population biologists, however, are more likely to view the risks posed by the unintended complex interactions that may result from uncontrolled introgression of genes into other species. They may also be more likely to focus on the possibility of harmful mutations of inserted genes, competition and breeding with wild species, and negative effects of insecticidal GEOs on nontarget organisms such as birds and pollinating insects.[53] Additional scientific information—generated by both groups of researchers in enormous and growing quantity—may consequently reinforce value disputes and competing interests rather than harmonize them.[54]

These tendencies also can occur when local knowledge clashes with scientific knowledge. Brian Wynne cataloged the contrasting knowledge bases of sheep farmers in Umbria, United Kingdom, with scientists studying the radioactive fallout on the farmers' pastures after the 1986 Chernobyl meltdown.[55] The scientists assured the local farmers that their sheep would be fine a few weeks after the fallout was assimilated into local soils and excreted by the sheep. The farmers, referring to a similar event in 1957 when a military installation dump was incinerated, were skeptical. And in fact the scientists' soil models did end up misspecifying the impact on the sheep because they assumed the wrong soil type. The sheep were rendered worthless to the farmers because the radioactivity never decayed according to the models. Knowledge generated by the sheep farmers reinforced their skeptical view of the government and its ability to look out for the locals' welfare. Knowledge generated by the scientists reinforced their desire to fix the model to create something that accurately modeled the impact on the sheep. The new input of realizing the wrong soil type only widened the gap between the different groups.

Biases in Knowledge Generation

Systematic biases that arise in the way we investigate or frame problems can make us overlook, neglect, or purposefully exclude some types of information. We cover three biases here: the rise of benefit-cost analysis and expert valuation; the preference for generalized versus contextual information generation and analysis; and the neglect of local, traditional, and indigenous information. These biases affect the type of information that is generated as inputs into the environmental decision-making process and make it difficult to satisfy the comprehensiveness, dependability, relevance, and openness criteria.

Benefit-Cost Analysis and Expert Valuation   To illustrate the deep difficulties of even the seemingly most basic knowledge related to environmental regulation, we can examine the knowledge needs of benefit-cost analysis. After all, what is more straightforward than balancing the sum of benefits of a proposed regulation against its costs? Formal benefit-cost analysis, as a specific economic approach that requires the monetization of benefits and costs, was developed in the early 1950s on the premise that it would bring rationality and consistency to government investments in water projects. Economists and international development agencies subsequently extended it to projects of all sorts, from investment in highways to educational investments in "human capital." The use of benefit-cost analysis throughout the U.S. federal government was mandated in President Ronald Reagan's 1981 Executive Order 12291 "Federal Regulation," and reinforced by President Bill Clinton's 1993 Executive Order 12866, "Regulatory Planning and Review."[56] Since then, all subsequent federal directives on how to implement benefit-cost analysis have reinforced the necessity to conduct systematic valuation and have promoted the extension of valuation to the projected consequences of the regulations under consideration.[57] These trends are not limited to the United States. In Europe, the expansion of environmental concern has prompted many efforts to develop and implement similar valuation techniques.[58] Through the efforts of powerful international entities such as the United Nations Food and Agriculture Organization, the World Bank, and the regional development banks, as well as of bilateral donors, many developing countries have been incorporating valuation in project and program appraisal methods.[59] Although the formal assessment of net benefits of policy options rarely dictates the policy choice, these assessments are common, and policymakers are increasingly under pressure to take heed of them. Benefit-cost analysis is very straightforward when the costs are monetary (government expenditures) and the benefits are economic goods sold in markets (maintenance of a recreational fishery). The analysis is more difficult when the benefits are not marketed (survival of an endangered species). Economists have displayed considerable ingenuity in assigning values to these non-market goods, including the intangibles associated with them (value to the public of keeping a species from extinction). We use the term *expert valuation* to describe the whole range of these valuation techniques, recognizing that some benefits are far easier to value than are others.

Expert valuation of public preferences is increasingly entrenched as a means for generating information as a policy input.[60] Supporters of valuation techniques place a premium on giving technocrats power in decision making, while painting members of the public as ignorant of risk, overly emotional, easily manipulated, and incapable of realistically assessing risk probabilities.[61] Because environmental policymaking calls for knowledge about stakeholders' values and preferences, gauging these values and preferences is a central analytic requirement. Although very few people are "antienvironment," decision makers need to know the importance of environmental goals for stakeholders who also have many other possible priorities: economic production, expansion of housing opportunities, or merely holding onto the money that would be spent for environmental protection or conservation projects. This challenge has generated a proliferation of research and methodological developments.[62] Economists have recently made methodological advances in capturing these trade offs through "revealed-preference" or "stated-preference" approaches using a range of methods tied to econometric analysis or survey techniques.[63]

For the purposes of information generation, benefit-cost analysis and expert valuation raise problems on several fronts in knowledge generation. Perhaps most important, expert valuation may supplant the direct expression of citizens' policy preferences, thereby keeping important information from entering the decision-making process. Knowledge generation in such cases is not sufficiently comprehensive or open. Conventional valuation techniques do not seek to know what *policies* citizens prefer, but rather how citizens value the possible consequences of policies. One risk posed by expert valuation to the expression of public input is that the input may not reflect the public as members of a community interested in expressing community values and policy preferences, but rather treats the public as passive objects for the experts' assessment. Another risk is that the methods may isolate the preferences for environmental outcomes from other factors that the public may wish to take into account. In short, expert valuation is a technocratic vehicle for generating information about public preferences and may preempt more robust forms of public input in environmental policymaking while also presenting decision makers with a particularly narrow sense of the public interest and preferences.[64]

The rise of benefit-cost analysis and expert valuation also favors particular forms of information, most notably quantitative approaches over more qualitative and rights-based appeals.[65] A status hierarchy in terms of how knowledge should be generated places quantitative, benefit-cost data in highest regard, which again poses a challenge in meeting the comprehensiveness criterion. Benefits and costs of finite magnitudes run counter to the logic of demands couched as absolute rights, such as the right to be free from pollution or the right a species has to survive. The assertion of rights is essentially a demand that denies the relevance of benefit-cost analysis; therefore, such an assertion cannot be represented with a finite valuation. For instance, in creating the 1970 Clean Air Act and the 1972 Federal Water Pollution Control Act, Congress explicitly rejected a benefit-cost approach to goal setting. Instead, the Clean Air Act prioritized the protection of human health, and the Federal Water Pollution Control Act emphasized achieving fishable and swimmable water quality without consideration of the benefit-cost balance. The 1990 amendments to the Clean Air Act require "maximum achievable control technology" even if the costs of employing the technologies exceed the benefits. The Clean Water Act requires the best available *economically achievable* technology for reducing toxic emissions. Although this criterion seems to balance benefits and costs, it falls far short of a societal benefit-cost analysis because the social benefits of controlling some toxic discharges may still exceed control costs even under the criterion of being economically achievable. This tangle of legislative provisions requiring that some notion of maximum protection trump the benefit-cost analysis and of executive orders requiring that the benefit-cost analysis be undertaken has placed the EPA and other environmental agencies in a very awkward position.

Valuation and benefit-cost analysis are also subject to the question of whether environmental values as captured by any technical valuation approach are stable enough and consistent enough with how people think to be meaningful. This query in turn calls into question the ability of this sort of new information to satisfy the dependability criterion. Benefit-cost analysis presumes that the relevant stakeholders hold relatively stable values. Yet Mark Sagoff has argued that the application of benefit-cost analysis fails to convey the intensity of commitment and how preferences are alterable, especially in a democratic context. Sagoff argues that "[l]ike actual markets, democracy does not take preferences as they come but alters them; for example, it subjects them to public scrutiny and debate. . . . The values emerging from democratic decision-making are supposed to differ from those entering it; the capacity of political debate to transform views even lends legitimacy to the political process."[66] As a consequence, the data that are generated from a static benefit-cost analysis and from the expert-valuation process may not be valid or reliable.

Finally, expert valuation may undervalue ecosystem services, thereby calling into question the dependability of the data generated as an input in the decision-making process. Agencies and policymakers generally regard stated-preference approaches (e.g., contingent valuation) as less rigorous than revealed-preference approaches (e.g., hedonic pricing), even though a stated-preference approach may do a better job of capturing behavior that reflects public welfare rather than individual private interest ("public-regardedness").[67] This methodological bias is currently reflected in the discrepancy between the proliferation of articles on stated-preference approaches and the secondary status that stated-preference results are typically accorded in actual applied valuation efforts. It is also reflected in the perspectives of the individuals within agencies charged to use benefit-cost analysis. Douglas Hall, deputy administrator of the U.S. National Oceanographic and Atmospheric Agency, stated in 1995 that "while we firmly believe that CVM [contingent valuation method—a common stated-preference technique] is a reliable economic tool, it has been seldom used and is of less significance to the natural resource damage assessment process than the debate regarding it would indicate."[68] Leonard Shabman and Kurt Stephenson explain the underuse of stated-preference approaches by noting that "only when a reasonable consensus and confidence develops among decision makers over the usefulness of any technique will the technique play a significant role in the collective choice process."[69] This tendency may seem to reflect a choice by policymakers, but they typically form their judgments on technique through signals from the experts.

Generalized and Contextual Knowledge Generation   Different methods for identifying, measuring, and analyzing information influence which information ultimately is viewed as most important and therefore most likely to be used in a decision process. One strategy for agencies to manage information from diverse sources is to try to aggregate, generalize, or homogenize, and many methodological approaches strive for aggregated measures that neglect differences.[70] These approaches include surveys, interviews, content analysis, analysis of economic choices, and quantitative indicators—all of which are used to gain a better understanding of the public's values and objectives. Information-generation and analysis methods inherently reflect assumptions about the data. For instance, conventional correlation and regression analysis is frequently used to analyze data on values and objectives. The objective of using more conventional statistical analysis is that it looks at how one variable, measured across the entire sample, relates to the other variables similarly measured. Thus, it yields overall patterns; for example, wealthier people tend to value ecosystem preservation more highly than do lower-income people. An alternative approach (referred to as "Q analysis" to distinguish it from "R analysis," or the conventional "Pearson *r*" correlation coefficient) is to use factor analysis to discover different subsets of individuals within the entire group that hold similar and dissimilar views. It is a more contextual mode of analysis that can provide researchers, policymakers, and practitioners with information about how public values and objectives are perceived by various subgroups, facilitating the identification of similar perspectives or views within each subgroup.[71] If a researcher uses a methodological approach or technique that supports aggregation and generalization, then a more contextual analysis of the variation within the data set is precluded. Focusing on either generalized or contextual information generation to the exclusion of the other makes it difficult to satisfy the comprehensiveness and dependability criteria.

Although generalized data help further understanding about broad trends, they tell us little about the prevalence or intensity of divergent perspectives. They can obscure points of conflict and may lead to false beliefs or expectations about agreement on goals or objectives. Aggregated data can also hide possibilities for consensus among otherwise divergent viewpoints, thus constraining opportunities for agreement. Yet generalized analysis is far more accepted in most social science circles, largely because it seems to capture overall patterns more comprehensively. A status hierarchy is implied, and scientists tend to seek credibility by complying with this hierarchy. This tendency reflects a penchant for "large n" samples, the desire to generalize to the entire population under examination, and a preference for familiar methodologies over unfamiliar ones.

As an example of the tendency to homogenize both criteria and relevant information, the Government Performance and Results Act (GPRA) of 1993 was enacted to improve the efficiency and effectiveness of federal programs by creating a system that establishes clear objectives for performance and measurements of program outcomes. The GPRA requires federal agencies to focus on specified program outcomes, quality service, and customer satisfaction by requiring strategic planning and performance measures based on identified objectives.[72] It brings to the forefront the importance of determining what an agency values within a framework of explicitly detailed values and objectives. Such legislation presumes, however, that values and objectives are held uniformly and are easily measured to facilitate clear feedback for improved program performance. Dealing with directives such as the GPRA creates challenges for environmental and natural-resource agencies that must distill measurable and tractable values and objectives from among many competing options. Moreover, the impetus to find a single dominant value or objective fails to reflect the complexity embodied in environmental decision making and management. The drive to homogenize values and objectives does a disservice to what may be clearly distinctive groups of values and objectives, thereby inhibiting more dependable data generation.

Multiple methods of inquiry reveal different perspectives about values.[73] A more complete understanding of values can result in better trend descriptions, less erroneous diagnosis of problems, and fewer misspecifications of alternatives. Appreciation for the diversity of perspectives about values and objectives reveals the weaknesses in policies such as the GPRA that oversimplify how to hold agencies accountable. Better understanding of the values and objectives of environmental management can lead to a more accurate understanding of current conflicts and enhance the capacity to mediate future conflicts.

Local, Traditional, and Indigenous Knowledge   In environmental decision making, centralized, conventional scientific information is often privileged over local, traditional, or indigenous knowledge. Bruno Latour's definition of science entails ideas that are generated and circulated globally through journal articles, equations, maps, charts, and the interaction of international scientific communities.[74] This conventional definition of science assumes that knowledge is not considered science if it fails to circulate in these ways. It also implies that conventional science is the only universally valid source of knowledge. Yet the superiority of scientific knowledge has now been called into question.[75]

A growing body of research has begun to challenge the primacy of conventional scientific knowledge and science-based technological practices in a variety of projects and points to the importance of local ways of knowing and relating to the natural world.[76] This change in view raises issues about accountability and the dependability of the information generated for policymaking. Experts can be wrong; the costs of policies based on their input can be heightened insofar as the experts are overconfident in their judgments, which can lead to inadequately hedged policies. Furthermore, local knowledge, based on closer monitoring of ecosystem behavior, can contribute to the creation of more sustainable environmental practices.[77] The exclusion of local, traditional, indigenous knowledge makes the dependability, comprehensiveness, and openness criteria difficult to satisfy.

The exclusion of other sources of environmental knowledge from the formal definition of "science" is paradoxically a risk for science itself. A sharp distinction between the presumably definitive knowledge generated by conventionally credentialed scientists and the "amateur" knowledge held by others may lead to the beliefs that science has to find all the answers and that if it cannot, it has failed. When science has not delivered definitive answers—as in the cases of Yucca Mountain or global climate change—citizens are likely to come to distrust experts, whether from government or industry. The insularity of conventional scientific research and the dissemination of its findings are also likely to deepen public distrust on the grounds that formal science is both flawed and undemocratic.[78] A healthier conception of knowledge generation would hold that there is a continuum of knowledge generation from the least formally structured knowledge based on practice to the most structured efforts carried out under the stringent protocols that credentialed scientists follow. So the question is not whether formal science is superior, but rather how formal science and other forms of knowledge can be most constructively integrated for policymaking.

Local, traditional, or indigenous knowledge is often defined as having a place-based or contextual character.[79] It includes knowledge about local context, specific characteristics, circumstances or events, and the experiential understanding of their meaning.[80] The development literature often defines this type of knowledge as "indigenous" because it implies a practice of knowledge making through experiential learning rather than through acquisition of information in a specific place.[81]

Starting around 1980, the shift toward incorporating indigenous or local knowledge in environmental and natural-resource management was a response to the emphasis in previous decades on centralized, technically oriented solutions for development. The latter efforts were seen as failing to improve the plight of the world's peasants and small farmers.[82] In reaction, local knowledge and institutions began to be seen less as obstacles to development and more as elements to be incorporated and included in development.[83]

The justifications for including local sources for knowledge generation in environmental decision making begin with the fact that in terms of the focus of attention, local knowledge often emphasizes lower-cost, more efficient intervention options.[84] In addition, because local knowledge is based on different methods of investigating reality, it can balance the tendency toward reductionism and professional biases. [85] Finally, local knowledge contributes additional and previously excluded voices, which can promote wider acceptance of decisions by fostering a hybridizing of professional discourse with local experience and by raising previously unacknowledged distributive-justice concerns facing disadvantaged communities.[86]

Excluding local, indigenous, or traditional knowledge can strongly affect the outcomes in environmental decision-making processes. In the U.S. context, the requirement that water-quality regulations be based on toxicology and on engineering assessments of the "best affordable technology" excludes the knowledge that the managers of aquaculture operations can provide on what standards are truly reasonable in light of the practices of keeping feed, waste, and hormones out of the emissions.

Of course, this sort of problem is not unique to the United States. For instance, the Narmada Dam controversy in India was sparked by opposition to the World Bank–funded project by local villagers who were to be resettled as part of the project. To address concerns raised by the locals, the World Bank established a first-ever Independent Review Panel, which found great disparities between the scientific data collected by bank professionals and the evidence given to the panel by the affected villagers in India. A second dam project was canceled in Nepal when feasibility studies indicated extremely negative ecological and social effects. The World Bank devised new policies and practices in 1998 that acknowledged the not easily codifiable knowledge embedded in indigenous practices, institutions, and relationships; it also devised assessment and consultation procedures to avoid the "Narmada effect." In addition to these World Bank reforms, several international agreements and programs—including Agenda 21 (1992), the Convention on Biological Diversity (1992), Forest Principles (1992), the Convention to Combat Desertification (1994), the World Conference on Science (1999), and the International Council for Science (1999)—developed provisions concerning traditional, local, and indigenous knowledge.[87] Within the United States, the community-based forestry movement has been successful in assisting in the passage of legislation that codifies tools such as "multiparty monitoring," which ensures that multiple views, such as those of practitioners, are included in the evaluation of forestry projects.

In some circles, there has been a tendency to romanticize local or participatory knowledge as a superior way of knowing.[88] But local knowledge alone is not sufficient for good decision making. It can sometimes be naive or even harmful to the environment. For example, commercial fishers often claim to have greater knowledge of fish stocks than do marine biologists. The fishers may indeed have relevant information, but they may know trends on a local rather than a global scale. At times, they also have a strong incentive to overstate the resilience of a given fishery so that their economic activity will not be curtailed by regulations.

Lack of Vision for the Generation of Public Input

Both the principle and the political advantages of policy responsiveness to the preferences and priorities held by the public have reinforced the importance of information about these preferences and priorities as a form of knowledge. It is not enough to assume that the public wants a cleaner and safer environment; environmental objectives entail trade-offs with other goals held dear by the public insofar as environmental protection requires restrictions or higher costs of certain economic activities and limits the range of personal action. Therefore, gauging how much the public values environmental safeguards and improvements is an integral part of both the formal and the informal evaluation of environmental policy options. On the formal side, certain environmental decision processes require, by law, direct public input in the vein of participatory democracy. Other decisions require that indirect assessments of public values be incorporated into technical assessments of benefits and costs. On the informal side, legislators and executive-branch officials are often keenly aware of and sensitive to "public opinion," whether expressed through opinion polls, letters to government officials, or stakeholder organizations.

That the public can contribute useful knowledge to environmental decision-making processes is today seldom contested. However, the increase in the many types of public-involvement processes and the knowledge generated from these diverse processes results in confusion over the purpose and intent of public input in environmental decision making.[89] Merely generating public input does not mean it contributes to better environmental decision making. The goal is to generate reliable information that is open, dependable, and suitably comprehensive.

Public participation can contribute to the creation of more informed policy by offering knowledge of local conditions not known to outside analysts or by providing information about public preferences and the existence and strength of interest groups. This information can be extremely important both in selecting politically viable policies and, once the policy is adopted, in securing public cooperation in implementation and enforcement.

Legislation promoting public participation in policymaking emerged in part out of the fundamental tensions that exist in administrative governance.[90] On the one hand, bureaucratic and subject matter experts are necessary for managing complex administrative programs, particularly for science-intensive areas such as the environment. However, the experts are not elected and do not necessarily have complete knowledge about public values or contextual conditions that can influence the analysis of policy problems and their alternatives. Greater public input means that the public can provide pragmatic support and substantive information to professional managers[91] and at the same time enhance social goals.[92] Moreover, rising education levels, increased availability of information about the environmental impacts of resource use, and increasingly savvy protest techniques have combined to make the general public a more formidable opponent when they are excluded from the decision-making processes that affect their lives.[93] In spite of the justifications for increasing public input, determining how to involve the public in more participatory decision-making processes or determining what structures and techniques facilitate effective public involvement remain a challenge.

Public participation refers to any of several mechanisms intentionally used to involve the lay public or their representatives in environmental policymaking.[94] These mechanisms can include policy dialogs, stakeholder advisory committees, citizen juries, facilitated mediations, public hearings, public-comment processes, regulatory negotiations, and many other modes.[95]

In the United States, the 1970s saw a flurry of statutes with nonbinding direct-involvement provisions, including a large portion of environmental and natural-resource legislation. The NEPA was typical of the legislation of that period. It dictated that all federal agencies that undertook any "actions significantly affecting the quality of the human environment" must prepare detailed statements regarding the "environmental impacts of proposed action" (2 USC, PL 91-190, Title I, sec. 102[c]). The call for public participation in the environmental impact statement process prescribed public hearings or the solicitation of written public comments or both. Likewise, in 1976 Congress enacted the National Forest Management Act (NFMA). This legislation represented one of the most significant and controversial efforts by any federal agency to incorporate public input into a decision-making process.[96] Rather than deferring to NEPA on the public-participation provisions associated with environmental actions, NFMA specifically required public input "in the development, review, and revision" of national-forest plans.

However, the experience with NEPA and NFMA has demonstrated that public input is not constructively used in most cases.[97] Usually flowing from legislative mandates, nonbinding direct public-input provisions such as NEPA and NFMA often fail to give bureaucratic agencies specific direction in how to handle public input or conduct public processes.[98] In an attempt to be comprehensive and open, they fail to be relevant. In the majority of cases, NFMA has not resulted in more constructive decision making; rather, controversy, conflict, and dissatisfaction have prevailed.[99] Frustration and disappointment with the public-involvement provisions have led some to advocate more selective public-involvement opportunities in national-forest planning and NEPA processes.[100] At the same time, there are experiments with even more sophisticated tools for eliciting public preferences, such as computer-based outcome visualization and participatory geographic information systems.[101]

The proliferation of nonbinding direct modalities has caused confusion over the purpose and intent of public input. Four distinct problems result: poor planning and program design, lack of experience in and appreciation for the complexity involved in soliciting input from the public, conflicting expectations about the outcome of public-involvement exercises, and failure to draw conclusions from the history of different types of participatory processes used in creating input.[102] For instance, when designing a program, managers may be confused about what function knowledge from public-input processes should play. Should the public expressions be considered equivalent to an informal referendum and thus be given equal numerical weight? Or should they simply considered as a nonquantitative portrait of the range of preferences? Public expectations may likewise differ from managers' expectations because nonbinding direct modalities may mislead the public as to how much weight these inputs will be given. In addition, various modalities of public participation do not convey public-preference information efficiently or effectively because public participation is not uniform and can be disorganized. Public-involvement processes are organized in dozens of different ways, varying from issue to issue and agency to agency. As a consequence, relevant publics do not know how to allocate their scarce time among the various issues of interest to them when it comes to many nonbinding direct processes. Other processes, such as deliberations over local zoning, are standardized and well understood, which allows local information to be elicited, allows the expression of preference, and gives the process a clear starting and ending point. Similarly, clear rules associated with referenda and initiatives explicitly dictate that majority rule determines the outcome. Clearer expectations by decision makers about nonbinding direct modalities of public can better channel efforts by the public for more constructive inputs.

The goal for the generation of public input should be for it to be open, dependable, comprehensive, and relevant. To date, this goal has remained mostly elusive.

Conclusion

This chapter has reviewed the ways in which knowledge generation can be problematic and offers specific categories and examples of these problems. As the categories and examples illustrate, knowledge generation in environmental decision making is not systematic. In the post–World War II era, we have seen a diversification of individuals, technologies, and institutions engaged in knowledge generation. Complexity and uncertainty make systematic and comprehensive coverage impossible. Professional, personal, and institutional biases contribute to incomplete knowledge generation. We often do not know what to do with the knowledge generated, as the example of public input clearly illustrates. Politics plays a role in shaping the values that are privileged in knowledge generation. And formal science, which has its own biases and susceptibility to political influence, is still privileged, even as new forms of knowledge are given more explicit roles in decision processes. All these factors combined mean that knowledge generation is not sufficiently comprehensive, dependable, selective, relevant, open, or efficient.

3

The Transmission and Use of Knowledge in the Environmental Policy Process

If knowledge is to have any influence on environmental policy, it must be *transmitted* from wherever it was generated or where it resides, and it must be *used* as an input in decision making. The transmission may begin from numerous possible sources—the scientific literature, the minds of experts, or the hearts of people who support or oppose a given policy. It may be conveyed by an equally diverse set of channels—technical journal articles, popular media, congressional testimony, or word of mouth at the local coffee shop. The uses of knowledge are also varied, from bringing an issue onto the active policy agenda to helping formulate policy options to choosing and enacting a particular policy and then evaluating how well it performed.

Just as the generation of environmental knowledge involves personal and financial costs, the transmission and use of knowledge are also costly. Relevant knowledge may be close to infinite, but because its transmission and use are costly, only some knowledge will actually influence policymaking. How, then, do transmission and use take place? What mechanisms are used to sift through all the relevant knowledge and determine what will have influence and what will never enter the process?

This chapter addresses the characteristics of knowledge transmission and use and identifies problems that these characteristics present for making environmental policy. Two themes run through this chapter. First, "filters" limit the comprehensiveness, dependability, and relevance of knowledge transmitted and used in environmental decision-making processes; second, the decision makers using knowledge rarely have good ways to evaluate its comprehensiveness, selectivity, and dependability.

Knowledge transmission and use are not value-neutral, comprehensive processes. Rather, they are selective in ways that privilege some participants and their values over others. Knowledge is transmitted and used within particular technical contexts, shaped by standards or rules that determine what sorts of knowledge are admissible and influential as well as the limitations posed by uncertainty and by scarce resources. These technical factors account for a narrowing of the pool of knowledge that actually becomes relevant in environmental decision-making processes.

Knowledge is generated in a political context, and this is also true of the transmission of environmental knowledge by individuals and organizations as they participate in the environmental policy process and use knowledge in making decisions. For example, knowledge can be used as a promotional strategy or tool. Legitimate uncertainty can be manipulated to discredit science or to justify inaction. Institutional interests can suppress, oversimplify, and distort scientific information.[1] One of the best-documented examples is the long campaign by the cigarette industry through most of the second half of the twentieth century to create the illusion of a scientific debate about smoking's health impacts, even in the face of overwhelming scientific evidence that smoking is dangerous.[2] Devra Davis shows how firms and organizations with economic interests in a wide range of environmental carcinogens used this same strategy. She writes of "the science of doubt promotion—the concerted and well-funded effort to identify, magnify and exaggerate doubts about what we could say that we know as a way of delaying actions to change the way the world operates."[3] This chapter explores how this politicization of knowledge in its transmission and use raises problems for policymaking and how it leads to policies that are not supported by the best available base of knowledge.

Challenges in the Transmission of Knowledge

Before knowledge can be applied to decision making, it must be transmitted. Because policymaking is done by people, knowledge consists either of what they know (expertise) or what they choose to learn or find out and deliberately insert into a given policy process. The transmission of knowledge into a given policy process entails both *screening*—some knowledge is not transmitted—and *framing*—shaping the way the issue is presented.[4] Both screening and framing limit the comprehensiveness of knowledge transmitted and used. They can be generally characterized as a selective "filtering" of knowledge as it is transmitted and used. The processes guiding the selectivity are often not explicit. Here we make them more explicit in the hope of drawing attention to the lack of transparency as well as to the impact on comprehensiveness.

We believe that there are four problems related to the transmission of knowledge: (1) the persistence of the privileged position of "science"; (2) the difficulty of coping with the diversification of knowledge-transmission vehicles; (3) uncertainty as a problem in knowledge transmission; and (4) the focusing of attention too narrowly through limited knowledge transmission.

The Persistence of the Privileged Position of Science

In the transmission of knowledge, expertise plays a strong role in screening and framing, so science has thus a particularly privileged position. The scientific community's views (in both the natural and social sciences) about the quality of various analytical techniques are very important in determining what types of analyses are believed to be sufficiently rigorous to qualify as inputs to environmental policymaking. Because different analytic techniques emphasize different aspects of environmental impacts (e.g., economic, health, aesthetic, or biodiversity), the canon of accepted methods has a significant but largely unrecognized effect on environmental priorities, how trade-offs between environmental protection and other objectives will be assessed, and what knowledge is passed on through the process. Tendencies toward "credibility seeking" and "certainty prejudice" crowd out knowledge that might otherwise be transmitted.

Whatever ambivalence and frustrations policymakers might have with science and scientists, the "scientific method" has significant framing effects on the transmission of knowledge. However, the influence of the scientific enterprise on policymaking is not a straightforward projection or transfer of scientists' understandings of knowledge generation, but rather a reflection of a complicated and conflicting set of conceptions of science—some simplistic and idealized, others very sophisticated. Major segments of the aware public and some policymakers embrace the notion that scientific "findings," once confirmed to the satisfaction of reputable scientists, can be taken as valid. Analysis and decisions can flow directly from these established findings. This notion ignores, of course, the omni-presence of uncertainty and neglects the questioning of the normative bases that have already gone into the generation, screening, and analysis of the knowledge. This questioning sometimes comes from within science itself, with one discipline questioning another discipline's methods and interpretations.

Knowledge is transmitted through a host of media, from discussions at the local barber shop or beauty salon to popularized television pro-grams on the fate of polar bears to highly technical peer-reviewed jour-nals. It is illuminating to contrast the implications of the most highly controlled medium—the technical, peer-reviewed journal—with the most open-access medium, the Internet. The more prestigious transmission media privilege particular types of knowledge and thereby particular sources. Publication (which is but one element of peer review) does not guarantee reliability, acceptance, or admissibility in the decision process.[5] But publication does increase the likelihood that substantive flaws in methodology or even errors in calculations will be detected.[6] Because certain transmission media, such as the peer-reviewed journal, are widely believed to ensure rigor, the kinds of knowledge that can pass this screen-ing and the experts seen as in command of this knowledge have an advantage in shaping perspectives and policies. Yet the culture, institu-tions, and rules that shape the transmission of knowledge run the risk of filtering out knowledge that policymakers should take into account. In some instances, well-grounded but innovative theories will not have been published.[7] Some propositions, moreover, are too particular, too new, or of too limited interest to be published.

The U.S. Supreme Court demonstrated an awareness of both the importance of the scientific peer-review publication process and the limi-tations of that process in the landmark 1993 *Daubert v. Merrill Dow Pharmaceuticals* (509 U.S. 579) decision on the admissibility of expert testimony and other scientific evidence. This ruling has arguably created a legal bias in favor of science over other forms of knowledge.

The Court's overall conclusion on peer review was that "the fact of publication (or lack thereof) in a peer-reviewed journal thus will be a relevant, though not dispositive, consideration in assessing the scientific validity of a particular technique or methodology on which an opinion is premised." It is striking that despite the inroads that "postpositivist" thinking has made in reconsidering the premises of falsificationist approaches to science[8] and the dutiful citations of the work of postpositivist scholars such as Sheila Jasanoff, Frank Fisher, Bruno Latour, Dorothy Nelkin, Brian Wynne, Ulrich Beck, and others, the Court adopted a very traditional view of how the scientific enterprise operates and how scientific findings should be screened. The decision stated that "scientific methodology today is based on generating hypotheses and testing them to see if they can be falsified; indeed, this methodology is what distinguishes science from other fields of human inquiry."

To determine admissibility, the decision called for "a preliminary assessment of whether the reasoning or methodology underlying the testimony is scientifically valid and of whether that reasoning or methodology properly can be applied to the facts in issue. We are confident that federal judges possess the capacity to undertake this review." The decision goes on to enumerate the multiple criteria of falsifiability and testability, known or potential rate of error, extent of peer review and publication, and "general acceptance" by the scientific community. Kenneth Foster and Peter Huber note that the criteria the Supreme Court established through the *Daubert* decision are "similar to those that scientists use to evaluate scientific evidence."[9]

A problem with the *Daubert* criteria is that they presuppose *a* scientific community and generally accepted methods for testing. Gary Edmond recounts the many conflicting viewpoints that persist in U.S. courts over the interpretation and application of the *Daubert* decision.[10] For example, the Ninth Circuit Court of Appeals did not adopt the Supreme Court's central emphasis on whether scientific conclusions had been tested, but instead focused on "peer review, publication and whether the evidence was designed for use in litigation."[11] The Tenth Circuit ruled in a prominent suit claiming damages from silicone breast implants that following standard scientific methodology is not enough to guarantee the validity of the conclusions.[12]

According to the *Daubert* decision, judges are not to "play scientist" by evaluating the content of knowledge. Yet the focus on the process (both reasoning and methodology) by which the knowledge is generated has elements of circularity. It presumes that science has clear criteria for establishing what forms of reasoning and what methodologies are valid.

Sheila Jasanoff notes that legal analyses of the issues of biotechnology regulation operate "from a perspective that [emphasizes] the forms of law over the substance of science," yet the forms of law require an assessment of the soundness of scientific procedure.[13]

If peer-reviewed knowledge generated by scientists has a privileged role in knowledge transmission, does this position diminish the role of local knowledge and of knowledge about the preferences of individuals and subgroups in society? As we noted in chapter 2, local knowledge suffers from biases against its generation in forms useful to decision making. When it comes to transmission, a problem posed by the *Daubert* doctrine is that it creates a legal bias in favor of formal science and against knowledge that has been generated through alternative, non-scientific means. For example, local knowledge made explicit but not cast into conventional scientific models entails high risks of delay and rejection as litigation proceeds. The seemingly objective *Daubert* doctrine is inherently political because it privileges certain values over others and screens certain types of knowledge out of the process.

This primacy of formal science in the United States has ironically encouraged policies that some regard as risky or even reckless. It appears that in the United States the implicit presumptions still largely reign that scientists are open-minded people acting in the public interest[14] and that policies that appear to be based on prior scientific work have well-balanced risks and opportunities. We have seen many billions of dollars going into the nuclear waste repository at Yucca Mountain; and genetically engineered organisms (GEOs) have been vigorously developed and applied in the United States,[15] in sharp contrast with western Europe. Compared to western European policymakers, U.S. policymakers appear to be much less constrained by the pessimism underlying the "precautionary principle,"[16] which requires that actors advocating a possibly harmful environmental action carry the burden of proof that such harm will not occur. Under this rule, actors advocating holding back on actions to avoid possible environmental harm do not have to prove their case. The precautionary principle—now part of European Union law—is intended to minimize the risk that environmental harm will come even if the estimated probability is low. In contrast, U.S. policymakers and the public often take expressions of uncertainty about knowledge as a sign of scientific failure or, at a minimum, of scientific weakness. The result of this view may be that the implications of uncertainty are ignored.

The intolerance of uncertainty, in any form, also works against most types of knowledge outside of the scientific paradigm. These prejudices reduce the opportunities to be precautionary, to weigh local knowledge, and to consider the intensity of public preferences.

This presumption seems to extend not only to the knowledge generated by scientists, but also to public acceptance of new technologies that have impacts on the environment. One might imagine that in a country as apparently health conscious as the United States, the concerns over genetically engineered crops, electronic emissions, and growth hormones used in milk and meat production would arouse far more opposition than they actually do. Yet compared to the public and policymakers in equivalently developed regions such as western Europe, the bulk of the American public and policymakers seems blithely unconcerned about these risks.[17] With reference to the issue of GEOs, Jasanoff notes "that the involvement of the courts in science and technology policy often reinforces dominant beliefs and institutional arrangements, which, in this [U.S.] society, include a well-entrenched faith in the progressive force of science and technology."[18]

The far weaker standing of the precautionary principle in the United States than in western Europe[19] regarding the impacts of technology is also a product of political forces that favor the transmission of knowledge to support this outcome. For example, biotech companies and megascale agribusiness mount highly effective lobbying efforts in the United States,[20] and agricultural exports provide one of the few bright spots for the U.S. trade balance. In the European Union, a number of environmental groups have long questioned GEOs and provide greater support for the precautionary principle. These filters for selectivity are trade-offs against the comprehensiveness of knowledge from more diverse sources.

Scientists themselves can filter other relevant knowledge out of the decision process. Their desire to be seen as credible plays into risk aversion when they are transmitting knowledge. We call this behavior *credibility seeking*. It occurs when the environmental considerations are especially difficult to study rigorously and therefore are underrepresented in the most respected transmission channels. Environmental scientists' behavior (whether in the biophysical or social sciences) in how they transmit their own knowledge has major impacts on restricting the availability of knowledge for use in the decision processes. The standing of different aspects of knowledge *within* the communities of experts shapes the acceptance and further transmission of particular kinds of knowledge, in turn signaling to policymakers which information warrants more serious consideration. Experts often suppress information or insights that they regard as less rigorous and therefore less scientifically defensible in order both to maintain what they view as the integrity of their disciplines and to protect their personal reputations. Or they may relegate such knowledge to a subsidiary status compared to apparently more rigorous findings, thereby signaling what policymakers should take into account. Moreover, scientific research, if it is to be published and applauded, typically has to break new ground in method, theory, or empirical findings. Yet the knowledge related to ecosystem sustainability is often mundane from a scientific perspective, involving intensive but routine monitoring.

To summarize, the privileged position of science means that the knowledge that is transmitted is not comprehensive. Other types of knowledge, including some forms of science, are filtered out during the transmission process. Certainty preference for peer-reviewed work and credibility-seeking behavior, among other factors, inhibit the comprehensiveness of the knowledge transmitted in the process, which also means that the knowledge that is transmitted is not as relevant, open, or creative as it might be.

The Difficulty of Coping with Diversification of Knowledge-Transmission Vehicles

The diversification of transmission vehicles for knowledge has matched the diversification of knowledge generators and the diffusion of the ability to generate high-level technical information. The rise of high-speed data processing and retrieval, graphics, the Internet, and the accompanying tools for information transmission and management have facilitated interaction among information providers, government agencies, interest groups, private corporations, researchers, and the general public on a scale unheard of even in the 1990s. The diversification of transmission vehicles creates a paradox—although information is more readily available to broad sectors of society, we have inadequate means to determine what should or should not be transmitted. The realm of comprehensiveness has expanded, but we have come no closer to understanding what constitutes dependability in transmission or how to be appropriately selective.

In particular, the World Wide Web, which first became available to the public in 1991, has become a powerful new tool for transmitting—some would say universally transmitting—all forms of information. According to a 2007 survey, 71 percent of American adults used the Internet, with the proportion ascending to 87 percent among persons eighteen to twenty-nine years of age.[21] There were differences by income, with 93 percent of households with annual incomes greater than $75,000 using the Internet, but only 55 percent of households with incomes less than $30,000. But the differences were even greater when Americans were stratified by levels of education. Ninety-one percent of college graduates used the Internet, but only 40 percent of persons with less than a high school education did. Half of U.S. homes now have high-speed broadband connections, and free broadband access is available at nearly all public libraries. Easy-to-use search engines such as Google and Yahoo offer access not just to email, but also to the rich content of the Web.

Internet journalist Kevin Kelly, referring to several ongoing projects to make all published books available in electronic form, writes: "The universal library of all books will cultivate a new sense of authority. If you can truly incorporate all texts—past and present, multilingual—on a particular subject, then you can have a clearer sense of what we as a civilization, a species, do know and don't know. The white spaces of our collective ignorance are highlighted while the golden peaks of our knowledge are drawn with completeness. This degree of authority is only rarely achieved in scholarship today, but it will become routine."[22]

Kelly's comment seems hyperbolic, but the amount of information transmitted through the Web is staggering. For example, users can read reports from the EPA, the National Research Council (NRC), trade associations, and a host of environmental organizations. They can browse environmental impact statements filed by the U.S. Army Corps of Engineers or by state and federal highway agencies. They can easily find data on emissions from individual power plants as well as on releases of toxic pollutants by specific industrial plants. On the political side, they can find politicians' voting records and even data on contributions to federal political campaigns, arranged by zip code. Virtually all academic journals are now available in electronic form. Many require subscriptions, but they can be accessed freely through universities and large public libraries. Several projects for the mass scanning of books are ongoing in important university libraries. When these books are available in searchable form, they will provide electronic access to an incredibly rich lode of knowledge. One of the newest—and wildly popular— features of the Web is any individual or group's ability to post still photos (Flickr) or video cam clips (YouTube) on the Web. This feature enables, for example, an environmental group to document erosion during a rainfall event at a construction site or a timber harvest and to distribute it to hundreds of activists.

Social-networking sites such as Facebook, Twitter, MySpace, and LinkedIn, among others, allow groups and individuals to share knowledge in new ways, often with a regional, national, or global reach. These networks distribute books, podcasts, video clips, personal observations, news stories, gossip, and broad content from myriad sources. Thousands can be reached in seconds as American (and other) publics become more versatile with information and additional portals are created to facilitate access. The costs for this transmission are close to zero. The 2008 Obama campaign's remarkable use of networking tools shows their power to identify and motivate volunteers and to raise funds.

A consequence of this expansion in the knowledge transmitted into the public domain is that we lack clear guidelines in how to be selective. How is the recipient to make quality judgments? The challenge is in how to identify reasonable criteria for dependability without becoming overly reliant, if not overly restrictive, on the canons of science and continuing to privilege the position of science in the more diversified world of knowledge transmission.

At one extreme, information available electronically can be of high quality and may even be peer reviewed. For example, the National Academies of Sciences makes available PDF (portable document format) versions of thousands of its books and reports. The consumer can almost instantly download the same material that can be purchased in printed form or consulted in a library. The same is true for statistical publications of most government agencies. At the other extreme, one might see on YouTube a video sequence of an apparent oil spill, yet have no guarantee that the stated time and place are correct or that contextual variables such as scale or elapsed time are accurate.

The real issues regarding the quality of electronic communication lie within these extremes. How much credence should be placed in a *Wikipedia* article, Google search, or first-person account of what someone experienced in her most recent visit to a national park? Many observers worry about the uncritical acceptance of electronic material.[23] But perhaps the opposite will be the case. In the past, printed material was sometimes accepted as factual even though it was not necessarily peer reviewed or even fact checked. The skeptical attitude engendered by the range of electronically distributed "knowledge" might lead to a salutary skepticism about all knowledge transmitted to the policy process: What is its origin? Has it been reviewed? What do other sources have to say on the same topic? Just as the awareness that counterfeit currency may be in circulation causes people to examine more carefully the banknotes they are given, the increased likelihood of encountering "bad" electronic information may lead to greater scrutiny of all information.

Falk Huettmann suggests using the Web to provide another level of quality control of information transmitted by scientists. He notes the widespread use of adaptive and science-based management in wildlife management but argues that "many decisions in this management field are still based on unsupported ideas, soft concepts, qualitative evidence, beliefs, and even myths and folklore that lack a true back-up assessment, validation with real data, and quantitative analysis available for a public review." He calls for data underlying decisions to be made publicly available through the Internet, but only those data sets that have been subject to peer review. He also argues that "each major wildlife management decision needs to add a standard management documentation system as a backup that clearly records what data and research were or were not available at that time and what the recommended research still needs to address in order to complete the data situation and to decrease uncertainty."[24] The diversification and universal availability of knowledge transmission guarantees greater uncertainty in how it can be dependably used.

Uncertainty as a Problem in Knowledge Transmission

As initially addressed in chapter 2, uncertainty is the engine of science: the excitement of the unknown or, at least, the not definitively known. It leads the way for intellectual curiosity and allows for the opportunity to make significant contributions. In diagnosing the sources of uncertainty—data limitations, underdeveloped theory, unknown weights to assign opposing effects, intrinsic randomness—scientists can focus on whether and how uncertainty can be reduced. From the perspective of science, uncertainty often means withholding judgment until more information or theorizing can be brought to bear.

In transmitting scientific findings, there is a tendency to emphasize disagreement or points of departure from existing data or theory. In addition to the previously mentioned incentives that place a premium on starting a scientific investigation by refuting or confirming what is already known, refuting what is known is much more professionally rewarding than confirming what is already known. This tendency is reinforced by scientists' inability or unwillingness to join in communicating the points where consensus or near-consensus exists. Some mechanisms for such communication do exist; for example, through the reports of the NRC, the U.S. EPA's Scientific Advisory Board, and the American Assembly, but for complicated reasons these communications are often overshadowed by messages that highlight the lack of scientific agreement.

At the same time, there is a credibility-seeking reluctance to transmit potentially challengeable knowledge. This can be seen in how the U.S. EPA shies away from the opportunity to highlight all the ecosystem benefits that can be captured with the complete range of valuation methods. In some instances, the agency simply excludes considerations that are not rigorously monetizable from the summary tables that balance benefits against costs. In other cases, it partitions the results into a "core" estimate based on the benefits derived from what the analysts consider to be the most defensible analysis (such as hedonic pricing estimates) and relegates additional value derived from the less defensible methods (such as contingent valuation estimates or nonmonetized benefits) to separate addenda. Therefore, the EPA often presents the benefits that can be inferred from private purchases of homes or from spending on family travel to parks or other locations with environmental amenities as the core valuation analysis, even though these methods cannot capture the value that people place on environmental benefits for the broader community or on the existence of ecosystem elements. These additional, nonmarketed ecosystem benefits such as community and existence values may be inferred from surveys (often through the contingent valuation approach), but they are presented as subsidiary considerations. Some of these additional benefit considerations may be monetized, but others frequently are not—they are simply listed as benefits, usually with a disclaimer statement that their value cannot be determined. These "icing on the cake" factors are invoked to bolster a benefit-cost analysis that in its quantified, monetized estimate may not be enough to justify the proposal to enact more stringent environmental regulation.

An example of this partitioning can be found in the EPA's background analysis to support more stringent restrictions on nitrogen oxide (NOx) emissions. Present analytical tools and resources preclude the EPA from transmitting the benefits of improved forest aesthetics in the eastern United States expected to occur from the NOx State Implementation Plan (SIP). This is attributed to limitations in researchers' ability to quantify the relationship between ozone concentrations and visible injury as well as in the limited quantitative information about the public's valuation of specific changes in forests' visible aesthetic quality. However, there is sufficient supporting evidence in the physical sciences and economic literature to support the finding that NOx reductions of the magnitude proposed in the SIP can be expected to reduce injury to forests and that reductions in this injury will likely have a significant economic value to the public.[25]

In this case, by neglecting to transmit some aspects of averted damage to forests as well as other nonmonetized benefits, the benefit-cost analysis was not decisive in terms of whether the annual benefits (estimated at between $204.1 million and $350 million) were indeed greater than the estimated annual costs of $335 million. Although the "supporting literature" is invoked to offset the fact that the monetized benefit-cost analysis cannot justify the rule, the take-away message is that "rigorous analysis" cannot justify the rule. The rule may be upheld, but the failure to support it on explicit benefit-cost grounds certainly weakens the support for future efforts to push for a more stringent rule. In a case like this, public testimony and letters and campaigns organized by national and local groups could supply policymakers with information about the values that cannot be quantified in the economic analysis.

The tendency toward risk-averse behavior in benefit-cost analysis also leads to the perverse choice to transmit findings derived from accepted applications in different contexts rather than findings from the current context that would have to be derived from more challengeable methods. For example, the survey-derived value of a day of hunting in one location may be applied to the value of a day of hunting in a second location. This "benefit transfer" runs the risk of transmitting erroneous knowledge based on a belief that rigor in previous knowledge generation will flawlessly transfer to a new context. The reasonableness of benefits transfer is, surprisingly, rarely challenged.

The upshot is that uncertainty in how knowledge will be used creates specific problems in knowledge transmission. Certainty prejudice, credibility seeking, and assumption drag all contribute to risk-averse behavior, thereby limiting comprehensiveness of the knowledge that moves forth in the decision-making process and resulting in knowledge that is of more limited relevance than it might be otherwise.

Focusing Attention Too Narrowly Through Knowledge Transmission
Knowledge not only reflects priorities, but also influences individual stakeholders and policymakers' priorities through its impact on the focus of attention. Policy agendas—the issues selected for focus in policy deliberations—do not emerge simply from the nature of the threats and opportunities faced by a society. Anthony Downs argued early in the rise of the post-1960 environmental movement that most key domestic problems are subject to an "issue attention cycle" where a problem "suddenly leaps into prominence, remains there for a short time, and then—though still largely unresolved—gradually fades from the center of public attention."[26] This was a brilliant insight that has proved to be true of many social issues. With respect to the environment generally (though not necessarily specific environmental issues), the fading away of interest that Downs predicted did not materialize. The difference was the persistence of environmental policy entrepreneurs, often operating through environmental nongovernmental organizations with impressive capacity to select and transmit knowledge, that has kept the environment as an active part of the policy agenda.

The focus of attention can also be crucial in shaping how environmental amenities will be prioritized. Consider some environmental services provided by the U.S. national forests: timber, recreation, education, and wildlife habitat. Information about a decline in wildlife would, in all likelihood, focus more attention on the issue of habitat and increase the weight of habitat concerns in decisions on forest use. And focus of attention is not simply a matter of information being "out there"—it is also a question of the intensity of efforts to transmit the information. The more stories on gray wolves that appear in the newspaper, the more likely people are to think about gray wolves and the issue of their reintroduction into areas shared by people and livestock. The media play an important role as a filter or amplifier of attention, and the information and knowledge that focus policymakers and stakeholders' attention have a major role in shaping the policy agenda.[27]

Two major characteristics of this filtering process tend to limit the comprehensiveness and the dependability of the knowledge being transmitted. Dramatic events often drive the focus of attention, particularly if they have strong visual attributes. Equally important, the focus of transmitted information is frequently motivated and controlled by individuals who combine passion for their subject with strong communication skills. Media coverage of environmental disasters—such as the 1960s mercury poisoning in Minimata, Japan, the 1969 Santa Barbara and 1989 *Exxon Valdez* oil spills, and the nuclear accidents at Three Mile Island in 1979 and Chernobyl in 1986—gave immediacy and focus to generalized pollution fears that already existed in the public subconscious. Hurricane Katrina in 2005 and other extreme weather events have given similar focus to the issue of global climate change (whether the dramatizing weather event actually was related to a climate trend or not).

Information transmitted through the media can be accorded a special status, even though it might be neither comprehensive nor dependable. For example, the 1989 "Alar scare" in which print and broadcast media gave wide publicity to a pesticide (daminozide) used in apple production (and subsequently banned by the EPA) is widely cited as an example of consumer and policymaker overreaction to a substance that actually posed little risk to humans—an overreaction that may have diverted attention away from much more dangerous substances.[28]

It is illuminating how some well-publicized events have led directly to the initiation of the policy process and to eventual policy change, whereas other, equally serious events have not. For example, the 1969 Santa Barbara oil spill led to a moratorium on offshore oil leases by the California State Lands Commission that would last sixteen years and that gave impetus to the passage of NEPA (1969) and the creation of the powerful California Coastal Commission (1972) through voter initiative.[29] In 1978–1979, it was revealed that houses and a local school at Love Canal (Niagara Falls, New York) had been polluted by toxic industrial wastes leaching from a long abandoned waste dump. This revelation was directly followed by the passage in 1980 of the Comprehensive Environmental Response, Compensation, and Liability Act (CERCLA), which created a federal mechanism to force cleanups of toxic and hazardous waste. In contrast, although Three Mile Island helped discourage utilities from proposing additional nuclear plants and led to bureaucratic reforms within the Nuclear Regulatory Agency, it did not lead to significant congressional legislative action.

The link between dramatizing incidents and policy initiation often requires the presence of policy entrepreneurs who seek to influence the policy process by political mobilization, often based on creative manipulation of the media. David Price and Anthony Downs first identified this role of the policy entrepreneur,[30] and J. W. Kingdon developed it more fully.[31] Policy entrepreneurs may be individual citizens concerned about a particular problem in their neighborhood or with special interest in a topic, or they may be organizations that range from neighborhood associations to national, professionalized entities.

A subset of the policy entrepreneur is the "knowledge entrepreneur."[32] This individual or organization attempts to control the flow of knowledge in order to set the policy agenda, define policy alternatives, and influence the selection of alternatives. They may even intervene after a policy is selected in order to influence how the policy is evaluated. As policymaking has become more technocratic, and as information generation and transmission have diversified, the space for knowledge entrepreneurs to exert influence has increased. What is transmitted and how it is transmitted are ultimately political decisions. The knowledge transmitted is accordingly not comprehensive, may not be dependable, and is undoubtedly selective.

Early examples of knowledge entrepreneurs include conservation advocates such as forester Gifford Pinchot, wildlife advocate George Bird Grinnell, and soil conservationist Hugh Hammond Bennett, all of whom were skilled at bringing environmental issues to the national consciousness and ultimately to policy. A key tool for these early knowledge entrepreneurs was the generation of interviews and magazine articles that would bring their causes to public attention. Rachel Carson, a very skilled writer as well as a scientist, used her books *The Sea Around Us* and *Silent Spring* to focus attention on the oceans and on ecological effects of the pesticide DDT.[33] In the case of Love Canal, housewife Lois Gibbs took up an issue affecting her own family, organized neighbors into the Love Canal Homeowners Association, then took the toxic waste dump issue national by founding the Citizens' Clearinghouse for Hazardous Waste. In California, environmental advocates such as Janet Adams, Peter Douglas, and Ellen Stern Harris moved the coastal development issue from a narrow focus on the 1969 Santa Barbara oil spill to a much broader agenda of dissatisfaction with coastal development, culminating in the 1972 petition drive and ballot initiative that created the California Coastal Commission.

At the national level, the role of knowledge entrepreneur has usually been performed by environmental advocacy groups, among them Environmental Defense, the Wilderness Society, National Audubon Society, Environmental Action, World Wildlife Fund, Natural Resources Defense Council, and Defenders of Wildlife, to name just a few. They are quick to use crisis situations or dramatic new scientific findings to transmit information, frame issues, and initiate the policy process, but they also commission studies of problems they believe are significant, then use the new information to place an issue on the agenda or to strengthen their promotional efforts.

Knowledge entrepreneurs are not necessarily pro-environment. In his comprehensive history of U.S. environmental politics between 1955 and 1985, Samuel Hays argued that "the control of information was perhaps the most crucial weapon used by environmental opponents." This was particularly true, he contends, as the locus of policymaking moved out of the realm of legislation into "the context of technical-scientific, economic and planning choices" by administrative agencies.[34] Adversaries of environmental regulation have regularly highlighted information to stimulate opposition to increasing regulatory burdens on various sectors of the economy. In some instances, they offer specific information on costs of particular regulations along with much more general antiregulation arguments to induce a generalized reluctance to regulate. For example, during the early years of the Reagan administration, the Council on Environmental Quality produced alarming assessments of the compliance costs that the Clean Air Act and Clean Water Act imposed on industry. This information was then widely circulated by business groups and was used to sustain a general concern over economic growth and the international competitiveness of the United States.

When housing costs were rising rapidly in the late 1970s, the National Association of Homebuilders and National Association of Realtors publicized studies that attributed a decline in housing affordability to local governments' "growth-control" policies, particularly in California. The National Land Rights Association (started in 1978 as the National Park Inholders Association) has periodically publicized what its members consider egregious cases of infringement of property rights in government acquisitions of new lands for conservation purposes. As housing prices in California reached astronomical levels in the early twenty-first century, opponents of land regulation publicized earlier studies of the impact of regulation on housing costs by such scholars as Bernard Frieden, David Dowall, and Randal O'Toole in an effort to link the issue of high housing costs in California to the state's relatively strict local and state regulations.[35]

Interest groups or stakeholders in this context generally focus on the knowledge most closely associated with accomplishing their goals, so the scope of their knowledge can be limited. However, within these limits they can have great depth of knowledge. These environmental opponents, like the environmental advocates, also transmit and filter knowledge, selecting information that will advance their own agendas.

Two specific ways of focusing attention on problems are state-of-the-environment (SOE) reports and release of newly available databases. As we detail later in this chapter, the knowledge transmitted in these forms is subject to political contestation, and policy entrepreneurs frequently use both forms.

SOE reports sponsored by government agencies or environmental groups identify or highlight issues that might not have been apparent previously. They can place certain environmental issues on the national agenda either by influencing the public directly or by moving issues onto the agendas of government agencies or of environmental advocacy groups.[36] Government SOE reports, issued annually by the Commission on Environmental Quality, were influential during the 1970s in putting issues on the national agenda and during the 1980s in furthering the Reagan administration's antiregulatory program by presenting estimates of the regulatory burden on the economy. Private organizations have produced scores of SOE reports, often on specific subjects such as the condition of the oceans or the management of protected areas. "Global environmental assessments,"[37] such as those concerned with climate change, forest and water resources, and transboundary movement of pollutants, have recently played a major role in international agenda setting. For example, assessments made as part of the negotiations leading up to the 2001 Convention on Long-Range Transboundary Air Pollution (LRTAP) had a major impact on both the convention agenda and outcome. Noelle Eckley Selin looked at the role of these assessments in determining how persistent organic pollutants (POPs) were treated in policymaking. She found that "LRTAP-inspired assessments helped put POPs onto the global agenda and framed the issue, mobilized additional participants, and provided bargaining focal points and road maps to a global convention."[38]

Some policies require information reporting for both monitoring and knowledge generation. What information is publicly released can be a political decision, as is highlighting of certain data in the media and by knowledge entrepreneurs once it has been released. A clear example of this relationship is the Toxic Release Inventory (TRI), established under the 1986 Emergency Planning and Community Right-to-Know Act.[39] The TRI is a publicly available EPA database that contains information on toxic chemical releases and waste-management activities reported annually by certain industries as well as federal facilities. Publicly available government databases such as TRI can focus attention as citizens and scientists learn of the toxicity of individual chemicals in their locale. Demands for managing those chemicals may then come onto the agenda. Thus, the reporting of toxic releases is both informative in terms of understanding environmental threats and relevant to corporations' reputations.[40]

However, the decision about which chemicals to track is itself contentious. Although some chemicals and wastes may be monitored, many equally or even more dangerous chemicals escape attention because their impacts have not yet been studied or because no advocacy organization has publicized them.

This relationship between knowledge and agenda setting is highlighted by the recent controversy over the TRI. In 2006, the EPA enacted a controversial rule change to reduce the TRI reporting burden. It is obvious that the higher-volume thresholds required for reporting toxic releases relieves companies of economic burdens, but they also allow companies to release potentially harmful toxics with less publicity. A less obvious but equally important point is that reducing the information on toxic releases makes it more difficult for epidemiological studies to connect concentrations of toxics with the incidence of disease, birth defects, and ecosystem changes. In reaction to the weaker requirement, the EPA's Scientific Advisory Board, comprising roughly forty natural scientists, social scientists, and legal experts, sent a letter in July 2006 to EPA administrator Stephen Johnson objecting to the reduction in required reporting. The letter argued that the changes may compromise the comparability and quality of the data in the TRI series. It also expressed concern that these proposed changes may hinder the advances of environmental research used to protect public health and the environment:

TRI data are widely used to evaluate changes in facility and firm environmental performance, to conduct risk assessments of changes in toxic release levels, and to conduct spatial analyses of toxic hazards. The TRI data provide the only reliable source of longitudinal data for this type of research. More than 120 scholarly articles have been published using TRI data to address a wide range of public-health, economic, and social science issues.[41]

This controversy underscores the political nature of deciding what will be transmitted and who will make the transmission decisions. The reporting of toxics should clearly be as comprehensive as is necessary to safeguard public health. However, it also needs to be selective because there is no end to chemicals that have some degree of toxicity in high enough concentrations. But what are the appropriate criteria for deciding on selectivity so that the data are deemed dependable in transmission and use? High human and fiscal costs associated with the transmission and use of data also create a need for efficiency. The need for openness is imperative if the data are to be viewed as credible.

Finally, in attempts to focus attention when knowledge is transmitted, the nuances of that knowledge are often lost. Knowledge may begin with a scientific study that generated huge amounts of raw data and has been written up in a lengthy technical report from which a short journal article is published. But it usually ends up in a one-paragraph summary in congressional testimony or as one of dozens of citations in a predecision analysis. This summary is then diffused among the general public through the media, perhaps through a television news report (rarely more than a minute in length), a newspaper article, or an Internet news item. The simplifying assumptions, restricted temporal or spatial scope, and purposes of the original research are easily shorn in each stage of transmission.

In summary, because not all knowledge generated is transmitted into environmental policymaking, the necessary filters privilege some participants and transmission processes over others. The transmission of environmental knowledge involves increasingly complex information that comes from an increasingly diverse set of sources. More people are qualified in terms of their skills, education, and experience to transmit and use knowledge. Likewise, the avenues for transmitting knowledge have diversified enormously with the advent of computers, mobile phones, and Internet-based tools. The expansion of the number of participants and avenues of transmission has created challenges in how to ascertain selectivity and dependability in what information should be used in specific environmental decision-making processes.

The trend toward complexity and sophistication in knowledge transmission seems to indicate that decision making simply needs more and better science. However, the trend toward diversification, particularly through the generation of "local knowledge" and recognition of its value, suggests that much broader selectivity criteria are needed. As we have seen, the choices we make about what knowledge is relevant and what should be allowed to influence policymaking depend on the importance accorded to expertise in general and to peer-reviewed science in particular. Also important is policymakers' capacity to respond reasonably to the existence of uncertainty and to the fact that a greater weight is typically given to costs and benefits that can be monetized.

The choices regarding what information is transmitted, what evaluation is assigned to that knowledge, and how dispositive the information will be deemed are inherently political choices based on various groups' beliefs, values, and relative power. As certain kinds of knowledge—whether science, local knowledge, or public preferences—are privileged in transmission, so too are the groups and interests that generate the knowledge and those that can use that knowledge to press for their preferred policies.

The Use of Knowledge

Once transmitted, how is knowledge actually used in policymaking? Policymakers use knowledge to define problems and lay out alternative courses of action, to choose a specific policy based on assessments of existing policy and projections of the likely consequence of alternatives, and to carry out the chosen policy, which may require abandoning existing policies.

We cover seven issues related to use of knowledge in the environmental decision-making process: (1) mandatory use of knowledge; (2) privileging of knowledge used; (3) uncertainty in using knowledge; (4) inadequate knowledge; (5) definition of objectives and consideration of alternatives; (6) implementation, evaluation, and termination challenges; (7) and the power dynamics and knowledge use.

Mandatory Use of Knowledge

Certain types of knowledge used in environmental policymaking may be mandated by law or regulation. The legal requirements and limitations influence what type of knowledge will or will not be considered in an environmental decision-making process. Once written into law, selectivity is ensured, but at the expense of comprehensiveness. For instance, a Section 7 consultation of the ESA restricts knowledge to the science of what is known about a threatened or endangered species or its habitat. Other data are deemed unnecessary if not based on the "best available science." More comprehensive use of knowledge, including public preferences about what to do about an endangered species or local knowledge about a species' habitat and behavior are not deemed relevant. This type of selectivity raises issues about the relevance of other types of knowledge to the decision process and why such knowledge should be excluded.

The U.S. Army Corps of Engineers is required to use benefit-cost analysis for each of its projects. For the project to move forward, it must have a benefit-cost ratio greater than one. This requirement was adopted for budgetary reasons and has probably had more influence on the Corps' impacts on the environment than have any regulations that were specifically "environmental." The upshot of this requirement is that in choosing projects, the Corps is especially interested in knowledge that might defend the existence of a set of possible benefits. The knowledge used under these conditions is much more likely to support the construction of a project rather than emphasizing any incidental destruction of resources caused by the project. Some types of knowledge will be used, but other types of knowledge will be excluded. This type of selectivity calls into question the dependability of the knowledge used. As the body of federal environmental law has built up over time, legal requirements have sometimes been inconsistent—the Clean Water Act enjoins against using benefit-cost analysis, but Executive Order 12866 requires that such analysis be conducted.

Some legislation has been enacted explicitly to force the use of knowledge with the specific goal of improving policymaking. For example, under the NFMA of 1976 all the national forests were intensively (and expensively) studied at five-year intervals. Public-preference information about how forests should be managed was also mandated. An assessment was done of all resources—including timber, wildlife, water, recreation, and wilderness—on both public and private forests. Public comments were collected about different management scenarios. Immense amounts of useful new information were generated, but the information was not used in a particularly constructive way. Those who wrote the NFMA expected that better information would cause better decision making and promote consensus. However, just the opposite happened: stakeholder groups looked selectively at the new information and publicized findings that reinforced their own points of view.[42] Rather than building a nationwide consensus on forest-resource use, the information generated was used as grist for continued disagreement. Additional knowledge, expensively generated and transmitted, turned out to be not the key to consensus, but became more political ammunition for the many stakeholders involved in the debate on how to best manage the national forests.[43]

The end results of these mandatory knowledge requirements are that other types of knowledge are ignored and limits are placed on the types of knowledge that can be used to make decisions about environmental issues. The legal requirements that call for selectivity over comprehensiveness raise important issues relating to the dependability and relevance of the knowledge ultimately used in these environmental decision-making processes.

Privileging of Knowledge Used

Formal science typically produces the most clearly privileged form of knowledge, reflecting the common expectation that science will play a straightforward role in a rational, linear decision-making process.[44] This expectation arises from a belief that science can and should drive policymaking. In this conception, science provided by experts can reveal the correct policy prescription that can be fed into a decision-making structure and implemented to resolve the problem. This model presumes that we know who will produce, transmit, and use knowledge; that the standards for evaluating knowledge are clear; and that uncertainties can be resolved or at least identified. It generally assumes that scientific knowledge is adequate and that this kind of information is the most relevant input into decision making. Both scientists and policymakers seek credibility through the use of science in these processes.

The privileging of formal science also arises in part because there are clear processes for creating and assessing dependability in science-based knowledge, whereas such processes available for local knowledge and public preferences are less developed. Formal science benefits from the fact that norms, contingencies, sanctions, and assets support it as a prescription for evaluation. Reliable work will be recognized as such through peer review, replication, and applications in varying contexts. Yet although this specialized knowledge production and transmission protocol is important, it is increasingly inadequate as both knowledge production and transmission continue to diversify. For local knowledge or public-preference-type knowledge, we lack alternative norms, contingencies, sanctions, and assets that can help us be selective. The predominance of and overreliance on science as a primary evaluation method may restrict the creative use of other types of knowledge in decision making.

Local knowledge is typically too contextually specific to be effectively subjected to replication; it is underspecified in terms of explicit, testable assumptions; and it is valued for its usefulness more than its truthfulness. It is no accident that the contrast between practical knowledge and formal science is parallel to the contrast between pragmatism (knowledge is useful insofar as it helps to understand and address a given problem) and the positivism that permits only empirically testable propositions. The propositional content of local knowledge may simply be untestable; for example, the explanation for a particular livestock-management approach may be, "My father and his father did it this way, and they knew what they were doing." The approach may in fact be a wise strategy, as evidenced by the fact that the ranch has survived through at least three generations, but whether it is or is not optimal or even close to it remains unknown. Formal science might propose comparing the success of the ranch with that of ostensibly comparable ranches, but definitive information may be lacking as to whether the comparability is valid. Or a municipal government may decide that an environmental policy is appropriate because it is locally accepted as just, politic, or simply psychologically satisfying. Or those affected may prefer one option entailing a greater scientifically estimated risk over another option that generates more dread even though its scientifically estimated risk is lower.

A far-reaching side effect of the deference accorded to formal science is that policymakers inherently privilege quantitative data over qualitative information in how problems are defined and addressed. Again, a status hierarchy is implied. Quantitative information and modeling are highly respected in most scientific fields, whether in the natural or social sciences. Giandomenico Majone wryly notes the "prevailing metaphysics, according to which the scientific character of a field is assumed to be in direct proportion to the degree of its mathematical formalization."[45] This assessment is applicable to both theory and measurements. For decades, climatological models and ecological analysis were not sufficiently developed to make credible biophysical predictions of outcomes needed to include ecosystem effects in the valuation and thereby to calculate ecosystem benefits and costs of climate change. Today, although ecologists, climatologists, and other natural scientists still bemoan the inadequacies of the predictive capacity of their understanding and models, they carry out analyses with these theoretical and data inputs and do not reject the results because of either's weakness.[46] It may well be that the investment of analytic skill would be more useful in addressing global climate change if it were to explore how to accommodate the multiple possible outcomes and the alternatives for addressing those challenges than if it were to try to wring all of the uncertainty out of models of an intrinsically uncertain future.[47]

In short, when we privilege science and quantitative data over other forms of knowledge and qualitative data, we narrow the comprehensiveness of the knowledge we use in decision making. When we limit the use of other types of relevant and dependable knowledge, we also limit both the range of considerations coming to the focus of attention and the depth of nuanced knowledge.

Uncertainty in Using Knowledge

Uncertainty impacts the uses of knowledge in different ways across the three arenas of advocacy, administrative and legal processes, and high-level policymaking.

In the advocacy arena, where knowledge is used to promote particular policies, there is a tendency to emphasize scientific disagreement instead of agreement. Criticizing one's opponents for the uncertainty in their knowledge is an obvious tactic. Less obvious is the impact that this tactic has on the focus of attention: it gives greater prominence to debates over the knowledge base than to debates over values at stake or to the compromise and negotiation needed to clarify and secure the common interest. Denouncing a position by alleging its lack of scientific soundness (or, at a minimum, that its knowledge base is not absolutely certain) distracts from the crucial challenge of developing hedging strategies to pursue the common interest in the face of inevitable uncertainty.

In the administrative and legal arenas, scientific disagreement due to remaining uncertainty reverberates in the policy process through the conflicts over credibility and admissibility as well as through administrators' avoidance of these conflicts. It may seem that admissibility is largely a judicial issue, but both the creation and implementation of laws and regulations have to anticipate court challenges. In a resource-constrained agency or organization, analysts, administrators, and activists often have neither the time nor the manpower to shore up challengeable findings or evaluative methods.

The hesitancy to use or give prominence to challengeable information and evaluative methods leads to delays in employing this knowledge until it has been legitimized through formal scientific and legal channels. One might argue that such hesitancy serves as a healthy filter for the use of knowledge. However, the uncertainty as to whether and when the knowledge has been "sufficiently" legitimized can lead risk-averse analysts and administrators to neglect it for considerable periods. The prejudice in favor of certainty again insinuates itself in obvious and subtle ways to circumscribe what kinds of knowledge are used and how they are used.

When it comes to decision makers' selecting of policies, the paradoxical impact of uncertainty on the use of knowledge is that it can lead to the extremes of either policy paralysis or excessive risk taking. For decision makers who—for political reasons—do not want to face the costs of environmental protection, it is often convenient to call for more research before costly programs are to be undertaken. The scientists' mantra "more research is needed" obviously feeds into this tactic. It is a convenient arrangement: scientists get more funding for further research, and the policymakers escape exposure for decisions that may alienate important political actors. As a consequence, uncertainty leads to procrastination in policymaking.

Yet insofar as uncertainty limits the predictability of policy impacts, it can also be the source for underestimating the negative consequences of policy actions. A particularly problematic scenario arises when uncertainty is high, but knowledge users are optimistic about the results of their actions. To the degree that existing ecosystems have been shaped to provide human benefits—after all, we have "coevolved" with nature[48]—the unpredictable impacts of human interventions on ecosystems are more likely to be adverse than positive. To be sure, if malarial mosquitoes were eradicated through unanticipated consequences of some human action, we all would rejoice, but for every such welcome consequence there are myriad unwelcome ones, such as inadvertently eliminating bees crucial for pollinating crops or bats that eat huge volumes of harmful insects.[49] An unpredicted consequence of preventing forest fires has been the pine bark beetle infestation that has greatly increased fire risks in the U.S. national forests. Yet policies with major impacts on ecosystems are often undertaken with severe underappreciation for these dangers.[50] Technical limitations in generating knowledge—much easier to identify than to overcome—result in inadequate incorporation of negative impacts of unknown or low-probability events and misestimation of physical and economic parameters.[51]

The reasons why the use of knowledge so often underestimates the degree of uncertainty are complicated. They begin with the failure of experts and knowledge entrepreneurs to transmit the degree of uncertainty. As mentioned earlier, signaling their ignorance is not something they relish, especially when the intended audience prefers certainty. By the time decision makers get policy relevant knowledge, it is often shorn of its caveats or any explicit statements of its questionable assumptions. Yet it is also true that decision makers frequently ignore expressions of uncertainty, anyway, for both psychological reasons and the need to be decisive when decisiveness is seen as a virtue.

Inadequate Knowledge

Once an issue becomes prominent on the policy agenda and the specific policy problem has been defined, legislative bodies and executive agencies often have only a short time to select among alternative policies. This brevity results in trade-offs between comprehensiveness of the knowledge available and the timeliness and efficiency of decisions to be made.

We have already mentioned that an alternative to making policy with inadequate knowledge is to postpone decision making until additional information can be collected. This delay can produce better policy, but it also means that the problem may fester unaddressed. The most obvious example is global climate change, where the costs of pursuing the wrong policy are extremely high, yet costs of inaction may be higher still.

The trade-offs among comprehensiveness, timeliness, and efficiency appeared almost immediately after the National Environmental Policy Act of 1969 was enacted, which required federal agencies to prepare environmental impact statements for major projects and policies. Some of the impacts simply could not be analyzed without new information.

For example, before the impact of a highway project on endangered or threatened species could be evaluated, a biological survey of the project area had to be done and a list of target species drawn up.

In some situations, sufficient information had been collected in advance of specific projects. The task was then to organize and transmit the information for use in the decision process. In these cases, agencies leveraged the data they already had on file about species, habitats, cultural resources, watersheds, and airsheds, and the information could simply be accessed when needed for an environmental impact statement. However, in other cases, information did not exist for specific species or archaeological resources, thereby requiring a case-by-case survey, which took time and cost money.

Several strategies exist to deal with the inadequacies of knowledge and the demands for timeliness in decision making. None is fully effective, however. Relevant knowledge may be collated, but there is rarely time to generate new knowledge. The classic legislative method of information gathering is the legislative committee hearing. Those testifying on environmental legislation are generally representatives of organizations that support or oppose the legislation, but they can also include experts from universities and think tanks. Persons giving testimony will often bring along detailed reports supporting their positions. It is not expected that policymakers will read these reports, but committee staff, many of whom have substantial technical expertise, frequently use them. The information often finds its way into the official committee report on the resulting legislation. These hearings provide an excellent venue for knowledge entrepreneurs to highlight—in a selective manner—information that will support their policy positions.

Where available knowledge is inadequate, policymakers' typical response is to set general directions and leave the details to a subsequent process, often administrative rule making. For example, when framing early air, water, and toxics pollution laws in the 1970s, members of Congress did not feel that they had enough technical information to set numerical standards. Congress left the strictness of the standard to later development by the regulatory agency, in the case of the Clean Air Act, or set a specific but very general standard, such as the fishable/swimmable standard in the case of the Clean Water Act. In either case, the EPA had to devote a great deal of its energy to formulating standards and then defending them in court. This detracted from its ability to implement policies and monitor results.

Another consequence of this delegation is that agencies such as the EPA cannot rely on the recognized democratic process to gain knowledge of public preferences. No matter what detail of preferences is provided in hearings or through documents gathered in the legislative process, administrative rule making by its very nature addresses issues on a level of specificity that the legislature has chosen not to resolve. Therefore, the legitimation of some public preferences over others that one might expect would come with legislative decisions is not forthcoming. Administrative agencies such as the EPA or the U.S. Forest Service are required to solicit information on public preferences, but they are left on their own to interpret what to make of these expressions. Thus, they face multiple levels of uncertainty in addition to the obvious scientific uncertainty: How should public preferences be determined? How will Congress and executive leaders interpret public preferences expressed in multiple ways as aspects of the public interest? How will the courts react to the next round of advocacy through litigation?

Biases in Definition of Objectives and Consideration of Alternatives
Putting a problem on the policy agenda is not the same as defining the objectives of policy. Knowledge entrepreneurs may have helped transmit information to create generalized public concern about toxic chemicals, but policymakers are more likely to face specific issues such as which agricultural chemicals should be banned or how much benzene a factory might be allowed to release into the environment. Knowledge users' needs differ from the focus of those who generate and transmit knowledge, and different policymaking processes call for different knowledge. The U.S. Department of Agriculture regulates agricultural chemicals, whereas the EPA limits toxic releases into the air, with major input from state pollution-control agencies. So the generalized concern over toxics becomes the subject of two very different decision-making processes that require different information and theories. The Department of Agriculture is interested in pesticide effectiveness as well as health risks; the EPA needs to know what impact the pesticide will have on downstream aquatic systems. The Department of Agriculture needs to know whether

genetically engineered plants will cross-pollinate other crops, jeopardizing their exportability; the EPA needs to know whether genetically engineered plants will escape to affect other plants or even ecosystems in adverse ways. Thus, how a problem is defined can influence what type of knowledge is most useful to decision makers.

What is measurable and operational from a knowledge-use perspective may not be most relevant for actually generating and transmitting relevant knowledge. Consider, for example, the problem of declining biodiversity. Policymakers and the public are by now well aware of the issue. The question is how to define biodiversity. From a scientific perspective, the definition should be operational, so the following largely unambiguous and (in principle) quantified definition has been conveyed to policymakers and has become the basis of the Endangered Species Act: the total number of species. Therefore, biodiversity conservation comes to be equated with preventing the extinction of individual species so that the total never falls. In fact, however, biological diversity can be defined in many ways—for example, as diversity of genes, species, assemblages, ecosystems, or ecological processes. And the dimensions of diversity can be defined in terms of variety, richness (number of different kinds of items found within a given area), or evenness (relative abundance of different kinds of items found within a given area).[52] The problem is that cataloging genetic material would be a Herculean task, and there is no straightforward, unchallengeable way to define assemblages, ecosystems, ecological processes, richness, or evenness that can be implementable from a knowledge-use standpoint. The U.S. ESA reflects one particular measure of biological diversity—the preservation of single species identified as rare and under threat of extinction—but neglects the other problem definitions of biodiversity decline that arguably may be of greater policy relevance. For example, an ecosystem's capacity to provide valued outputs depends on assemblages ranging from soil bacteria to pollinators. Several species often serve the same function within the ecosystem. An imbalance in the assemblage may be far more serious than the disappearance of a species. Once the problem has been defined as single-species management, both the universe of possible policies and the scope of relevant knowledge are also defined, which may limit the comprehensiveness of the knowledge used in a decision-making process.

Implementation, Evaluation, and Termination Challenges

Challenges with regard to the dependability and comprehensiveness of knowledge arise when there is a breakdown between who generates, who transmits, and who uses the knowledge. Applying a law or regulation to a specific environmental event or condition raises three challenges for knowledge.

Those who implement the prescriptions based on knowledge are rarely the same people who developed the knowledge. In fact, the two groups may consist of people with entirely different training, disciplinary orientations, and incentive structures. This difference raises the obvious challenge of effectively conveying knowledge and the routines for applying it, with enough information and guidance so that the applications can be sufficiently nuanced. The U.S. Army Corps of Engineers has had this problem in recent years as it has tried to offset the environmental damage caused by some of its water-resources projects by restoring environmental functions to nearby degraded land. Ecological restoration is a new and rapidly developing area within ecology. The Corps, skilled at engineering and even at avoiding environmental impacts, simply does not have adequate staff to implement and monitor ecological restoration projects.

Implementation also calls for more knowledge of human reactions to environmental policy than "environmental science" in its conventional definition typically provides. A policy, *if* fully enacted, may have the anticipated consequences of reducing pollution or preserving a species, but full implementation presumes that people subject to the policy will comply to a predictable degree. This expectation requires knowledge of the psychology of compliance, legal aspects of the consequences of noncompliance, and economic knowledge of the costs and benefits of different degrees of enforcement. Seldom does one person possess all the knowledge necessary to effectively implement a policy.

Perspectives among those who use knowledge are not monolithic. The presence of divergent perspectives poses challenges for agency officials who must implement management prescriptions. Prescriptions that are based on knowledge generated from aggregate data and generalized studies often overlook differences in the perspectives of those who implement policy and those who are affected by it.[53]

Dependably conveying knowledge from generation through transmission to use includes monitoring to assess whether the knowledge has proved relevant for ameliorating the given problem. For instance, developing effective implementation strategies requires stretching the range of environmentally relevant knowledge to encompass the factors that determine the degree of compliance with the rules. Many policy breakdowns can be traced to the failure to anticipate and overcome noncompliance. One of the major reasons why so many environmental agencies have had to shift from command-and-control regulatory approaches to more market-based approaches has been the belief that the latter will increase self-monitoring and voluntary compliance. The capacity for recognizing the need for new knowledge in evaluating the results of environmental decision making and for using it as a basis for terminating old policies and germinating new policies is often slow, incomplete, or nonexistent.

For several reasons, the accumulation of knowledge about how well a policy is working and new scientific discoveries about environmental systems do not in most cases cause the termination of old policies and the adoption of new ones. Because policymaking has costs, not least of which are policymakers and interest groups' time and attention, many policies are on a fixed schedule for review and revision. For example, once every five years Congress reviews farm subsidies and the conservation programs to which they are increasingly linked. Similarly, several years have elapsed between reauthorization and modification of the Clean Air Act and Clean Water Act, in part due to congressional committee schedules, in part to the emergence of new issues, such the Iraq War, which divert attention elsewhere.

Another reason for infrequent policy termination is that "policy learning"—the process that reveals the weakness of existing policies and management doctrines—tends to be very slow because of the buildup of interests with an economic stake in a given policy and the normal human tendency to resist admitting error.[54] A classic case is the Forest Service's longstanding reluctance to modify its policy of rapid suppression of wildfires, even after significant economic and environmental costs had been identified.[55] "Advocacy coalitions" reject knowledge that runs counter to their preferences and thus prolong the policy debates that may culminate in a policy change.[56]

A third reason for slow policy termination relates to knowledge itself. Thomas Kuhn's classic account of how the buildup of expertise among scientists makes them resist radical new theories has its counterpart at much more pedestrian levels.[57] If technicians who monitor drinking water are accustomed to testing for a certain list of chemicals, and they do so at the point at which the water moves from the water-treatment plant to the distribution system, they will not look favorably on the prospect of testing for additional chemicals in water from the taps of individual houses. Only if some dramatic new problem is suspected, such as lead leachate from household pipes resulting from use of certain water-treatment chemicals, will the testing method be modified.

Greater interest in setting the policy agenda, promoting policies, and establishing a prescription generally overshadows interest in actually implementing or evaluating policies. As a consequence, the role for knowledge in these later phases of the policy process is less emphasized than the role of knowledge in the earlier stages of the process.

Power Dynamics and Knowledge Use

Individuals and groups in many cases must have the technical skill to use knowledge. Information professions have mushroomed along with the diversification of skill sets required to use knowledge. Along with the proliferation of these professions, there has also been an increase in the technical proficiency required to utilize effectively the techniques to use knowledge.[58] The obstacles to using information from the Web, databases, geographic information systems, content analysis, computer models, and simulations lie less in physical access than in the skills necessary to find information in them and to utilize what is found. There are clear distributional consequences for those who possess access and the skills to utilize knowledge and for those who do not.

For example, it had long been a dream of urban planners to allow policymakers and citizens to visualize the results of alternative land-use policies, such as zoning or road construction. In the early 1980s, the Environmental Simulation Laboratory at the University of California, Berkeley, ran video cameras along tracks over tiny physical models of San Francisco and Times Square so that planners could see the results of alternative policies. Later, models were created with computer graphics, and the 1989 video game *SimCity* let players create their own environments. Today, interactive computer simulations are common tools not only for planners, but for the public in "visioning" exercises. These exercises allow citizens to create visual models of what a neighborhood might look like under alternative assumptions about density and building heights. Behind these models are algorithms that depend on the manipulation of enormous masses of information. In theory, using this kind of model can be as simple as playing *SimCity* (or the more recent environment-building games *Second Life* and *ActiveWorlds*). However, in some cases the model may contain a host of hidden properties. For example, a simulated building might cast a shadow, or it might not. The designer may determine this feature, and it is unlikely the user will notice it.

Another recent development has been the availability of technologies based on geographic information systems (GIS). GIS technology makes it possible to map complex data into easily understandable displays and to create predictive and optimization models for a wide range of environmental phenomena, which allows complex ideas to be represented visually for easier comprehension. For example, national and even local land-conservation organizations often use GIS to identify priority lands for protection, weighing parcels with criteria that can be changed with a keystroke. Efforts are being made to organize publicly accessible data sets that can be manipulated with GIS tools, including local and state wildlife and habitat databases. For example, the university-based Ocean Biogeographic Information System (OBIS)–SeaMap project has to date collected more than a million data points on sightings of marine mammals, sea birds, and sea turtles, spanning the years 1935 to 2007.[59] This information can be combined with data such as ocean temperature, shipping lanes, and fishing effort to find optimal designs for marine sanctuaries. Individuals can download data sets from the Web and can upload data they have collected.

Powerful information tools such as OBIS-SeaMap involve two issues, however. First, the GIS software programs needed to manipulate and map the data currently cost from $3,000 to as much as $30,000 each, although producers of these data sets are well aware of this limitation, and some are trying to link their information to Google Earth or to other free data-management and mapping tools. The second issue is much more difficult. Use of GIS programs requires a very high degree of knowledge not only about the software, but also about underlying physical and biological processes. Only highly trained people can use the available data, and only highly trained people can determine whether some other data user is adhering to accepted technical norms or not. For example, the OBIS-SeaMap data show very large numbers of sightings of some endangered whales. An unskilled—or malicious—user of the data set might map the data points and make the argument that these animals are abundant and need no protection. However, a whale biologist would understand that there may be multiple sightings of the same animal and that environmental conditions may lead even a rare species to congregate in a single spot. The problem is that although complex data can be universally conveyed, there are no universal guidelines for its use.

To use knowledge requires increased technical savvy to manipulate the tools that have emerged. These programs incorporate the designers' assumptions, but the user may be unaware of the hidden properties that affect the outputs from the programs. Information professions create programs to utilize knowledge, such as simulations, GIS interfaces, and so on. These tools also can be costly and require technical skill. Access to and the ability to utilize such knowledge effectively can create power differentials with consequences for who wins and who loses in environmental decision making.

Conclusion

As with knowledge generation, the transmission and use of knowledge are political phenomena. Various problems pose challenges to comprehensiveness, dependability, relevance, efficiency, and openness in knowledge transmission and use.

The diversification of transmission sources leads to greater difficulty in assessing comprehensiveness and dependability. Although tools such as the Internet have democratized transmission of knowledge, they have also created greater challenges in how to manage this knowledge for dependable use in environmental policy processes. Due to the diversification in knowledge transmission, uniform standards are lacking by which to judge what constitutes dependable knowledge. The amount of knowledge transmitted may have increased, but that does not mean the quality has increased or that it is relevant for specific problem contexts.

The privileging of formal science determines what forms of knowledge are most likely to be transmitted. It arises in part because there are in place clear processes for creating and assessing dependability in transmitting science-based knowledge—namely, the peer-review process—whereas the options for evaluating the dependability of local knowledge are less developed. Formal science works for the transmission of knowledge because we have a widely understood and accepted process for doing it. We do not have a parallel process in place for local knowledge. The consequence is that overreliance on formal science unnecessarily restricts the creative use of other types of knowledge in decision making.

Uncertainty contributes to risk-averse behavior in what types of knowledge are transmitted and through which channels it travels. Various filters in the transmission process—whether from legal, administrative, journalistic, regulatory or professional biases—limit the comprehensiveness of knowledge carried from generation to use. Credibility seeking and preferences for certainty influence what knowledge is transmitted. These professional biases are furthermore reflected in administrative and legal contexts.

A subset of policy actors, called knowledge entrepreneurs, specialize in transmitting knowledge into the policy process, providing a selective filter as they pursue their interests. They employ knowledge to pursue particular goals, and, in the absence of consensus among stakeholders on the priorities of these goals, this pursuit is political in the most fundamental sense of the term. Knowledge can positively or negatively affect intensity of demands, gain adherents for strategies, and create polarization. Individuals and groups disseminate knowledge to advance their own interests, policy preferences, and outcome preferences. Knowledge entrepreneurs further their own interests by seizing on focus events (e.g., an oil spill) and leveraging them to highlight a certain policy direction.

The underpinning of all these problems of transmission is its inherent political nature, even if some of the transmitters, such as formal scientists, do not regard it as such. Equally political processes are at work when knowledge is used. Mandatory uses for knowledge codified in laws and regulations specify which types of knowledge will be considered or not. Preferences for science and quantitative data are prevalent when knowledge is used in decision-making processes because they are seen to enhance credibility. Uncertainty is sometimes invoked for political reasons to delay decision making or to stimulate greater comprehensiveness in the knowledge that can be brought to bear on an issue, even though timeliness and efficiency are lost in the process. Knowledge likewise may be cited as being inadequate, even though the ability to reduce certainty in complex systems may be impossible. In both cases, more knowledge may not lead to consensus or even agreement; in fact, it may create greater divisiveness and disagreement.

4

How Knowledge Shapes the Environmental Policy Process

Knowledge is not only used in making environmental policy, but it can also change the policymaking process itself. As we have shown in chapters 2 and 3, the content of environmental knowledge impacts environmental decision making. For example, there is no doubt that the growth and dissemination of scientific knowledge about climate change and greenhouse gases has led to the Kyoto Protocol, ongoing international negotiations, and many other measures.[1] But the impacts of knowledge go far beyond their role as simply an input in policymaking. In this chapter, we show how the generation, transmission, and use of knowledge affects and in some instances distorts the policymaking process itself. In these cases, the standing of different forms and sources of knowledge shapes the arenas where decision making occurs as well as the very routines of decision making. In turn, these *governing biases* influence the participants involved in decision making, the skills sets that are favored in decision making, and the values and ideas that shape the outcomes from decision making.

The previous chapters gave many examples of how the generation, transmission, and use of knowledge impact policy outcomes. For example, the guidelines that govern decision making often explicitly call for particular types of knowledge. The policy process may also exclude certain types of information, as when the courts determine that expert judgments not based on peer-reviewed studies are inadmissible.[2] This determination has the same consequence of privileging participants and institutions in the policy process itself.

In some cases, however, the type of knowledge required for the knowledge processes utterly transforms the processes of decision making itself. Consider the 1981 presidential Executive Order 12291, "Federal

Regulation," which required benefit-cost analysis of regulations that exceeded certain impact thresholds. This requirement meant that a new set of agencies and people with a new set of skills became a major part of the policy process.[3] Participants lacking the ability to perform or at least understand benefit-cost analysis were now at a disadvantage relative to those comfortable with this economic technique. Keep in mind, however, that the impetus to require benefit-cost analysis would not have been plausible without the prior technical development of benefit-cost techniques.[4] An enormous literature addressing such issues as how to discount benefits and costs occurring in the future, how to decide whose benefits should have standing, and so on made benefit-cost analysis far more rigorous (although still not as rigorous as its adherents would like to argue). This accumulated methodological knowledge, not specifically developed for regulatory impact assessments by the U.S. federal government, enabled benefit-cost analysis to be adopted and in an important sense made it difficult for the federal government to resist requiring it.

As this example reveals, the impacts of knowledge on the environmental policy process itself are typically subtle and hardly recognized by those involved in the process, which makes the influences of these governing biases all the more entrenched because the dynamics often go unnoticed. In essence, the preconceptions of what knowledge ought to be and what decision analysis ought to be used constitute a frame that is often unchallenged.

The potential impacts of knowledge on the environmental policy process can be characterized along two dimensions. One dimension covers the different *arenas* through which initiatives to create or change laws, regulations, and practices affecting the environment can be pursued: levels of government (local, state, national) and branches or types of governmental institutions (legislative, executive, judicial, bureaucratic, regulatory). In the following section, we detail four patterns associated with how knowledge alters the arenas where policymaking occurs. First, the legitimacy or credibility of knowledge can impact the jurisdiction where an issue gets traction. Second, in some instances, knowledge demands have been used as a justification for centralizing policymaking at higher levels of government. Third, based on the knowledge participants possess, they may "venue shop" for the arena where their issue will receive the most responsive hearing.[5] In all of these cases, knowledge dynamics transform the arena where decision making occurs. Fourth, the prevalence of some analytical routines has made these techniques more central to decision making, while also shifting the locus of decision making from legislative to administrative arenas.

A second dimension of how knowledge affects the policy process itself covers *participants' status and power*. Both status and power can be changed by knowledge dynamics. When particular forms of knowledge make it compelling to use particular decision processes, the prevalence of these processes grants standing to some individuals, but not to others. In some cases, standing is ceded based on process participants' knowledge or expertise. Likewise, standing may be granted only to people directly harmed by environmental deterioration or to a broader set of stakeholders. In both cases, the knowledge leveraged in these processes alters who has status and power to participate in decision making. Another aspect by which participants' status and power may be altered is how their skills and strategies for knowledge acquisition and processing are valued. These skills and strategies include decision routines that influence how knowledge is packaged or even what kind of knowledge is relevant.

In the subsequent section, we cover patterns associated with how knowledge shifts the balance of power among participants in environmental decision making. First, we address how knowledge impacts the standing of individuals, organizations, and agencies. Second, we turn to how specific participants' knowledge based skill sets result in the privileging of these skills and participants in decision making. Third, we look at the role of competition and professional rivalries and how these dynamics can alter institutional processes in policymaking. Finally, we explore how systematic demands for types of knowledge result in the devaluation of nonexpert based input.

The Impact of Knowledge on Shifting Policymaking Arenas

The availability of sufficiently credible knowledge is often one of the criteria used for deciding *whether a particular arena is legitimate for policymaking*. Also, the political feasibility of using specific knowledge in a given political arena rests on whether the available knowledge can mobilize enough commitment within that arena.

Environmental advocates, industry representatives, and government officials face a situation of partially constrained options in deciding on the arenas through which they can pursue their policy initiatives. Of course, existing constitutional provisions, laws, regulations, and judicial doctrines set some limits on this discretion, and political considerations also restrict what is feasible. Nevertheless, some degree of discretion often remains: initiators may be able to choose among municipal, county, state, or federal levels, where they may be able to direct their efforts to elected executive officials, executive agency administrators, regulatory commissioners, legislators, or judicial officers.

Skepticism about the reliability of particular forms of knowledge also influences the environmental policy process through limitations of admissibility. Laws and legal doctrines that exclude particular kinds of information, analysis, and argumentation arose out of legislators' or jurists' conviction that those forms of knowledge can erode the policy process—for example, by confusing the deliberations through the introduction of "junk science." As our previous review of the *Daubert* decision indicates, court doctrines in particular exclude forms of testimony that do not meet certain scientific standards. Yet this exclusion also extends to prior decision stages, insofar as legislators and regulators need to anticipate legal challenges that may focus on the acceptability of the knowledge on which their analysis and decisions are based.

When knowledge is limited by legal rules of admissibility, the inadmissible information, analysis, conclusions, and recommendations may not be able to reach policymakers. In short, the knowledge restrictions embedded in these decision processes reduce the comprehensiveness of available knowledge and whatever creative thinking the excluded knowledge may have stimulated.

Another form of skepticism focuses directly on the considerations that particular forms of knowledge are expected to emphasize. Certain extremely important statutes, such as the ESA, do not permit benefit-cost analysis to be taken into account, presumably out of the belief that the rights to species survival may be undermined by the seductive logic of putting human monetary considerations above respect for nature. The Clean Water Act also does not permit benefit-cost considerations and simply mandates that waters be "fishable" and "swimmable." The Clean Water Act was one of the earliest (1972) of the modern environmental statutes, and this lack of a balancing criterion may reflect legislators' belief that clean water is an absolute human right.

Knowledge and Jurisdictional Shift

The availability of credible, admissible knowledge can serve as a switch point for establishing jurisdiction, in terms of both government levels (local, state, national) and the institutions within a given level. The rising status of benefit-cost analysis has advanced the importance of technical, bureaucratic agencies in making or influencing environmental policy decisions. For example, as the valuation of ecosystem services becomes more credible as a means of capturing both tangible and intangible benefits, the agencies mandated to conduct formal benefit-cost analysis become more prominent and their input more difficult to ignore. By the same token, the bureaucratic agencies mandated to oversee the use of these analyses become pivotal. Thus, the Office of Information and Regulatory Affairs (OIRA) of the U.S. OMB has become increasingly influential as the enforcer of methodological standards.

The way that knowledge can influence the level of government deemed appropriate for managing particular environmental issues is illustrated by the conflicts in the United States over which arenas are appropriate for determining whether and how to regulate greenhouse gas emissions. During the George W. Bush administration, some initiatives to regulate greenhouse gases existed at the local, state, and regional levels. Boulder, Colorado, had its own carbon tax; the Regional Greenhouse Gas Initiative emerged as a cooperative effort by northeastern and mid-Atlantic states to reduce carbon dioxide; New Jersey made a commitment to stabilize greenhouse gas emission reductions at 1990 levels by 2020. Yet the federal government attempted to block state-level greenhouse gas regulations.

The State of California, already given special status in the Clean Air Act because Californian automobile emission regulation preceded the federal government's, has the right to petition the EPA to impose more stringent emissions standards on vehicles sold in California.[6] In addition, other states can adopt the California standards once EPA permission is granted. California had received numerous prior waivers for tightening emissions standards to curb conventionally defined pollutants, such as fine particulates, but not to limit greenhouse gases. Under the George W.

Bush administration, however, the EPA refused to act on California's petition for permission to enforce a 2002 California law imposing more stringent auto emissions standards. The Clean Air Act required only that the EPA administrator determine that the California petition was not based on reckless analysis. As the evidence of climate change mounted and the Bush administration "admitted" that climate change is a problem, the basis for dismissing the petition eroded. Left without the argument that the California analysis was flawed, Administrator Stephen Johnson simply refused to take action on the petition. California and other states took their grievance to the Supreme Court, where it is likely that the states would have prevailed. In the event, the election of Barack Obama, committed to greenhouse gas regulation, resolved the conflict.

The resistance to *nationwide* greenhouse gas regulation was signaled by the EPA's 2003 announcement, under orders from the George W. Bush White House, of its determination that it did not have authority to regulate greenhouse gas emissions. The EPA invoked the argument that greenhouse gases were not pollutants as specified by the Clean Air Act. In response, twelve states (including California), three cities, and thirteen nongovernmental entities sued the EPA to force regulation of carbon dioxide emissions from automobiles.[7] With appellate court decisions taking different sides on the case, the dispute went to the Supreme Court. As knowledge regarding the impact of greenhouse gases on Earth's temperature became more credible, the Supreme Court in 2007 ruled that greenhouse gases in high concentrations do constitute pollutants, and therefore the EPA can regulate them. The EPA began to promulgate rules to this effect in case it would be required to do so by court directive, new legislation, or a shift in the administration's stance. Greater certainty in science, complemented by experiences with and observation of the consequences of climate change, transformed the arena where policymaking takes place. In 2009, after the Obama administration assumed office, the EPA indeed declared greenhouse gases to be pollutants and moved forward to regulate them.

At the same time, the U.S. Congress took up the issue of regulation of greenhouse gas emissions on its own, making this regulation a direct matter of legislative action. The 2009 movement to the legislative arena was predicated on the replacement of Representative John Dingell (D-MI), chairman of the House Energy and Commerce Committee, by

Representative Henry Waxman (D-CA). In representing an automobile-manufacturing state, Dingell had not been enthusiastic about raising auto emission standards. Waxman, representing a coastal district with minimal dependence on the auto industry, and his colleagues successfully passed a clean energy and climate bill in the summer of 2009, at which time the Senate Environment and Public Works Committee was slated to take up the issue under the direction of Chairwoman Barbara Boxer (D-CA). The Obama administration soon thereafter raised the corporate average fuel economy standards, and Waxman began moving forward major legislation on climate change and energy production.

In short, increasingly credible knowledge on global climate change forced changes in the arenas of environmental policymaking, spurring legislative action and contributing to the decisions to give jurisdiction over greenhouse gases to the EPA at the national level and to California and other states willing to adopt the California standards. One insight to be gained from this episode is that the venue for greenhouse gas regulation and therefore the scope that such regulation can have depend on what scientific determinations are accorded standing. Yet the acceptance of scientific judgments, such as whether carbon dioxide is a "pollutant" at high concentrations even if it clearly is not at lower concentrations, depends on the value determinations of whether the economic costs of regulating emissions are justified by the hoped-for reduction in global climate change. The question of which arenas have the authority to enact policies on greenhouse gas emissions hinges on a complicated mix of the credibility of knowledge (Do greenhouse gases really pose a significant threat?), jurisdictional battles, judicial doctrines, and interest-based politics.

Centralizing Tendencies

The California greenhouse gas–regulation case demonstrates that knowledge can trigger shifts to decentralized arenas. In other instances, there has been a tendency to use knowledge as a justification for centralizing policymaking at higher levels of government (i.e., from the local to the state level; from the state level to the national level). In these cases, the driving assumption is that more centralized forms of government are more capable of managing certain problems based on the need to satisfy knowledge demands.

If decision makers are wedded to the scientific management approach mentioned in chapter 2, the primacy of high-level knowledge dictates that decisions are made through top-down, bureaucratic, expert-driven institutions. Officials at the top make important decisions based on highly technical input; decisions flow down the bureaucratic chain of command and are implemented by people on the ground.

Thus, the practice of scientific management often creates a bias in favor of centralized government control of environmental and resource management. Scientific management is both a simplification strategy and a control strategy. Confidence in generalized scientific principles, as opposed to the more modest belief in the need for contextualized experimentation, implies that the centralized authorities can formulate prescriptions that will serve all.

Top-down policymaking based on overly generalized scientific propositions creates a number of perverse dynamics that must be overcome to implement policies that can maximize the sustainability of ecosystems and resource endowments.[8] For instance, the assumption that general rules should prevail often contributes to perverse learning, especially misgeneralization from past experiences to current and future contexts. When scientists, analysts, and policymakers assume that correct policies are straightforwardly derived from correct knowledge, the explanations for policy failures may be assumed to lie in the recalcitrance of affected publics or in the incompetence of the agencies responsible for implementation. Although this assumption may be very convenient for the policymakers, it is a severe limitation to the evaluation and improvement of policy choices.[9]

Such reductionist thinking sometimes provokes the adoption of resource-management doctrines or heuristics that ignore crucial specific circumstances of particular cases with regard to key operational assumptions necessary for centralized decision making. For example, the doctrine of "maximum sustainable yield" for renewable resources such as timber or fish requires determining the level of extraction that will not jeopardize the stock's capacity to replenish itself and taking into account other factors, such as weather and disease, that may affect the stock. As doctrines become entrenched, they may be accepted as scientific wisdom, even if they are oversimplified, disconnected from ultimate goals, or impervious to new knowledge. The maximum sustainable yield doctrine, widely assumed to be self-evidently valid, is based on the often unexamined assumption that the initial species mix of the stock to be managed is the optimal one. Therefore, embracing the doctrine precludes considering the possibility of reconstituting the resource base.

Once a doctrine becomes embedded in the policy or practices of an institution, it is especially difficult to entertain new knowledge that challenges the wisdom of the organization's past and current leadership. For example, the doctrine of forest fire prevention was so entrenched in the U.S. Forest Service that the growing scientific understanding of the negative consequences of eliminating fires from forest ecosystems was disregarded for decades.[10]

Public-management experts recognize that although some public policies should be formulated and enacted at the highest levels of government, other policies should be handled at lower levels. For environmental protection, the rationales for national control are strongest when impacts spill over from one state to another or when relevant expertise is so specialized, as in the case of nuclear-waste management, that national control is likely to be more effective. Yet decentralized control is justified when regulation must be adapted to local circumstances and different local preferences, going beyond national policymakers' capacity to tailor the application of national policies adequately or to plumb community preferences effectively.

Particular forms of knowledge can also induce centralization of decision making by defining problems broadly in light of highly aggregated information. If information gathering concentrates on national rather than local trends, diagnoses are more likely to be defined on that same broad level; the generation of solutions will tend to reflect the same breadth; and national policymakers will see themselves as the appropriate decision makers. Furthermore, as knowledge becomes more esoteric, the perception (whether valid or not) that officials at lower levels of government are less well equipped to address complex environmental issues becomes more prominent. This perception reinforces the widespread tendency among people, especially those with a certain level of expertise or experience, to believe that authority in their own hands is more reliable than authority in others' hands. Ronald Brunner documented this tendency in U.S. energy policy following the "energy crisis" of the mid-1970s.[11] Despite the opportunity for myriad local innovations, the federal government tried to centralize energy programs, leading to overly generalized policies and the neglect of promising local innovations. Some local communities, presuming that energy policy was a national rather than local issue, did not explore local policy options.[12]

This centralization tendency is further reinforced by the standards prevailing within science itself. A fairly widespread perception of science is that broader, more general theory is better than narrower theory. General theory tends to be reductionist theory because more complex theory entails configuring multiple elements, which focuses attention on the fact that in different contexts the configurations will be different. One implication of this high regard for grand, simple theory is the tendency to apply very broad diagnoses to policy problems, to seek information on large, aggregate scales, and, in turn, to generate broad prescriptions that overlook contextual differences.[13] The presumption that follows these solutions is that interventions are applied most effectively by a higher level of government.

Consider, for instance, how the demand for science can play out under the practice of ecosystem management, wherein demands for knowledge privilege certain types of institutional arrangements. Ecosystem management is potentially another form of knowledge demand that can lead to greater centralization, thus shifting the arena of decision making if higher levels of government are believed to be more proficient in the collection of such data. In its healthiest form, ecosystem management approaches the complexity of systems and the need to view them holistically by making governance jurisdictions correspond to ecosystem boundaries, increasing the levels of coordination, and combining multiple information sources from across the ecosystem.[14] Ecosystem management may also alternatively be interpreted as an argument for placing the main emphasis on information gathering and analysis. As Hanna Cortner and Margaret Moote have observed,

Ecosystem management requires understanding and tracking vast amounts of information, from ecological structures, processes, and stressors to ecological indicators and social values. . . . Society needs to consider all the effects of its management decisions: on downstream ecosystems, global economies, and local communities, to name a few. This requires an extremely broad geographic focus. Understanding the potential effects of decisions also requires information on the detailed aspects of ecosystem functions at site specific locations.[15]

Therefore, as knowledge discovers ecological connections spanning larger geographical areas, the argument for more centralized control grows stronger. Yet the risk is that policymakers may think ecosystem management requires that the highest government level dominate, even where it is not appropriate. The promise of ecosystem management is that if it is conjoined with adaptive management, it can incorporate local knowledge and local decision making, but transboundary issues can still be addressed at more centralized levels. Central policymakers often have a vested interest in increasing their jurisdiction, and the ecosystem philosophy may provide a convenient rationalization for this institutional end.

Venue-Shopping

When a degree of discretion exists in the choice of arena, those interested in launching a policy initiative may have the opportunity to generate or disseminate knowledge that steers the initiative into the arena that holds the greatest promise of their success. This "venue-shopping" refers to the strategic placement of policy issues at various levels in the federal (or state or local) governance hierarchy in light of institutional biases that favor some interests over others.[16] Venue-shopping may also extend to choosing one branch of government—executive, legislative, or judicial—over another. Advocacy groups, often including environmental scientists, sometimes take advantage of the fact that the perception of impending environmental crisis can elevate decision making to the legislative level, resulting in strong policies that favor environmental protection. At other times, they may find their advantage lies in the courts. In this manner, knowledge is leveraged strategically to shift the arena of focus for political advantage.

Various characteristics of knowledge are likely to make a difference in this respect. The content of the knowledge may focus on selected facets of environmental problems, with the effect of prompting action by different agencies or branches of government. For example, scientists who note habitat destruction in a particular location may undertake research on the causes of the degradation. They may find acid rain is at fault, which may imply that existing laws need modification and therefore that legislative initiatives are called for. Or research may focus on effects, such as the reduction of fish and wildlife populations, the possible disappearance of economically unimportant species, or the deterioration of water quality—all of which would require different executive agencies to address the effects.

The research may focus on different scales, prompting action by local, state, or national leadership to take up the corresponding issues. For example, research on ecosystem changes in a lake within a single state may trigger action in the state policy arena; a broader multistate watershed study may trigger national as well as state action.

The research may also be transmitted through selected media with different degrees of alarm, prompting different policymaking institutions to become involved. Many cases demonstrate a common though not universal pattern: knowledge that conveys a crisis flows first through popular media, mobilizing legislative action that results in broad and often incoherent laws, which then makes the judiciary the arena of environmental disputation. If an issue reaches a high enough level of public concern, elected officials feel compelled to take action. Therefore, one institutional impact of environmental knowledge rests on how much urgency it evokes, which in turn depends on how it is generated and transmitted.

The following examples illustrate how knowledge that conveys extreme threat pushes the decision making up to elected officials. Regarding biodiversity, the 1973 ESA was a straightforward national response to the dire warnings of species extinctions conveyed by Rachel Carson's *Silent Spring* and a spate of newspaper stories about the endangered status of charismatic species such as the Bald Eagle and the mountain lion.[17] No formal benefit-cost analysis was conducted. The resulting federal law—very species-oriented—was not a matter of reacting to technical studies about the decline in biological diversity, but rather to the much more urgent evocation of crisis.

The heavily publicized Love Canal tragedy (reviewed in chapter 3) and other high-profile land and sea contamination cases similarly led to the 1980 CERCLA legislation. David Lannetti notes that in addition to Love Canal,

High profile incidents cited by Congress in proposals for hazardous waste legislation included: the disposal of 17,000 drums of hazardous waste in the "Valley of the Drums" outside Louisville, Kentucky; the discharge of kepone, a hazardous insecticide, into the James River in Virginia; the polychlorinated biphenyl

(PCB) contamination of the Hudson River in New York through the discharge of electric insulating fluid by General Electric; and the contamination of Michigan livestock through ingestion of cattle feed contaminated with polybrominated biphenyl (PBB), a fire retardant.[18]

Lannetti adds that "the possibility of new federal legislation governing the release of hazardous substances gained acceptance in Congress after a series of major maritime oil spills resulted in the passage of federal bills governing oil spills and chemical wastes."[19] It is instructive that the actual incidents triggering federal action were often very specific and very local, yet there was a presumption that the key to preventing future incidents was necessarily federal.

Some scientists, dissatisfied with the pace and stringency of environmental regulation, have acted on the principle that dramatic pronouncements will drive the process to examine environmental risks in greater depth. The escalating debate on whether to regulate Bisphenol A, a compound found in plastic items ranging from baby bottles and sports bottles to microwave oven dishes and children's dental sealants, is an illuminating case in this regard (see chapter 6).

Moving issues into the national arena for a policy response is part of a long-observed pattern of issue expansion.[20] In the cases documented here, knowledge played a catalytic role in expanding the political debate to a wider arena. If knowledge does not elicit an adequate response when it is first transmitted, advocates have an incentive to switch arenas, thereby altering the policymaking process itself.

Analytical Routines and the Arenas of Policymaking

The rise of some analytical routines has not only made some of these techniques more central to decision making, but also altered where authoritative decisions will be made. Let us revisit the development and uses of benefit-cost analysis. Richard Stoll has demonstrated how the Supreme Court–imposed criterion of "reasoned decision making" has been bringing benefit-cost analysis closer to being a requirement for passing this test. He assesses two important cases decided in 2000: *American Petroleum Institute v. EPA*, involving a rule to regulate wastewater from petroleum refining and *Chemical Manufacturers Association v. EPA*, involving a rule to impose "maximum achievable control technology for hazardous waste combustors." He concludes that for both cases the District of Columbia Circuit Court vacated the EPA rules "because EPA's decision-making process did not adequately evaluate benefits in light of costs."[21] Despite the EPA's legislated mandate to impose *non*-benefit-cost criteria in the Clean Air Act, the Clean Water Act, and CERCLA, not only does the sway of benefit-cost analysis raise its own status, but its credibility can supplant agency jurisdiction in favor of judicial authority.

The OIRA, especially under John Graham, a noted advocate of the use of economics in regulatory decision making who was controversially appointed in 2001 by George W. Bush, greatly increased the number of regulatory proposals rejected through a "return letter" requiring modifications by the regulatory agency. Sally Katzen, who had headed the OIRA for five years under the Clinton administration, observed that "the cynical view would say that insisting on the best science is just a way of raising the bar and letting fewer regulations get through."[22] Although OIRA officials insist that they are upholding scientific standards, the opponents of OIRA oversight object that the office is derailing legislative mandates by requiring "rigor" that in key cases is unattainable.

In 2007, an amendment to Executive Order 12866 added a new requirement that a regulatory agency demonstrate that the regulation corrects a market failure.[23] A subsequent hearing by the U.S. House of Representatives Committee on Science and Technology, Subcommittee on Investigations and Oversight examined the argument that

OIRA has been using its circulars to force agencies to analyze and reanalyze the information underlying and supporting proposed regulations. Now, with the amended Executive Order, OIRA is putting in place an economic criterion—market failure—for regulation and guidance that may have nothing to do with the values established in statute. This effort is coming with no consultation or input from Congress. Further, by making the regulatory policy officer a more empowered gatekeeper, with political allegiance to the President, it raises the chances that the agencies themselves will find it hard during the Bush years to get regulatory proposals started or completed simply to submit them to OIRA for review. Congress did not empower agencies to protect public health and safety simply to then sit on its hands to see all Congress appropriates for regulatory-relevant science and the legal authority seated in agencies be trumped through a sweeping Executive Order.[24]

Imagine—as a thought experiment perhaps less outlandish than it might at first seem—that the systematic, fully explicit, monetized benefit-cost analysis of environmental regulations was regarded as simply infeasible.

This judgment would be based on recognition of the problematic methodological assumptions, the irreducible uncertainty of risks, and the inevitable neglect of some of the intangible benefits and costs. Under this scenario, the insistence on analytical rigor of the economic analysis would be misplaced. We would not see an OIRA, often with an antiregulation agenda, holding back the approval of regulations on the grounds that the analysis behind them is insufficiently rigorous.

What might replace benefit-cost analysis? We might see more doctrines based on meeting thresholds, as was the case with the U.S. Clean Water Act. When the original Clean Water Act and Clean Air Act were being drafted, Congress did not know how to set the standards. It took two tacks: for the Clean Air Act, it mandated that the EPA formulate regulations on ambient levels safe for people and vegetation, a task which occupied the agency for more than twenty years. But for the Clean Water Act, Congress simply fastened on the threshold of making rivers and lakes "fishable and swimmable." In some cases, the costs of bringing rivers and streams into compliance with this standard are far greater than the benefits that would accrue; in other cases, the standard is too modest from a benefit-cost perspective.

As it is, we see a continual struggle. On the one side are those who wish to bring legislation or the interpretations of legislation through the regulatory and judicial processes in line with the benefit-cost criterion. They require credible knowledge as inputs to the analytical process and credible analytic routines to justify their actions and influence. They may be pursuing negative policy objectives, such as limiting regulation, or they may simply believe that benefit-cost analysis is the best way of securing allocative efficiency across programs. On the other side are those who doubt that the benefit-cost analysis (and the valuations on which it is often based) can adequately capture the full scope of environmental benefits, those who believe that the rights to environmental protection should prevail even if the costs exceed the benefits, and those who oppose other elements of the agendas of the benefit-cost advocates. Anyone who asserts a right to environmental protection is rejecting the primacy of benefit-cost considerations: the essence of a right is that the protection ought to be afforded regardless of the costs.

Put another way, knowledge can play different roles in invoking particular laws and regulations and in determining how they will be applied. Benefit-cost analysis and expert valuation require highly knowledge-intensive inputs. The rights-based doctrines, as enshrined in the Clean Air Act and the Clean Water Act, also require environmental information, but of a different nature and for different purposes. Thus, there are reciprocal relationships among knowledge, the policies that require it, and the institutions mandated to use it.

By the same token, insofar as the existence of sufficiently credible knowledge (including analytical routines) privileges particular laws, the application of these laws privileges the knowledge on which they depend. The standing and perceived legitimacy of these analytical routines and knowledge over others alters the relative balance of power for specific statutes or regulations and thus for the arenas that take jurisdiction over the issue.

The Impact of Knowledge on Participants' Status and Power

The nature of credible, admissible knowledge shapes the relative potency of different skills required for actors to be effective in influencing change in the relevant policy processes. Technical science and decision-supporting techniques have deepened as the number of doctorates in environmental and related sciences has increased, the publications on environmental science and policy have proliferated, and various analytic approaches have gained more respectability and credibility. Environmental advocacy organizations have become more professionalized, calling for different skill sets. As the efforts to strengthen or block environmental initiatives have shifted arenas, some types of mastery over environmental knowledge have also become more prominent. Within most arenas, competition pits government units against one another and nongovernmental groups against other nongovernmental groups. The availability of credible knowledge can provide organizations with the wherewithal to play a prominent role in the decision-making process. Knowledge of high standing can also elevate the officials and experts who rely on this knowledge or are respected for their mastery over it.

Standing in Policymaking

Standing influences different participants' authority in environmental policymaking. Although standing has a formal, legal meaning, in practice what gives individuals, government agencies, and other organizations standing includes the credibility and availability of the knowledge at their command. For example, although the NRC of the National Academy of Sciences has no formal policymaking authority, its reports are afforded great credibility and deference in policymaking because the panels are composed of foremost experts in the field under scrutiny. By being in possession of the best knowledge, these experts provide privileged standing to council panels and the influence they bring to bear on policy.

Other agencies and organizations may specialize in specific types of knowledge, which then accords them standing within a given policy arena. For example, the U.S. FWS cannot have credible influence in formulating regulations on agricultural runoff or play a role in natural resource damage assessment and restoration efforts without a wide base of knowledge. It must have data on actual contaminations and assessments of the toxicity of various contaminants. It must rely on theories about the impacts of sediment disturbance on the release of toxins and the possible toxin-produced fish mutations. The agency collects some of this information in the course of its normal work, but other data require special studies (and the financial resources to perform them). Thus, the availability of knowledge can have a major impact on the influence the agency can exert, even within its central area of expertise. The budget for conducting or gathering knowledge therefore becomes a critical resource for agency influence.

The standing of different aspects of environmental knowledge within communities of experts shapes the acceptance of particular kinds of environmental knowledge, which in turn signals to policymakers which information warrants more serious consideration. Experts, both to maintain what they view as the integrity of their disciplines and to protect their personal reputations, shy away from sharing information or insights that they regard as less rigorous and therefore less scientifically defensible. Or they may relegate such knowledge to a subsidiary status compared to apparently more rigorous findings, thereby signaling to policymakers what they should take into account. Thus, the expectations and behavior of environmental scientists, whether in the biophysical or social sciences, about the standing of knowledge has major impacts on restricting the availability of knowledge for use in the decision-making processes.

Skills and Analytical Routines

As different professional knowledge bases, analytical routines, or technical proficiencies are favored, different value sets will influence what type of knowledge is privileged in decision routines and outcomes. The range of credentials at play in influencing environmental policy has greatly expanded. For mobilizing people to press for particular policies, skills in communications and public relations have become important; for drafting ever more complex regulations and engaging in litigation, legal credentials have gained status. Perhaps the most striking rise in prominence has been among experts credentialed in economics, computer modeling, and statistics. Quantified, monetized information on benefits and costs alters the constitutive basis for environmental decision making by giving greater weight to formal benefit-cost analysis, which in turn gives greater influence to the specialists, especially economists, who are able to perform such analyses and have the credibility to insert them in policymaking. Economists are not the only technical experts privileged by advances in knowledge. The greater standing of atmospheric and oceanographic information as needed inputs for climate-change predictive modeling increased the authority of scientists skilled in these areas, and their huge data needs have swelled the budgets of some data-gathering agencies at the expense of other agencies.

A very wide range of *evaluative analytic methods* aid in making decisions by analyzing aspects of the environment and, in some instances, aspects of human preferences regarding the environment. Among the most prominent are:

• methods to guide and assess whether rights-based rules should be invoked, as in whether species are in danger of extinction

• valuation techniques that estimate willingness to pay for or willingness to accept environmental changes

• benefit-cost analyses that systematically identify, monetize, and calculate the net benefits of changes expected to result from particular policy options

• habitat equivalency analyses that estimate how much restoration would compensate for the loss of environmental services following toxic dumping or accidents[25]

• quantitative optimization models that estimate the optimal mix of effort or investment

• ecological footprint analyses that rank land-use alternatives in terms of how efficiently (in terms of various inputs) they produce valued outputs, such as timber, recreational opportunities, and ecosystem services

• methods for eliciting and evaluating "local knowledge," such as participatory research and local resource-use mapping

• methods for eliciting and evaluating information on public preferences, including polling, analysis of written comments, and facilitated public meetings

These evaluative methods are part of the mutually reinforcing process through which knowledge determines the very structure of the environmental decision-making process. Each evaluative method relies on particular information. For example, habitat equivalency analysis requires projections of how long it would take to restore a damaged ecosystem and estimates of the value of the curtailed ecosystem services. Each method also takes particular considerations and types of policy appeals into account. For instance, emphasis on ecological functions that can be quantified privileges them as compared with the less-measurable aspects, and it often emphasizes the goal of maximizing aggregate utility rather than observing rights. The use of particular evaluative methods will increase the power of those who operate them and thereby their priorities and preferences. For example, ecologists and toxicologists are pivotal in determining whether the thresholds that trigger rights-based rules will be invoked; valuation requires natural scientists to project the biophysical impacts of particular options and social scientists to elicit how people perceive and regard these changes in terms of monetary trade-offs. Habitat equivalency analysis requires biologists to understand the biophysical characteristics of habitats and economists to gauge the costs of forgone benefits until the habitat is restored. The ecological footprint analysis[26] requires engineers and economists to take into account human production as well as biologists to assess biophysical capacities and outcomes.[27] Psychologists, survey specialists, and political scientists are often central to the tasks of eliciting and interpreting public input.

The rise of the disciplines of conservation biology and ecology has reinforced the consideration of ecological factors in environmental policymaking, thereby requiring natural scientists' expertise. The projection of biophysical consequences is the initial input in benefit-cost analysis of environmental changes. In addition, some of the key evaluative concepts of these disciplines—such as biodiversity indicators, energy balances, and ecosystem-collapse risks—do not translate into benefit-cost terms, placing the economist alone at the interface with policymakers.

It is a commonly held fallacy among environmental activists that benefit-cost analysis is always biased against environmental protection. In fact, *if* the environmental benefits are sufficiently captured, benefit-cost analysis can identify when existing environmental regulations permit pollution despite the fact that environmental costs exceed the benefits. For example, although the Clean Water Act is often viewed as a bulwark against the environmental offenses of polluting industries, it calls only for the use of the best "affordable" antipollution technologies, even if the pollution damage still exceeds the costs of control. In such cases, a benefit-cost analysis would call for shutting down the polluting activity.

Competition and Professional Rivalries

Political motivation to influence policy outcomes has impacts on the standing of different aspects of environmental knowledge because those interested in effecting particular outcomes have an incentive to discredit the methods, theories, and findings that will weaken support for these outcomes. The tactic of hiring "dueling experts" to question the science, consistency, or completeness of an opponent's analysis in order to undermine the preferred outcomes is well known.

The desire for a privileged position in decision making is manifested through competition and professional rivalries. Competition among groups of specialists often hinges on whose expertise is perceived as most relevant in the decision-making process. Jockeying to demonstrate which knowledge base is most important or to create a favored status for one group of participants over another can result in changes in decision-making processes that formally demonstrate a privileged status.

Consider, for example, the rivalry among specialists in the confrontation between ecologists and the U.S. Forest Service regarding the agency's commitment to ecological sustainability. The essential issue is the degree of influence that ecologists and ecological knowledge have in Forest Service planning. The Forest Service's Committee of Scientists was reconvened in 1997 to provide guidance for the issuance of new planning regulations for the agency. Originally created to provide guidance for the formulation of the 1976 NFMA, the thirteen-member Committee of Scientists comprised subject-matter experts from all disciplines relevant to forest management. Following two years of meetings, the committee released a report in 1999 that established "ecological sustainability" as the Forest Service's guiding principle.[28] This pronouncement followed contentious debates within the committee over whether a tripartite measure of sustainability—ecological, economic, and social—should prevail. [29]

In 2000, the Forest Service proposed new planning guidelines consistent with the primacy of ecological sustainability However, in 2005, after a change of administrations and new appointments, the Forest Service issued new regulations, which immediately drew the ire of conservationists and the community of biological scientists. As a 2005 article in the journal *Conservation Biology* notes,

In January 2005, without convening a Committee of Scientists, the Forest Service issued a new set of regulations . . . [that] only minimally address ecological sustainability, failing to recognize that it is foundational to social and economic sustainability, and [that] greatly diminish public empowerment in the management of their lands. Specifically, the new regulations eliminate as a goal the obligatory protection of biological diversity, eliminate the requirement to prepare environmental impact statements...and reduce the role and influence of science in the development and implementation of forest plans. . . . The 2005 regulations completely eliminate the requirement that forest plans maintain viable populations of vertebrate species, along with the requirement that management indicator species be designated and monitored. In their place, the new regulations allow for unlimited discretion to "provide for ecological conditions to support a diversity of native plant and animal species in the plan area." This language does not provide a measurable, or enforceable, standard . . .[30]

The authors (two biologists and a legal scholar) frame the conflict in terms of scientists and the public versus the bureaucracy. They bemoan the demotion of ecological sustainability from its former status as the fundamental management objective, accusing the Forest Service not only of inappropriately downgrading the objective, but of failing to recognize the scientific wisdom that ecological sustainability is a requirement for socioeconomic sustainability. The Forest Service's adoption of new regulations without convening the Committee of Scientists is cast as a violation of both scientific responsibility and legislative mandate. According to the authors, it also contravenes the foundational legislation that provides public access to the authoritative decision-making process and reduces both public oversight and scientists' capacity to determine whether Forest Service practices adhere to the "best available conservation science."[31]

The article reflects an effort to use ecological science to challenge agency decisions at the bureaucratic level for violating policies established through legislative decision making, which also required public accountability. This critique revives the criticisms that motivated the NFMA in the first place. The authors make it clear that they believe the bureaucracy's disregard for legislatively mandated requirements for sound science and public accountability justifies a court challenge.

The relative balance of power of ecologists in the debate waxed and waned. The planning regulations were still under court challenge in 2009, in part due to the concerns about the role ecology should plan in national-forest planning. The end result was to shift the locus of policy-making from the administrative to the judicial realm. Judges will be the final arbiters of what constitutes the most legitimate knowledge base for national-forest planning.

Expert versus Lay, Activist, and Interest-Group Input

The privileging of some sources of knowledge runs the risk of displacing other sources of knowledge. As more precise measurement techniques are favored (whether they are actually more precise or not), they elevate experts over lay people, activists, and interest groups, as has happened in a succession of quantitative models of resource management, from optimization models in the 1970s to GIS-based models today.

In 1979, the Forest Service designated the Forest Planning (FORPLAN) Model as the "required analysis tool" for forest planning.[32] It was the successor to earlier timber and watershed models, but it had the virtue of considering trade-offs among a wide range of forest outputs. Because these outputs were measured in different units (e.g., acre-feet of water, cords of pulpwood, recreation visitor-days), elaborate valuation studies were conducted to reduce incommensurables to a common unit, an imputed dollar value. FORPLAN fed off the information generated by the diverse informational inputs required by the relevant federal legislation,[33] including public hearings and the collection of comments to draft plans for each of the National Forests. Yet FORPLAN also influenced the type of information generated and used. For example, qualitative information and local site-specific information were less desirable than information that matched FORPLAN's output categories and areal units of observation. In 1989, Alan McQuillan judged,

FORPLAN cannot adequately handle spatial relationships . . . Game animals move between ridge tops and creek bottoms; soil erosion, like water, flows from upslope to downslope; certain areas can be seen from the highway and others are obscured by topography; if a certain area is logged, then adjacent timber needs to be left standing to provide for reseeding, and so on. However, the spatial nature of these relationships shields them from the vision of FORPLAN. In a roadless drainage, timber stands cannot be scheduled for logging unless roads can be built for log hauling. However, if the forest plan allocates a critical entry point to the drainage to remain in roadless condition, then road building cannot proceed anywhere. This logic escapes FORPLAN.[34]

Moreover, the use of FORPLAN minimized stakeholders' effective participation. The FORPLAN process invited participation, but the participants were presented with bulky documents that offered what appeared to be a most rigorous and scientific investigation and ranking of policy options. To be sure, the valuation of outputs such as timber supplies and recreational opportunities reflected stakeholders' preferences, but the model took into account neither the stakeholders' *policy* preferences nor the importance of interaction. By the late 1980s, the overall planning effort was a clear failure, and FORPLAN was eventually abandoned. McQuillan concluded that "it appears that the designers of the forest planning process never recognized this need [to restore public trust in the forest planning process]. Instead, they perceived an overriding need to determine the optimal, socially efficient forest plan. . . . [T]hey adopted a sophisticated 'black box' model (FORPLAN) which is not only inaccessible to many of the agency's own professionals, but also beyond the general reach and scrutiny of an intelligent public."[35]

The patterns prevalent in FORPLAN are evident today in the use of valuation techniques. To the degree that expert valuation gains acceptance and prominence, the clear message is that public preference can be represented without direct public expression of policy preferences. Several background points are necessary to explain this view.

The expression of preferences directly from private actors can be seen as part of the traditional "politics of the policy process," in which individuals and groups let their preferences be known to influence government policymakers. These preferences are expressed in terms of both outcomes ("We want swimmable rivers") and concrete policy preferences ("We want that paper plant closed down; we want marshes to be restored, paid for through bonds"). Granted, several U.S. laws provide opportunities for direct public input into environmental policymaking. The NEPA of 1969 requires public hearings and comment periods for federal actions that significantly affect the environment, and the EPA's Scientific Advisory Board committee meetings are open to the public and must accommodate public comments.

However, experts and policymakers may be interested only in finding policies that satisfy their outcome preferences, even if the public does not prefer these policies per se. For example, the former may believe that higher gasoline taxes are the best way to satisfy the preference for less air pollution, even if the public (or certain segments of it) would prefer a policy of tighter regulation of factory emissions. In such a scenario, the expert valuation of public preferences may reflect the public's priorities regarding the outcomes of air pollution levels (typically cast in terms of willingness to pay for a given reduction in pollution) rather than the public's preference for ways of achieving such outcomes. Unlike direct public participation in policymaking processes, during which any citizen, in principle, can exercise voice, the dominant expert-valuation approaches sample either consumer behavior ("revealed preferences") or stated opinions of a sampling of citizens. If the approach is to make inferences from the preferences revealed through purchases of houses, payment of entry fees at parks, and so on, the stakeholders' inputs are purely passive; in fact, the stakeholders are probably unaware that their economic behavior is being assessed to gauge their valuation of environmental services. If the approach is to establish values through the "stated-preference" approach of asking a sample of stakeholders about their willingness to pay, the public's input is also only partial and, because the questions are formulated by the valuators, passive as well.

The fact that the standard approaches to expert valuation capture outcome preferences but not policy preferences is, in some circles, a great virtue rather than a limitation. Credible knowledge about the public's outcome preferences derived through these standard approaches is regarded as more genuinely reflective of the "true" values held by all stakeholders than are activists' expressions of policy demands. According to this perspective, determining stakeholders' values through inferences drawn from active citizen participation is a poor way to gauge these "true" values because participation reflects exposure to possibly distorted appeals to support particular policy initiatives. A highly influential manifesto by Nobel Prize laureate Kenneth Arrow and eleven other prominent economists argues in favor of expert valuation and benefit-cost analysis in these terms:

Whenever possible, values used to quantify benefits and costs in monetary terms should be based on trade-offs that individuals would make, either directly or, as is often the case, indirectly in labor, housing, or other markets. Benefit-cost analysis is premised on the notion that the values to be assigned to program effects—favorable or unfavorable—should be those of the affected individuals, not the values held by economists, moral philosophers, environmentalists, or others.[36]

This statement denies the standing of the public's political input in expressing policy preferences and, for that matter, of interest-group input as well. John Loomis similarly argues that "valuation studies have the potential to provide an effective way to diminish the often bemoaned role of 'special interests' in the current policy process."[37]

Others, including some economists, not surprisingly reject this anti-politics stance as both unjustified and quixotic. Ethicist Mark Sagoff labels this position as strikingly nonreflexive.[38] It fails to see that activism is an indication of intensity of commitment. Most fundamentally, it rejects the legitimacy of the promotional function of the policy process and the ability of policy entrepreneurs and persons in leadership positions to convince the public to change their values. Sagoff argues that both markets and democratic decision-making inevitably and legitimately shape values. If one accepts this premise, it calls into question the validity of preferences inferred from valuation approaches that ignore the socio-economic contexts in which they are shaped. Economists Leonard Shabman and Kurt Stephenson similarly argue that values are and should be shaped by the policy discourse: "When residents enter the polling booth, they face the similar [willingness to pay] question not as a purchaser of reduced flood risk, but as a city citizen. This makes the search for a 'true,' 'correct,' or 'unbiased' benefit estimate a futile one. Indeed, different benefit estimates from different techniques are not to be explained away, they are to be expected."[39]

Conclusion

In chapters 2 and 3, we addressed the problems associated with generating, transmitting, and using knowledge in policymaking processes. In this chapter, we brought to light how knowledge impacts the policymaking process itself. These governance biases are often taken as incidental side effects, if they are noted at all. We feel they deserve explicit attention because they have profound impacts on the institutional processes of decision making.

The two institutional dimensions most affected by knowledge are, first, the arenas where policymaking takes place and, second, the status and power of various kinds of participants in the policymaking process. Political actors undertake to shift these institutional foundations where policymaking occurs. Participants sometimes use knowledge to alter the level of government addressing a given issue or the branch of government taking action. Advocacy groups venue-shop based on their knowledge of institutional biases and institutional accessibility. The privileging of specific knowledge bases, analytic routines, or skill sets likewise elevates or lowers some participants over others. What is perceived as credible or legitimate at one point in time may change in the future. Requirements for the use of certain types of knowledge in a decision process, such as administrative requirements for benefit-cost analysis, may bias the use of some information over other information, with the concomitant result of favoring some participants and some considerations over others.

5

The "Ecology" of Knowledge and the Environmental Policy Process

We can adopt the metaphor of ecology to understand the interplay of the generation, transmission, and use of knowledge as well as the broader impacts of these processes on the policymaking process itself. Each element of this complex system influences each other element. This chapter lays out the interconnections and assesses the opportunities for improving environmental decision making in light of the rigidity that might arise from the fact that these aspects are so intertwined.

Four fundamental patterns can be found:

• The generation, transmission, and use of knowledge reinforce one another by elevating the standing of and demand for knowledge that is created or invoked in each of these functions.

• Different laws, executive orders, court decisions, regulations, and decision processes take different approaches in the use of knowledge, reflecting different normative principles regarding the appropriateness of basing environmental decisions on utility calculations, fairness, or rights.

• When the application of knowledge through particular environmental decision routines (laws or regulations) results in consequences that key actors find unacceptable, they will try to modify or reject the knowledge or the decision routines to blunt these consequences.

• The world of science and the world of advocacy intersect with different objectives and standards, requiring various forms of mediation.

The Mutual Reinforcement of Knowledge Generation, Transmission, and Use

The bottom-line use of knowledge is an authoritative decision by governmental officials to adopt new laws or regulations, to judge whether a particular law or regulation should be invoked, or to carry out the application of that law or regulation. Much of the knowledge that goes into these decisions has been transmitted—and filtered—through several stages.

In the previous chapters, we artificially applied divisions between the generation, transmission, and use of knowledge to elaborate on their functions in environmental decision processes. Although these functions are analytically distinct, the exercise of each actually involves the others. Each will shape the conduct of the other two, as illustrated in figure 5.1.

To understand these particular interrelationships, it is useful to map out the decision process in abbreviated form. Knowledge used in environmental decision-making processes is created by several different types of sources, and it is transmitted initially through various media (journal articles, experience, training manuals, the Web, extension materials, social networking, news media, and immediate word of mouth). A vast

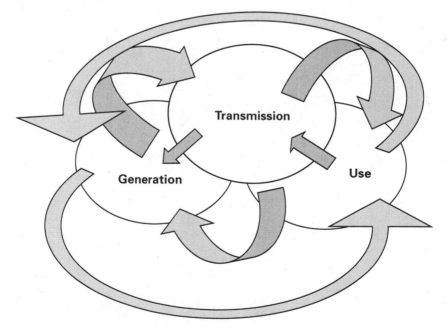

Figure 5.1
Ecology of the generation, transmission, and use of knowledge in the environmental decision-making process.

amount of knowledge—whether sound or not—is "out there." When an environmental issue comes onto the active policy agenda, a "predecision analysis" is conducted—within government agencies or by entities contracted by government agencies and various stakeholder groups. This analysis uses existing knowledge, but it also creates new knowledge in the form of its own synthesis, findings, and recommendations.

For example, an analysis prepared to consider more stringent regulation of the development and use of GEOs will rely on the existing knowledge of plant genetics and on engineering studies regarding the effectiveness of containment, but if the analysis concludes that more stringent regulation is not justified, this conclusion in and of itself constitutes new knowledge for the environmental decision-making process.

It deserves emphasizing that the multiple participants in these processes also interact and give rise to interdependencies of their own. The overall quality of the policy outputs depends on the interdependencies throughout the process. Generators, transmitters, and users may have little awareness of or interaction with each other and no knowledge of the role that others play in the larger picture, or they may have tight links with each other.

Generation Entails Transmission

A very common side effect of the generation of knowledge is the transmission of prior knowledge because formal science relies very heavily on the cumulative development of data and theory. Therefore, the scientific generation function invokes prior studies, often many of them. In invoking these studies, the new study, if it is respected because of its own content or where it is published, legitimizes these prior studies. This legitimation is reflected in the importance that citation counts play in rewarding research and scholarship.[1] In other words, the generation of current environmental knowledge transmits and adds to the credibility of the previous studies on which the new studies are based.

This same sort of relationship holds for applications of knowledge in the predecision analyses that bridge knowledge generation and authoritative decision. For example, the EPA's regulatory impact analyses base much of the analysis on the data, theory, and valuations derived from previous studies. As we explore in greater depth in chapter 6, one of the most striking, though problematic, examples is the regulatory impact analysis for the 2002 concentrated animal-feeding operations rule, which required a valuation of the consequences of more stringent regulation of the waste disposal of large livestock and poultry operations.[2] The analysis applied a twenty-year-old valuation undertaken in the 1981 report *An Experiment in Determining Willingness to Pay for National Water Quality Improvements*.[3] In essence, the use of the Mitchell-Carson study (even though it was designed for totally different purposes) transmitted and legitimized that study for contemporary use, despite the qualms that others have expressed about its continuing relevance.[4]

There is often strong path dependence once a prior study or finding has been invoked in the generation of new environmental knowledge. That is, an earlier work that is subsequently used in one new study is more likely to come to the attention of others and is more likely to be regarded as acceptable for further use. This tendency is known as the "founder effect."

Some knowledge pathologies can arise from the founder effect. One is that prior studies will come to be accepted as gospel, but sight of their limitations in both quality and scope of reasonable applicability is lost. Another is that if a flawed data set or empirical study seems authoritative and is the best available, it will have a disproportionate impact on subsequent work. For example, Kate Showers argues that a widely used 1977 Food and Agricultural Organization soils map for Africa "demonstrate[d] how scientifically accepted techniques of data manipulation can create apparently authoritative misinformation and perpetuate stereotypes about Africa." In this case, a generalized map prepared from very limited field data "became the basis for all subsequent African continental soil maps" and was used to construct subsequent "crisis narratives" about the prospects for African food production. Showers complains that a "tradition of unquestioned expert opinion combined with the authority of science" caused this map to be accepted while local and indigenous systems of knowledge about soil were ignored.[5]

The use of knowledge in making environmental policy decisions requires that the knowledge be conveyed through additional analysis in order to work out the details for its application to the specific case at hand. In general, we would expect the analysis to add to the visibility and credibility of the knowledge on which it is explicitly based. The use of an earlier estimate or study or model implies that it is relevant and sound.

Use Requires Transmission and Often New Generation

For knowledge to be used, it must be effectively transmitted. So far we have presented the dynamics that raise the standing of information as it is generated, transmitted, and applied to policy decisions. Yet some knowledge comes to be discredited or simply neglected. Effective transmission means overcoming challenges about the knowledge. The challenges may question the validity of the knowledge by attacking its substance, the methodology by which it was generated, or its relevance to the case at hand. Critics may also challenge the standing of knowledge generators or the legal standing of the knowledge itself. Data can always be questioned in terms of accuracy or whether the measurements are meaningful. Challenges to the bottom-line assessments of the magnitude and valuation of environmental effects occur all the time. For example, any estimate of the risks involved in allowing fish waste to escape from aquaculture operations can be challenged as being too high or too low, just as any assessment of the health hazards of cultivating genetically engineered plants can be questioned.

Challenges to knowledge occur in research settings and publication outlets, bureaucratic agencies, legislatures, and courts. The bases of these challenges differ across the types of institutions involved in generating, transmitting, and using environmental knowledge. Within universities and other conventional scientific research settings and transmission media, substance and methodology are most likely to be challenged, although on occasion the standing of the source of the knowledge is also relevant and thus can be challenged. In bureaucratic, legislative, and judicial arenas, challenges to substance and methodology are typically presented by experts with credible credentials who assert opposing data, models, or interpretations. At the same time, the admissibility of the knowledge depends on legal doctrines that go beyond whether the knowledge is perceived as sound.

More up-to-date studies by credible experts sometimes supplant earlier assessments. The effectiveness of this replacement depends on whether the defenders of the earlier studies respond by questioning the assumptions or methods of the later studies. When this push-back does occur, as in the case of the skeptics of global climate change, it typically requires institutions—seen as reflecting scientific consensus—to overcome the stalemate of "dueling experts." For climate change, the Intergovernmental Panel on Climate Change has played this role.

Amid serious concerns about GEOs exacerbating consumer allergies or becoming destructive elements within natural ecosystems, the U.S. National Research Council convened several committees to assess the health and environmental risks of using GEOs.[6] The United Kingdom's Royal Society did the same.[7] Reviewing the scientific claims asserted in the literature *and* noting the lack of serious problems in farming and human health attributable to the rapid expansion of GEOs in the United States and the United Kingdom (e.g., no rise in allergies that can be attributed to GEOs), these committees of eminent scientists placed these risks into the broader context of ecosystem interactions. For example, they noted that people "eat the DNA" of other organisms all the time; this consumption does not change the consumer's genetic makeup, and there is no reason to expect that GEOs will be different in this respect. In this way, the use of knowledge required effective transmission of hundreds of studies reviewed by the panels and at the same time called forth the generation of new knowledge provided by the panels' syntheses of the existing knowledge.

Transmission Legitimizes and Encourages Generation and Use

For many environmental scientists in both the biophysical and social sciences, publication in peer-reviewed journals is the sine qua non of professional respect and advancement. Just as a citation in a credible communication medium rewards those responsible for the communication, a publication conveying new knowledge in such a medium is also rewarding—typically even more so. Therefore, opportunities to publish or convey knowledge credibly expand the incentives for scientists to generate knowledge in forms consistent with these types of transmission.

A prime example of this stimulus from expanded media can be found in the growth of "ecological economics" and the publications that serve the ecological economics movement.[8] Since 1989, the journal *Ecological Economics* has been publishing interdisciplinary articles, many with heterodox economics that would not be accepted in the mainstream neoclassical economics journals. On the basis of the citation counts that determine the journal rankings to which economists pay a lot of attention, *Ecological Economics* has achieved a middling rank[9] and is certainly a respectable publication outlet for environmental economists and others writing on the intersection of natural and social systems. *Ecological Economics* publishes more than 20 articles in each of its twelve issues annually. With more than 240 articles per year, the journal clearly provides a major venue for articles that would find a greater challenge to be published in other respectable journals.

Use Encourages Creation and Transmission of New Knowledge

In chapter 2, we observed that a great deal of knowledge is created by government-funded science. Although some of this expenditure is meant simply to advance the state of knowledge in general, much of it is the direct result of prior policymaking. Legislators typically write laws that include general goals or statements of intent, leaving administrative agencies to promulgate detailed regulations. But the agencies sometimes have an inadequate scientific basis for doing so, particularly in situations where their rules are likely to face court challenge.

A notable example is the Clean Air Act of 1970, which (among other things) directed the EPA to identify air pollutants that damaged human health. The act itself identified neither the chemicals nor the levels of concentration that would pose threats to human health. Among the obvious targets was ozone, a component of photochemical smog. But what concentration of ozone is dangerous? Should the standard be for a one-hour, an eight-hour, or a twenty-four-hour exposure? And should the protection be for the average healthy adult or for "sensitive populations" such as children, the elderly, and asthmatics? Since 1970, EPA has spent millions of dollars on ozone exposure studies on people and animals, and the general outcome has been to move the presumed safe-exposure level to lower concentrations. A chain of research resulted in the EPA's setting of the first ground-level ozone standard in 1971 and of revised standards in 1979 and 1997. Even at this writing, there is debate between the EPA's political leadership and its own Scientific Advisory Committee over how far the ozone standard should be lowered from its current 0.08 parts per million, with the committee contending that "there is an urgent need to fund more research on the effects on sensitive subpopulations of low levels of the photochemical oxidant mixture for which ozone is used as a surrogate."[10]

Laws, Regulations, Processes, and "Ecological Niches" of Competing Principles

Environmental policies may be based on different normative objectives or criteria. These principles for deciding on environmental policies compete, just as different species compete for territory and food supplies. They also fit different ecological niches. The relevance to knowledge is that different principles call for different types of knowledge, and one principle may explicitly prohibit the consideration of a type of knowledge that another principle uses. In addition, knowledge is sometimes employed, rejected, or distorted to alter the consequences of applying the principle that is formally required under the governing laws or regulations.

The principles underlying environmental laws can be divided into three broad categories. One is what Richard Posner calls "value maximizing"—philosophically harkening back to Jeremy Bentham's "greatest good for the greatest number" utilitarianism.[11] This principle is technically reflected most prominently by benefit-cost analysis, but some consideration of overall benefits and costs is present in virtually all deliberations over the passage or amendment of environmental legislation.

The second principle is fair distribution of benefits and costs. Of course, very different standards of fairness exist.[12] Many concepts of fairness presume that a fair distribution of benefits and costs ought to be pursued even if it means that overall utility is not maximized. Other concepts argue for maximizing total utility, then finding a fair way to redistribute the new, larger quantity.

The third normative principle is observances of rights, which are protections or prerogatives that have been accepted as appropriate even if their specific applications neither maximize society's utility nor meet any particular standard of fairness. If a particular right appears to be especially compelling in existing circumstances, then it may be enshrined in legislation. For example, the prerogative to pollute within the existing laws and regulations is by definition a right if it is accepted as appropriate to uphold even if the costs to society far outweigh the benefits and lead to patently unfair outcomes. It is thus a "property right." There are, of course, also rights to be protected from pollution or other environmental threats.

Even if actors agree that a particular broad principle is appropriate, how should the principle be applied? Even if all agree on the primacy of fairness, what is fair? If all agree on pursuing maximum utility, which option will do that? If all agree on the primacy of rights, whose rights should be upheld? Although these philosophical discussions are important, here we are more interested in the fact that each of the three principles calls for and gives standing to different types of knowledge in environmental decision making.

These principles create different demands for knowledge in terms of both the complexity of the knowledge required and the nature of the information and theory. For example, Lisa Heinzerling points out that technology-based standards (i.e., "best available technology") such as those adopted by the Clean Water Act do not require the detailed knowledge of pollution impacts that the earlier water-quality-based standards required.[13] The technology-based standards at least partially and indirectly reflect benefit-cost considerations because they limit regulation to technologies that must be affordable by some users in order to be developed and available. The earlier water-quality standards reflected a rights conception—that the public ought to be guaranteed a particular standard of water quality regardless of the costs—but the knowledge demands were regarded as onerous.

Each of these principles has its own logic and advocates, and many policy debates pit one principle against the others. For example, a debate over whether current pollution levels ought to be lowered through more stringent regulation brings property-rights arguments into conflict with fairness arguments and with the benefit-cost principle of calibrating the permissible pollution level according to the balance of health benefits and economic costs. From time to time, circumstances will make one principle particularly compelling to policymakers. Thus, when instances of blatant unfairness emerge, as in the many cases where environmental justice considerations are raised, a prescription to reinforce some criterion of fairness of outcomes will seem more compelling. When strong evidence of inefficiency becomes prominent, utility maximization may dominate. Rights considerations may dominate when existing policies or practices are seen to threaten fundamental liberties or entitlements.

The result is that U.S. environmental policy is governed by a set of laws, regulations, and processes that formally or informally enshrine conflicting principles. In contrast to the rules that apply benefit-cost criteria, the Clean Air Act and Clean Water Act protect the public's right to enjoy clean air and water. CERCLA recognizes the rights of people living near a damaged habitat to have that habitat restored; in effect, this law gives standing to the habitat and its ecosystem, while at the same time reflecting a fairness doctrine that those in closest proximity to a damaged ecosystem should be able to enjoy the ecosystem's amenities in the future. CERCLA requires restoration of that habitat even if the restoration costs exceed the sum total of benefits.

It is striking that for all the technical cachet of benefit-cost analysis, few of the important U.S. environmental laws call for decisions to be made according to formal benefit-cost criteria. The Toxic Substance Control Act and the Federal Insecticide, Fungicide, and Rodenticide Act do require the EPA to balance benefits and costs.[14] Yet some of the most important environmental laws—including the ESA, the Clean Water Act, and many of the provisions of the Clean Air Act—do not specify that a benefit-cost balance should determine the stringency of the regulations, let alone serve as a trigger for action in particular instances. Many laws and regulations do require actions to be triggered by other sorts of findings: noncompliance, dangerous levels of environmental hazards, and threats to conservation goals. For example, if a species' population is found to be so low that the threat of extinction exists, the ESA is invoked.

It is inevitable that the outcomes of applying any one of these principles will prove to be unacceptable to particular actors. Perhaps they see a policy that purports to pursue a "fair" distribution of benefits and protections as instead treading on rights that ought to be protected. Or others see a policy that upholds a particular right as patently unfair or excessively costly. In reaction to their dissatisfaction with these consequences, some actors will try to change or block the applicability of the laws or regulations that others maintain are appropriate.

Blunting the Implications of Laws and Regulations

When an environmental law or regulation results in a rule or specific application that some actors regard as unacceptable, their maneuvers to negate these results can have major impacts on the standing of particular forms of environmental knowledge. Recall from chapter 4 that the OIRA within the federal OMB can derail regulatory initiatives that in OIRA officials' judgment do not meet the quality standards of its benefit-cost analysis. The privileging of benefit-cost analysis and of OIRA come from presidential Executive Orders 12291 and 12866, which require this analysis for any rule that has substantial economic impact. OIRA is permitted to trump rules that are based on principles other than aggregate maximization of costs and benefits.

The strategic impact of these executive orders should not be overlooked. A U.S. Government Accountability Office (GAO) assessment of OIRA's impact concluded that from mid-2001 to mid-2002, OIRA's actions delayed or excluded provisions of six of the fourteen rules that the EPA proposed.[15] Although nothing in OIRA's explicit mandate permits it to formulate environmental rules, there is strong evidence that it not only delayed or blocked rule formulation, but also forced modifications in the rules, presumably through agencies' acquiescence in order to get OIRA to permit the rules to go forward. For example, David Driesen analyzed the twenty-five cases of OIRA intervention that the GAO deemed led to significant changes during that 2001–2002 period and found that in twenty-four of these cases, the changes reduced the stringency of the regulations that the proposing agencies had submitted.[16] OIRA has even been able to insert benefit-cost analysis as the trigger for applying regulations based on different principles. Heinzerling notes that in 2002 OIRA created a "compliance alternative" that would exempt power plants from more stringent restrictions on cooling-water-intake fish kills if a benefit-cost assessment of a facility shows costs exceeding benefits.[17]

The Toxic Release Inventory issue mentioned in chapter 3 also offers an example of how efforts to blunt the impact of laws based on particular principles can influence the standing of knowledge. The TRI was established on a rights basis (the public's "right to know"), but in some quarters it is regarded as failing a benefit-cost standard because of the burden placed on the firms required to report their toxic releases. The controversy over which toxic substances and their volumes require monitoring and reporting reflects the clash over these principles. The outcome of the controversy determines how much knowledge will be available to expand our knowledge of public-health risks of the burgeoning number of potentially toxic chemicals.

The Science and Advocacy Worlds

Like settled areas and the wilderness, the world of environmental science and the world of environmental advocacy converge in a sort of "exurbia." Policymakers and policy analysts live in this exurbia where the two worlds overlap and sometimes clash.

When two worlds intersect, boundary institutions and actors play a crucial role. The main thrust of the work on boundary organizations relevant to knowledge and policy has focused on the collaborative contributions of such organizations as agricultural extension services, the National Research Council, and the now defunct Office of Technology Assessment. David Guston, one of the best-known advocates of viewing these institutions as boundary organizations, argues that "the presence of boundary organizations facilitates the transfer of relevant and usable knowledge between science and policy."[18] Yet Thomas Gieryn and many other observers point to the fact that boundary organizations are also involved in contestation over what science is credible and deserving of use.[19] In fact, a whole chain of organizations is involved in judging, contesting, and transferring knowledge between science and policy. Not all of this knowledge is relevant and worthy of use, and these organizations suppress some relevant and worthy knowledge. In our concluding chapter, we assess the potential of these boundary organizations for overcoming some of the problems in how knowledge is used in the environmental policy process.

6

The Consequences of Knowledge Problems in the Environmental Policy Process

The problems with knowledge in the environmental policy process have very real consequences for the people who experience and are affected by them. The previous chapters were meant to be theoretical, although we cited many examples ranging from climate change to national-forest management to acid deposition. In this chapter, we lay out the many problems that can plague the role of knowledge in the environmental policy process and then illustrate how some of these problems are present in contemporary environmental decision-making settings. These cases are typical of various environmental problems that face society. One can choose almost any current environmental issue and subject it to analysis according to the problems summarized in our previous chapters. In this chapter, we move beyond the theoretical detailing of the problems and demonstrate through the application to three additional case studies a more systematic and comprehensive approach to understanding problems that occur in knowledge processes. These applications provide insight into how we might begin to imagine more constructive relationships among different knowledge types and remedy the dysfunctions that currently afflict environmental decision making.

All of the problems covered in chapters 2, 3, and 4 are summarized in table 6.1. There are some commonalities across the categories, and they deserve some discussion before proceeding to the analysis of the case studies. Some problems are more prevalent across categories than others and demonstrate more entrenched dysfunctions in knowledge processes. Problems with uncertainty prevail in generation, transmission, and use. And the privileged position of formal science and biases for some types of knowledge over others likewise pervade the knowledge processes.

Table 6.1
Summary of Problems with Knowledge in the Environmental Decision-Making Process

---

Problems with Generation of Knowledge
Diversification of knowledge generation
Complexity and uncertainty
Biases

- Biases in favor of benefit-cost and expert evaluation
- Biases in favor of generalization and against contextual knowledge generation
- Biases against local, traditional, and indigenous knowledge

Lack of vision for public input

Problems with Transmission of Knowledge
The persistence of the privileged position of science
Diversification of knowledge-transmission vehicles
Uncertainty as a problem in knowledge transmission
Attention focused only on specific areas through knowledge transmission

Problems with Use of Knowledge
Mandatory use of knowledge
Privileging of knowledge used
Uncertainty in using knowledge
Inadequate knowledge
Unsound definition of objectives and consideration of alternatives
Implementation, evaluation, termination challenges
Skewed power dynamics and knowledge use

Impacts on the Environmental Decision-Making Process
Shifting arenas of policymaking

- Credibility of knowledge
- Centralizing tendencies
- Venue-shopping
- Analytical routines

Participants' status and power

- Standing in policymaking
- Competition and professional rivalries
- Experts versus lay, activists, and interest-group input

Interconnections among Knowledge Generation, Transmission, Use, and Impacts
Generation, transmission, and use reinforce one another by elevating the standing of knowledge created and invoked in each function.
Various laws, executive orders, court decisions, and regulations take different approaches in the use of knowledge, thereby reflecting different normative principles.
Key actors try to modify or reject knowledge they find unacceptable and thus blunt its consequences.
Science and advocacy require different forms of mediation.

Diversification of sources is present in generation and transmission. It is arguably the diversification of sources in generation and use that contributes to greater uncertainty and threatens the privileged status of science. As more knowledge generators enter the process and there are more ways to transmit knowledge, questions arise about the uncertainty of the knowledge needed or generated and about the uncertainty of the knowledge transmitted. There has been a tendency to fall back onto the protocols of science to deal with uncertainty in both generation and transmission, which has had the twin consequences of potentially excluding other relevant knowledge and placing unrealistic expectations on what science can deliver effectively in environmental decision making.

Klamath River Case Study

In early 2001, Oregon's Klamath River basin faced forecasts of severe drought. In a drought year, the Klamath basin is typified by too many claimants for too little water.[1] Farmers, Native American tribes, wildlife advocates, and downstream salmon fishermen all clamor for their portion of water. In April 2001, the U.S. Fish and Wildlife Service and the U.S. National Marine Fisheries Service (NMFS) were required to submit biological opinions as part of a triggering of Section 7 of the Endangered Species Act of 1973 (ESA).

The ESA was written and implemented as the most powerful environmental law to protect threatened and endangered plants and animals and their habitats in the United States. The ESA clearly requires detailed knowledge of the location of thousands of species, their current populations and population trends, and the nature and extent of threats to species survival. Specific provisions in the law require that "the best scientific and commercial data available" be used to inform policy direction. Thus, ESA Section 7 states that federal agencies must consult with the U.S. FWS or the NMFS before taking action so as not to jeopardize listed species or their habitat. In these cases, the FWS or the NMFS or both issue a "biological opinion" that identifies the probable influence of the proposed activity on the species in question. The statutory requirements for a single-species approach to biodiversity conservation, however, mean that knowledge generation focuses on narrowly collected biological information to the exclusion of other types of knowledge relevant to species recovery.[2]

In the Klamath case, the FWS and NMFS claimed in final biological opinions that the U.S. Bureau of Reclamation's proposed 2001 Annual Operations Plan for water release into the Klamath River would jeopardize two endangered species of sucker fish in Upper Klamath Lake and threaten coho salmon downstream. The consequence of the biological opinions was to give preference for the water to the fish over the farmers in this drought year.

Local farmers disagreed with the findings. They assailed the ruling and the science on which it was based in order to blunt its consequences on their livelihoods. According to their knowledge of the water flows and species in the region, more water might potentially harm the fish. Mortality among the suckerfish, they recalled, was greatest during years when water levels were highest. Moreover, denial of water would be economically devastating for their farming communities. However, their knowledge was not considered relevant, so it was not transferred to or used in the final decision. Under the constraints of the ESA, the biological opinions forced the Bureau of Reclamation to give most of the available water to the endangered fish. Withholding the water from the farmers, as predicted, had dire economic and social consequences.

Controversy over the generation, transmission, and use of science in the biological opinions led to claims of "junk science" and "combat biology" in the media, with all sides recruiting their own scientists to promote respective interest-group positions.[3] Key questions were whether the local knowledge provided by the farmers had value and whether the government-provided scientific information was unassailable. The media storm led to requests by the George W. Bush administration for a study by the NRC. In February 2002, an interim report from the NRC concluded that there was "no substantial scientific foundation at [that] time for changing the operations of the Klamath Project." It also importantly concluded that the Bureau of Reclamation's original plan of providing water to the farmers was "also unjustified."[4] Most of the required data were missing, and the limited data available showed no consistent relationship between annual water levels and flows in the basin and annual fish kills. There were not enough data to validate giving the water either to the fish or to the farmers. Thus, no action could be justified based on the best available science. Nevertheless, the 2001 Annual Operations Plan wreaked havoc on local economic interests and everything else that depended on irrigation water, including migratory wildfowl and bald eagles that lived on irrigation runoff.

In the following year, the opposite situation prevailed. Farmers used their knowledge and political influence to secure the support of the Bush administration to protect the farmers' interests. In 2002, the Bureau of Reclamation ruled to allocate the majority of the water to the farmers. Native American activists, suckerfish advocates, and downstream fishermen were outraged and warned of dire consequences for the fish. The farmers' interests prevailed. That fall, thirty-three thousand migrating and returning salmon perished. The fish died when they were crammed together in a smaller number of pools under low water conditions and naturally occurring infections were spread epidemically.[5]

In this case, knowledge was constrained by both the statutory authority in the ESA and the political maneuverings of the Bush administration. The focus remained on water levels to the exclusion of other ecosystem components that also were essential to the system's recovery. Relevant knowledge from economic, cultural, ecological, and social interests beyond the endangered species could not be transmitted to or used by decision makers. Data on water levels and fish kills were insufficient to support a decision of more or less water allocation to the endangered fish in 2001. Of course, the NRC was able to take several months to evaluate the science relating to the fish species, a luxury not afforded to the NMFS and the FWS biological scientists who were up against pressing deadlines. The final NRC report was not completed until 2003. Although the NRC was clearly comprehensive in its analysis, its report was not timely, efficient, or particularly relevant to decision makers when they were formulating the 2002 Annual Operations Plan.

After the release of the NRC study, local fisheries biologists attacked it as being overly simplistic and undermining the credibility of much of the science that had been conducted in the region. Instead of creating greater clarity about future alternatives and contributing toward consensus, the report made matters worse by creating a more hostile environment for scientists and fueling antiscience sentiments.[6]

Among other items addressed in the final report, the NRC suggested a more holistic ecosystem-based approach to restore the entirety of the system under collapse. Recommended actions included dam removal, fisheries restoration, and systematic improvements to water quality and quantity.

Until 2008, the tensions in the Klamath basin continued to run high. Neither the farmers nor coastal fishermen nor tribes saw fit to move beyond litigation to get what they wanted. In 2008, however, the various sides finally came together in the Klamath Basin Restoration Agreement.[7] The agreement includes twenty-six agricultural, environmental, tribal, fishing community, and federal and state organizations and agencies. One of the benefits of creating a group to include all stakeholders— beyond the scientists, lawyers, and bureaucrats who had been the primary participants in 2001 and 2002—was the opportunity to introduce other salient knowledge into the decision-making process. Power rates, kept low by hydropower, were important to farmers and other residents. Klamath tribes wanted the right to buy back their homelands. Many people wanted to restore nonendangered fish such as Chinook, steelhead, and lamprey, in addition to other threatened species, to the basin. Working with biologists, hydrologists, and engineers, local stakeholders leveraged their existing and historical knowledge to formulate collective understanding of a workable model for the region. The final goal is to remove four dams, strengthen the natural stocks of fish species, establish reliable and ecologically viable water and power supplies to sustain agriculture and wildlife refuges, and enable the Klamath tribes to buy ninety thousand acres of land.

The Klamath case study demonstrates several problems with knowledge process and their consequences, as detailed in table 6.2. Beginning with the generation of knowledge, it illustrates that very little new knowledge was generated. The FWS and NMFS synthesized and summarized most of the existing knowledge in biological opinions in a very short time. Even though there were diverse sources to generate knowledge, the focus was mostly on the science provided through biological opinions. There was a clear bias against local, traditional, and indigenous knowledge. In addition, there was lack of vision in how public input could have been used in this process. Intense preferences for different policy directions were not channeled constructively. The complexity of the case most likely contributed to great uncertainties that were difficult to reduce, as demonstrated by the NRC report. Nonetheless, uncertainty

Table 6.2
Summary of Problems with Knowledge in the Klamath Basin Case Study

---

Problems with Generation of Knowledge
Diversification of knowledge generation: Any sources of knowledge were allowed, but science was favored.
Complexity and uncertainty: The complexity of the situation created great, perhaps irreducible, uncertainty.
Biases against local, traditional, and indigenous knowledge: Local and tribal knowledge were ignored.
Lack of vision for public input: Intense public preferences were not channeled constructively.

Problems with Transmission of Knowledge
The persistence of the privileged position of science: Science was the knowledge that was transmitted.
Focusing attention through knowledge transmission: The focus on science limited how other knowledge could be used or how the problem could be framed.

Problems with Use of Knowledge
Mandatory use of knowledge: The ESA constrained what knowledge was allowed to be used.
Privileging of knowledge used: Science was the preferred form of knowledge.
Uncertainty in knowledge used: All sides used uncertainty to favor their position.
Power dynamics and knowledge use: Knowledge was used to exclude participants; those with biological or legal skills were initially favored.

Impacts on the Environmental Decision-Making Process
Participants' status and power

• Standing in policymaking: Lawyers and scientists were elevated in standing.
• Competition and professional rivalries: Different scientists competed over whose knowledge was best.
• Experts versus lay, activist, and interest-group input: Expert knowledge was favored over other forms of knowledge.

Interconnections among Generation, Transmission, Use, and Impacts
Generation, transmission, and use reinforced one another by elevating the standing of knowledge.
Uncertainty biases were exacerbated at each phase in the process. The privileging of science was reinforced at each stage of the process.
Key actors tried to modify or reject knowledge they found unacceptable and thus blunt its consequences. When science suggested the fish should be favored, the farmers attacked the science.

---

continued to be treated as something that could be addressed in spite of the complexities detailed by all who were participating in the decision.

The NRC also synthesized existing findings, but it took nearly two years to do so. In the meantime, decision makers had to proceed with water releases. Policy cannot always wait on certainty. The NRC concluded after the fact that not enough was known at the time to justify a decision one way or the other. This conclusion was impractical from a policy standpoint because decision makers needed to move forward.

Knowledge transmitted and used was constrained by the ESA's legal requirements—only biological opinions were allowed. Farmers' and fishers' local knowledge was not transmitted. The privileging of science led to a framing of the problem that limited the alternatives that could be explored. This limitation led to the initial failure in being able to address the problem of the ecosystem as a whole and framed the debate solely as a zero-sum game between farmers and fish advocates. Key participants were excluded unless they were part of the legal process.

Different interest groups used different knowledge to support their individual perspectives. This use led to claims of "junk science" and "combat biology." Scientists were recruited to support a given interest group's position. More science did not lead to agreement on what should be done. All sides exploited the uncertainty.

The ESA's legal biases constrained which participants had standing. Scientists and lawyers were initially given greatest standing. Competition among different scientists led to jockeying for position to establish standing. The NRC emerged as the group that was given greatest deference in this status hierarchy, and its experts were given greater standing than farmers and tribal members.

The knowledge generated was reinforced in transmission and use, and all of it was constrained by the ESA. Scientists and interest groups immediately sought to reject science that did not support their positions in order to blunt its consequences for their respective groups.

In 2008, many participants in the Klamath basin controversy began to engage in a collaborative working group that looked at the problems in their watershed from an ecosystem perspective. This more comprehensive approach used knowledge hybrids and leveraged science, local knowledge, and the preferences of the people most affected by water-allocation decisions. A more durable solution can emerge from this approach, provided adequate funding is supplied for the extensive restoration needed in the region.

Bisphenol A Case Study

The still-unresolved debate on whether to regulate Bisphenol A (BPA)—a compound found in ubiquitous plastic items ranging from baby bottles, sports bottles, and microwave oven dishes to children's dental sealants, lenses, CDs, and DVDs—highlights how uncertainty and conflicting scientific standards inhibit policy response. BPA has a low acute toxicity but is a known endocrine disruptor,[8] which means that BPA can mimic the body's own hormones. The concern is that the chemical may cause negative health effects, especially in long-term, low-dose exposures. BPA also has some odd characteristics and may be more dangerous at very low exposures than at high ones, especially for young children. The uncertainties associated with its peculiar dose response make it fodder for immense controversy. In recent years, several governments issued reports that explored the safety of BPA. There is little to no consensus on whether BPA should be regulated. Much of the controversy stems from how the knowledge about BPA has been generated and used; the scientific literature is in disagreement or has reported conflicting results. Experiments were conducted with different protocols, which reduced the usefulness of comparisons. Disagreement among scientists and regulatory agencies has thus left the consumer with little guidance.

In 2008, the U.S. Food and Drug Administration (FDA) asserted that baby bottles that contain BPA were safe. This proclamation was triggered by reports in 2007 casting doubt on the safety of BPA, leading to heightened concern by environmental groups and the public.

In 2007, the Center for Evaluation of Risks to Human Reproduction (CERHR), part of the National Institute of Environmental Health Sciences, convened an expert panel and conducted an evaluation of the potential for BPA to cause adverse effects on reproduction and development in humans. CERHR's purpose is to provide a timely, unbiased, scientifically sound evaluation of the potential for adverse effects on reproduction or development resulting from human exposures to substances in the environment.[9] Thirty-eight experts convened by the CERHR issued a consensus statement that concluded that average levels of BPA in people are higher than those that cause harm to animals in laboratory experiments. However, the statement did not call for the immediate ban on BPA for specific uses, but rather advised consumers to be aware of the potential risk and called for more studies.[10]

At that time, Steve Hentges, a spokesman for the plastics industry, stated that the results of the expert panel were "completely at odds with the findings of every governmental scientific body that has reviewed the same science." He accused the scientists of being "self-selected," of having "made their views known in the past," and of having conflicts of interest because they had previously studied BPA effects and had already taken advocacy positions.[11] The industry essentially argued that a fair assessment of the balance of scientific opinion required the judgment of new experts who would take a fresh look at the existing knowledge.

Following the expert panel, another CERHR twelve-person panel was appointed to review the relevant literature on BPA. This review resulted in a two-year evaluation of the very limited number of available human studies but more than one thousand animal studies of BPA's effects. The panel concluded that the only conclusive data in all the studies were those that showed effects on the brain, behavior, and the prostate gland. The panel found that a significant portion of the literature was not able to be fully considered due to a variety of limitations in how the various studies were carried out. The final peer-reviewed report, issued in 2008, expressed "some concern" about the effects on the brain, behavior, and the prostate gland in fetuses, infants, and children.[12] The same report identified "minimal concern" for effects on mammary gland and early onset of puberty in females. It concluded that there were still many areas of uncertainty and that significant data gaps still needed to be filled.

Environmentalists were discouraged with what they considered weak recommendations by the CERHR in the preliminary report issued in 2007, which were repeated in the final 2008 report. "Only the chemical industry agrees with the decision that BPA has little or no human health risks. That by itself should speak volumes about the corrupted process endorsed by the panel today," said Dr. Anila Jacob of the Environmental Working Group, a consumer advocacy group.[13]

Since the release of the 2008 CERHR report, the National Toxicology Program and the National Institute of Environmental Health Sciences have identified future research and testing activities. Working in collaboration with the Centers for Disease Control and Prevention, academic investigators, and the FDA National Center for Toxicological Research, the National Toxicology Program and the CERHR seek to reduce uncertainties and research gaps to provide clearer understanding of the threat that exposure to BPA poses to public health.[14]

In April 2007, Health Canada, the Canadian governmental department responsible for national public health, released a Draft Screening Assessment for BPA and concluded that the chemical may pose some risk to infants. Minister of Health Tony Clement stated at that time, "We have immediately taken action on Bisphenol A, because we believe it is our responsibility to ensure families, Canadians and our environment is [*sic*] not exposed to a potentially harmful chemical."[15]

In response to the CERHR and Health Canada announcements in 2007, the FDA declared that it would form an agencywide BPA task force to review concerns raised by the CERHR study. According to the FDA at that time, "There is a large body of evidence that indicates that FDA-regulated products containing BPA currently on the market are safe and that exposure levels to BPA from food contact materials, including infants and children, are below those that may cause health effects."[16] In its August 2008, the FDA issued a follow-up draft report that the small amounts of BPA that leach out of food containers do not threaten children or adults.

Other countries have found BPA to be safe. In January 2006, German regulators carried out a scientific assessment of the studies on BPA and came to the conclusion that the presence of BPA in polycarbonate bottles "poses no health risk to babies and infants during normal use."[17] Also in 2006, the European Union's Food Safety Authority found that low-dose effects of BPA in rodents were not demonstrated in a robust and reproducible way, so they could be used as pivotal studies for risk assessment.[18] In 2007, Japan recommended against regulating BPA also on the grounds that animal studies provide inconclusive evidence of human risk. In 2009, Australia and New Zealand affirmed the safety of BPA. Food Standards Australia New Zealand stated that it "concurred with the conclusions reached by the US FDA and the [European Food Safety Authority] that the levels of exposure are very low and do not pose a significant health risk."[19]

Undeterred by findings in other countries, the Government of Canada announced on October 17, 2008, that it was drafting regulations to prohibit the importation, sale, and advertising of polycarbonate baby bottles that contain BPA. Scientists concluded in their assessment that BPA exposure to newborns and infants was below levels that could cause negative effects; however, due to the uncertainty raised in some studies relating to the potential effects of low levels of BPA, Canada sought to take action to enhance the protection of infants and young children.[20] As of 2009, bans on baby bottles that contain BPA are also under consideration in Washington State, Minnesota, and Connecticut.

In October 2008, an independent scientific advisory panel criticized the FDA's assessment that BPA is safe, saying it failed to take into account numerous scientific studies and came to faulty conclusions.[21] Under greatest contention were the standards that applied to how the research was carried out. The independent panel contended that the FDA and the European Food Safety Authority relied on two industry-funded studies but rejected hundreds of independently replicated studies that followed accepted scientific practices and contradicted the industry-funded research. The scientists claimed that the FDA's rationale "ignores the central factor in determining the reliability and validity of scientific findings, namely independent replication."[22] In April 2009, the FDA announced that it would revise its draft assessment and take into account additional studies as it continued to research BPA.

In the meantime, the six largest manufacturers of baby bottles have said they will stop U.S. sales of bottles made with BPA.[23] Sunoco Inc. announced that it will no longer sell BPA to companies for use in food and water containers for children younger than age three.[24] Wal-Mart Stores Inc., Toys "R" Us, CVS, and other major retailers announced plans to phase out products containing BPA.[25] Nalgene agreed to stop using the plastic additive in its products.

U.S. consumers are currently left on their own to decide how to understand the conflicting scientific findings and interpretations. Advice for concerned consumers ranges from one end of the spectrum to the other. The FDA Web site states, "At this time, FDA is not recommending that anyone discontinue using products that contain BPA while we continue our risk assessment process. However, concerned consumers should know that several alternatives to polycarbonate baby bottles exist, including glass baby bottles." But the National Toxicology Program's Web site cautions: "Some animal studies suggest that infants and children may be the most vulnerable to the effects of BPA. Parents and caregivers can make the personal choice to reduce exposures of their infants and children to BPA, for example by opting for glass, porcelain or stainless steel containers, particularly for hot food or liquids."[26]

The BPA case study illustrates several challenges concerning knowledge in decision making, as noted in table 6.3. Enormous amounts of science, literarily more than one thousand peer-reviewed articles, have been generated to try to understand the effects of BPA on animals and humans. Policy certainty on how to regulate BPA is no clearer today than when the first report on it was completed. Regulatory agencies have had the task of assimilating and synthesizing findings of the existing knowledge on the topic. Greater weight has been given to peer-reviewed research than to anecdotal stories. Public input has come primarily in the form of comments on draft reports of the summaries of research.

The standards used to create "science" in the BPA case have been assailed. The individuals creating science have been attacked. The veneer of "independent," "unbiased," and "scientifically sound" studies and panels has been insufficient to keep the panels' findings from controversy. Uncertainty is cited as the problem. Continual emphasis on comprehensive reviews of science is invoked as the solution to identifying a regulatory solution.

Environmentalists and the chemical industry alike have used results of science to move their respective agendas forward. The media and Web sites have been the favored vehicles for moving respective interest-group agendas forward. Different interest groups attempt to focus attention in different policy directions. Environmentalists wish to see greater regulation of BPA, whereas the chemical industry wishes to preserve a useful tool in its commercial kit. Peer-reviewed literature has been the primary path by which knowledge has been validated. There has been little to no discussion of how to find alternative modalities of knowledge generation, transmission, and use in this decision process.

When results were used to move a contested agenda forward, opposition groups attacked not only these results, but also the methods of research and the individuals who conducted the research. Claims of conflict of interest were rampant.

Table 6.3
Summary of Problems with Knowledge in the BPA Case

Problems with Generation of Knowledge

Complexity and uncertainty: Complexity over dose responses and physical interaction in young and old age groups complicates certainty claims.
Biases

• Biases in favor of generalization and against contextual knowledge generation: Generalizable, peer-reviewed studies have been favored over anecdotal claims.

Lack of vision for public input: Interest groups and citizens have significant preferences, but knowledge generated to include such preferences has not been gathered.

Problems with Transmission of Knowledge
The persistence of the privileged position of science: The peer-review process has been the favored transmission vehicle.
Diversification of knowledge-transmission vehicles: The Web, news media, and the peer-review process have been utilized to transmit knowledge.
Focusing attention through knowledge transmission: Interest groups have attempted to focus attention on different aspects of the problem through the knowledge transmitted—consumer protection versus unwanted and unnecessary regulation.

Problems with Use of Knowledge
Privileging of knowledge used: Science has been most favored in decision making, human versus animal studies are more favored, and studies that follow specific protocols are favored.
Uncertainty in using knowledge: Uncertainty in existing knowledge has led to calls for additional knowledge to be generated for use in the process.
Inadequate knowledge: Existing scientific knowledge is inadequate for current regulatory purposes.
Definition of objectives and consideration of alternatives: Alternatives are defined based on the knowledge that is used in the process.

Impacts on the Environmental Decision-Making Process
Shifting arenas of policymaking

• Venue-shopping: Decision making is shifting from the federal level to the state and local levels.

Participants' status and power

• Standing in policymaking: Scientists are accorded greatest status in decision making, and some scientists are higher on the status hierarchy than others.
• Competition and professional rivalries: Scientists attack each other and their respective science to achieve greater standing.
• Experts versus lay, activity, and interest-group input: Expert input is favored over other types, which are marginalized.

Table 6.3 (continued)

Interconnections among Knowledge Generation, Transmission, Use, and Impacts

Generation, transmission, and use reinforce one another by elevating the standing of knowledge created and invoked in each function: Science and uncertainty reinforce each other.

Key actors try to modify or reject knowledge they find unacceptable and blunt its consequences: Interest groups and scientists attack the foundation of science in an attempt to blunt the consequences of the information on decision making to favor their preferred outcome.

Science and advocacy require different forms of mediation: Advocacy and science are intertwined with little recognition.

Despite the conflict over the state of the knowledge, consumers needed to decide whether to use or not use baby bottles that contain BPA and the industry needed to decide whether to continue producing BPA and products that utilize BPA. Several private companies have opted not to use BPA. Consumers have looked for alternatives to existing products that use BPA. This action suggests that the market, producers, and consumers "vote with their feet" when it comes to uncertainty and regulatory decisions.

Canada has opted to take the precautionary principle route due to young children's vulnerability. The United States, Japan, the European Union, Australia, and New Zealand are less risk averse in how they interpret or use the knowledge.

Scientists are the privileged actors with standing in this case to the exclusion of many lay activists who claim BPA causes reproductive problems. Because regulation has been slow in coming through the FDA, many states have begun to take action to regulate BPA. In this arena of policymaking, unresponsiveness to the existing knowledge on BPA has led some activists to move to the state or municipal level to get action. Venue-shopping is alive and well given the controversies over BPA. Various scientists have attacked one another in an attempt to gain greater standing of their knowledge and how it will affect policymaking. Experts and scientists are at the top of the hierarchy in terms of who has greatest standing among the many participants in the process.

In the regulatory arena, science is the standard, which creates a feedback between what kind of knowledge is generated, transmitted, and used. Other types of knowledge are excluded.

Interest groups (environmentalists, industry) found the conclusions regarding how knowledge would be used unacceptable and attacked the basis on which the knowledge on BPA was generated. There has been no attempt to integrate explicitly the spheres of science and advocacy, although such integration is happening implicitly in every step of knowledge generation, transmission, and use.

Greater acknowledgment of the stakes and of the incorporation of local knowledge and public preferences might create more site-specific regulatory solutions. This shift is beginning to happen at a state level in the United States. The market, consumers, and producers likewise needed to move forward in the face of uncertainty, which has led to a more precautionary approach among all parties. The specter of lawsuits and liability down the road perhaps colored BPA producers' actions. In light of existing peer-reviewed literature that does suggest a connection between human health and BPA, especially among young children (Babies! Who would want to risk that in court?), risk-averse producers are more likely to adopt a more precautionary approach.

Concentrated Animal-Feeding Operations Case Study

The problems of the transmission and use of knowledge through the decision-aiding tools of valuation and benefit-cost analysis are vividly illustrated by the EPA's efforts to undertake an impact assessment of proposed regulations for the waste of concentrated animal-feeding operations (CAFOs).[27] The effort is a striking example of undervaluing environmental benefits, thereby weakening future efforts to justify more stringent regulations of the expanding "farm factory" operations.

Since the early 1990s, environmental groups have been bringing lawsuits against the EPA and large-scale CAFOs, which have grown enormously in size and number, currently exceeding fifteen thousand operations. Although many of the lawsuits were initiated by environmental activists (e.g., Sierra Club chapters and the Natural Resource Defense Council), public attention was greatly heightened by mid-1990s hurricanes that led to hog-waste lagoons spilling over into streams and rivers and to other high-profile, alarming cases of water contamination. The courts ruled that existing regulations did not fulfill the requirements of the Clean Water Act to protect waterways from three risks: wastewater pollutants from normal operations, the use of manure as fertilizer, and discharges caused by storm waters.

Under a consent decree, the EPA and the Department of Agriculture spent two years assessing the benefits and costs of various alternatives and developing a draft rule proposal in December 2000. EPA managers and analysts knew that the provisions of the Clean Water Act, in the version then in force, would dictate the outcome of the rule, but it took another three years before the final rule was published, following more data collection, solicitation of public comment, and analysis of alternative options.

The Clean Water Act, as interpreted by the court, dictated that a more stringent rule than had existed before would have to be adopted, regardless of the benefit-cost analysis, and yet Executive Order 12866 required that the benefit-cost analysis be undertaken as part of the regulatory impact assessment for any rule that would entail costs more than the $100 million threshold to make it a "significant regulatory action."[28]

The CAFO regulatory impact assessment was undertaken in a politically charged atmosphere regarding the rigor of benefit-cost analyses of federal regulations. As mentioned in chapter 4, in 2001 John Graham was appointed as the administrator of the OIRA within the OMB. OIRA's mandate includes policing the quality of regulatory impact assessments and remanding these assessments back to the agencies for revision if OIRA deems them inadequate. According to a GAO review, in the one-year period (July 2001 through June 2002) before the release of the CAFO rule, OIRA had judged four hundred regulatory rules to be inadequately assessed. The GAO reviewed a subset of eighty-five of these cases and reported that of all the cases that the OIRA challenged, the EPA's rules "were most often significantly changed" due to the OIRA intervention.[29]

This seemingly innocuous assessment role empowers OIRA to block or delay new regulations, ostensibly on technical grounds. However, the concern on the part of advocates of stronger regulations, in both the environmental and nonenvironmental spheres, has been that OIRA will use its technical role as a pretext for a general attack on more stringent regulation. The heart of the problem is that no benefit-cost analysis is immune from critique. No prediction of impacts or valuation of benefits and costs can be guaranteed to be comprehensive and accurate. Therefore, it is impossible to determine whether an OIRA rejection of a particular regulatory assessment is motivated by the straightforward objective of quality control or the ulterior motive of undermining the movement toward stricter regulation. In fact, the distinction itself may be unclear. The adequacy of an impact assessment may be sufficient to an advocate of regulation who sees a greater risk of consequences from no regulation than from regulation, but not to the skeptic of the virtues of stricter regulation.

Despite Graham's prestigious academic pedigree (he was the founding director of the Risk Assessment Center at the Harvard School of Public Health), environmental groups strenuously opposed his appointment. His own publications included sharp critiques of benefit-cost analyses that supported stricter environmental regulation; he had argued that the net benefits of some of these analyses had been exaggerated by their neglect of risks and costs beyond the environmental factors. Taking these nonenvironmental factors into account, Graham asserted, would have shown that some proposed environmental regulations have higher costs than benefits.

Graham's analytical approach was in turn criticized as having "a perspective on the use of risk assessment and cost-benefit analysis that would greatly jeopardize the future of regulatory policies meant to protect average Americans. He advocates an analytical framework that systematically reinforces the worst tendencies of cost-benefit analysis to understate benefits and overstate costs. As head of OIRA, he would be in a position to impose this approach throughout the government."[30] A letter to the Senate from fifty-five specialists in environmental science and policy, including some of Graham's own colleagues at the Harvard School of Public Health, asserted that "Professor Graham's controversial risk management methodology discounts the real risks of well-documented pollutants such as dioxin and benzene, and makes use of extreme and highly-disputed economic assumptions. Professor Graham has shown his willingness to over-ride health, safety, environmental, civil rights, and other social goals in applying crude cost-benefit tools far past the point at which they can be justified by existing scientific and economic data."[31]

An additional factor that caused concern for advocates of stricter environmental regulation was the OIRA practice, required by Congress, of inviting "nominations" from nongovernmental groups to examine particular regulations and impact assessments. According to the GAO review, most of the nominations were submitted by George Mason University's Mercatus Center.[32] George Mason and the Mercatus Center are fairly closely associated with the laissez-faire, antiregulation Austrian school of economics, and the three Mercatus Center board members with government experience all served as Republican appointees.

In this contentious atmosphere, it is no wonder that EPA had little incentive to engage in the potentially risky effort of measuring and presenting the full range of benefits and costs of CAFOs in an explicit, quantitative manner. The CAFO regulatory impact assessment did not venture into the minefield of trying to be comprehensive in projecting the consequences of the waste and in valuing these consequences. The EPA embraced the strategy that Herbert Simon labeled "satisficing": instead of striving for the outcome with the maximum benefit, the EPA chose an option that would reach an acceptable but hardly optimal level regardless of the uncertainties that can lead to different outcomes.[33] Thus, the EPA devoted just enough resources to make quantitative estimates of the rather obvious benefits and costs. Whereas the total cost of limiting the release of waste by the large-scale CAFOs was estimated as $289 million annually, the estimated annual benefits were reported as "$204+ [B] to $340+ [B]." The "[B]" represented benefits that were not monetized, including the important benefits of reducing the risks of eutrophication and pathogen contamination as well as the "human and ecological risks from antibiotics, hormones, metals, and salts."[34] The fact that the benefit estimates were presented within a broad range left little room for criticism that the monetized benefits might be beyond this range—leaving aside the problem that other benefits were excluded from the analysis. Yet with the estimated costs above the midpoint of the range of explicit benefits, the rule seems at best only weakly justified by the analysis, undercutting any future efforts to press for a more stringent rule.

In addition, instead of attempting a new analysis to value the CAFO benefits, the regulatory impact assessment invoked a well-known if highly limited earlier study. Robert Mitchell and Richard Carson, iconic experts in valuation methodology, were extremely well known for their classic 1989 text *Using Surveys to Value Public Goods: The Contingent*

Valuation Method.[35] More than 2,800 articles and books have cited this text, and it won the 1998 Association of Environmental and Resource Economists "Publication of Enduring Value" prize. In 1993, Carson and Mitchell had also published a well-received article in *Water Resources Research* on the application of their "contingent valuation" survey of a national sample to determine the "average American's" willingness to pay for water of "drinkable, swimmable, and boatable" quality. Although the article was published in 1993, the survey had been conducted in 1983. In the CAFO assessment, the dollar figure was adjusted for inflation and changes in income levels, but the survey's application was obviously problematic for the context two decades later. Nor were the purposes of the original survey relevant to the CAFO issue. The EPA Scientific Advisory Board Committee on Valuing the Protection of Ecological Systems and Services noted that "the Mitchell-Carson study used in the CAFO rule was not intended to apply to specific rivers or lakes."[36]

The use of the Mitchell and Carson's "ladder" of drinkable, swimmable, and boatable water quality also led the water-modeling effort to rely on a compatible but overly simplistic model.[37] The EPA Committee on Valuing the Protection of Ecological Systems and Services noted that

[t]he desire to use value estimates from the Carson and Mitchell study apparently also influenced the choice of ecological models used to predict water quality impacts. In both the CAFO and aquaculture assessments, EPA chose to use the QUAL2E water quality model . . . apparently because it could readily be linked to this valuation study. Although this model can estimate the interactions among nutrients, algal growth, and dissolved oxygen, it is not capable of ascertaining the impacts of total suspended solids, metals, or organics on the benthos and the resulting cascading effects on aquatic communities that might have important water quality impacts.[38]

Thus, even for the limited set of ecosystem services for which these assessments provided monetized benefits, the benefit estimates were not very reliable.

The EPA Water Office's management of the valuation effort resulted in the use of a model that excluded the effects of animal wastes on air pollution[39] to the neglect of the important benefits of reducing the emissions of ammonia, sulfur oxides, and greenhouse gases. The balkanization of the Water Office and the Air Office was only part of the problem;

there was also scant motivation to incorporate air-quality benefits when even important water-quality benefits were given short shrift.

Finally, the CAFO analysis, as reported in the OIRA regulatory impact assessment, made no mention of the public input presumably provided by the elaborate public-comment apparatus that contributed to the lengthy and expensive preparation of the CAFO rule. Local knowledge was neglected in favor of national-level models and parameters despite the fact that CAFO emissions have highly distinctive, localized impacts.

The weakness of the 2003 CAFO rule is reflected by both the muted response from CAFO operators and the strong objections from environmental groups. The farm factory industry filed some lawsuits challenging the EPA's authority to impose all of the provisions of the 2003 rule, and in 2006 the Second Circuit Court of Appeals ruled in favor of the industry. Yet the environmental groups petitioned for a reversal, and by 2008, again under court order by the Second Circuit Court, the EPA made the CAFO rule more stringent by requiring the submission of detailed nutrient-management plans.[40] The modification entails even higher costs, reducing the rationale for further strengthening the rule without a fair assessment of the total benefits. In this context of policymaking through litigation, there is even less incentive for an environmental agency to spend staff time and financial resources (even the half-hearted impact assessment cost roughly $1 million in payments to external contractors and consultants) or to take on reputational risk through a truly ambitious assessment of benefits.

Much like the previous two case studies, the CAFO example includes several prominent problems with knowledge processes, as detailed in table 6.4. CAFOs involve both air and water pollution and illustrate the complexity as well as the uncertainty that surround the ability to understand the full effects of both types of pollution. These two factors make knowledge generation difficult and even more challenging to integrate when it is used for decision making.

The biases in favor of benefit-cost analysis and expert knowledge to fulfill the mandatory use of benefit-cost analysis under OIRA's critical eye required time-consuming generation of knowledge and quite limited transmission of knowledge that would have strengthened the case for a

Table 6.4
Summary of Problems in the CAFO Case Study

Problems with Generation of Knowledge
Complexity and uncertainty
Biases

- Biases in favor of benefit-cost and expert evaluation
- Biases in favor of generalization and against contextual knowledge generation
- Biases against local, traditional, and indigenous knowledge

Lack of vision for public input

Problems with Transmission of Knowledge
Uncertainty in knowledge transmission

Problems with Use of Knowledge
Mandatory use of knowledge
Privileging of knowledge used
Power dynamics and knowledge use

Impacts on the Environmental Decision-Making Process
Shifting arenas of policymaking

- Venue-shopping
- Analytical routines

Participants' status and power

- Standing in policymaking
- Experts versus lay, activist, and interest-group input

Interconnections among Knowledge Generation, Transmission, Use, and Impacts
Generation, transmission, and use reinforced one another by elevating the standing of knowledge created and invoked in each function.
Different laws, executive orders, court decisions, regulations took different approaches in the use of knowledge, thereby reflecting different normative principles.

---

more stringent rule. The mandatory use of benefit-cost analysis in a context of limited analytic resources led to heavy reliance on national-level information and models, which minimized the extent that local knowledge and more contextual knowledge were generated or used in the process. An enormous volume of public comment developed during the CAFO process, but it is unclear how or if the comments were considered in the final decision, demonstrating a lack of vision for the role that such input can play in the decision-making process.

Credibility-seeking behavior, legal biases, and the founder effect factored into which information was transmitted in this case. Uncertainty in knowledge transmission contributed to the type of information within the benefit-cost analysis that was moved forward. Because quantification and monetization were regarded as essential, some aspects of the case, especially those related to the full accounting of the benefits of more stringent rules, were undervalued. Obsolete valuation through benefits transfer was undertaken because the benefit-cost analysis was not determinative of the imminent decision to accept the rule. These faulty assumptions embedded in the obsolete numbers were dragged forward to affect other aspects of the analysis.

The knowledge that was used privileged some participants over others and demonstrated the power dynamics that are at work when specific types of knowledge are mandated for use. The overall impacts on the policy process were, first, to shift the policymaking arena to OIRA and, second, to delay the eventual CAFO rule. Some of the analytical routines used in the CAFO benefit-cost analysis were elevated above others, thereby reinforcing an already-existing status hierarchy. Some participants, especially experts, were elevated in their standing, whereas others—including lay participants, activists and interest groups—were lowered in theirs.

The CAFO case study illustrates how the generation, transmission, and use of knowledge reinforce one another by elevating the standing of the knowledge created and invoked in each function. Different normative principles were at work when benefit-cost rules were utilized than when the rights framework of the Clean Water Act was used.

7

Insights and Recommendations

This concluding chapter begins by summarizing the insights we have gained from examining how knowledge is generated, transmitted, and used in the environmental policy process, and it ends with our recommendations for improving the process. The first half of the chapter accounts for why environmental decision making is plagued by a host of problems related to the knowledge processes, and the second half offers strategies for addressing these problems. We reimagine the role for knowledge in policy making, taking into account twenty-first-century realities and arguing for a more realistic appraisal of the limits of and capacity for inserting knowledge in environmental decision making so that it can better serve the common good. In particular, this appraisal means taking into account the political as well as the technical processes associated with creating and compiling scientific, local, practical, and values-based knowledge.

In thinking about the roles of science and politics in making policy, most people (and most scholars) assume there is a distinct boundary between the two. This dichotomy also is one of the reasons local knowledge and public preferences are neglected in decision making. Science is seen as a source of rationality and efficiency, but politics as a necessary evil that leads to inferior choices and considerable delay. Knowledge related to local causes and consequences or distributional concerns occupies a questionable middle ground. In contrast, we regard the boundary between science and politics as permeable and often indistinct throughout the policy process. Scientific knowledge is used politically, and science itself is often driven by politics. Moreover, politics has the potential to incorporate alternative knowledge into the process.

Rethinking Assumptions

We begin by looking at false assumptions that often influence the knowledge processes. In the previous chapters, we demonstrated how the policy process often ignores, distorts, or misdirects knowledge. One of the reasons for these problems is that we have unrealistic expectations and faulty understanding of the role that knowledge plays in environmental decision-making processes. Many of the Progressive Era and post–World War II assumptions about how the knowledge process works no longer apply, given the changing social context in the twenty-first century.

Policymakers should not expect science alone to lead them to an inevitable convergence to the optimal policy. Even solid progress in environmental science does not reduce the fundamental differences in the values and priorities held by different stakeholders. We accept Roger Pielke's trenchant observation that "science is a determining factor in decision-making only when there is very little political conflict."[1] Therefore, formal science should be appreciated and used not as the major driver of environmental policy, but rather as one of a number of factors that contribute to the difficult task of balancing interests and aspirations to serve the public good. Science is important, but it is not the only important piece of knowledge.

A major finding of the previous chapters is that interest-driven behavior ("politics" for short) is pervasive in the generation, transmission, and use of all knowledge—science and alternative forms alike. This does not mean that everyone is self-serving; people pursue "interests" on behalf of the single individual (themselves), but also on behalf of others ranging from family to nation to humankind in general. The failure to acknowledge the pivotal role of professions, organizations, and individuals results in cumulative dysfunction from knowledge generation to transmission to use. Increases in knowledge do not necessarily make decision making easier. And more knowledge, even entirely new knowledge, does not necessarily induce contending groups to move toward agreement. In short, knowledge does not resolve conflicts over the environment, even if it does play a pivotal role in value-based controversies. When hidden under the veneer of "science," "objectivity," and "peer review," politics in these processes is played out in hidden ways. When not made explicit, the biases of personal, professional, and institutional interests influence how knowledge is generated and transmitted, which in turn influences how knowledge is incorporated into policymaking itself. It is important to make the biases more explicit in order to help us be more conscious of values we are favoring and why we do so, and then we must create personal, professional, and institutional responses to incorporate these values in a more transparent way. In a world where it is impossible to be comprehensive in the knowledge involved in decision making, the only choice is to be clear about what influenced the selection of the knowledge that is used. This clarification should entail what was included as well as what was excluded. Reimagining boundaries means being explicit about how biases influence the knowledge generated, transmitted, and used. Creating checklists also can make participants systematically aware of how such biases may be influencing selectivity.

These processes also require a continual effort in knowledge integration, including both knowledge among the amazing range of scientific disciplines relevant to the environment *and* alternative knowledge relevant to finding stable political solutions. Integration is unfortunately not as highly valued as specialized knowledge generation, especially in the culture of formal science. We need to explore whether it is possible to elevate the roles of existing institutions with professional cultures that do value knowledge integration or it is necessary to create new institutions. Educational institutions need to recognize the value of integration, train students in it, and restructure professional rewards to provide incentives consistent with this proficiency. These initiatives include better preparation of government personnel and the public to engage in these processes. We need to build the scientific and political literacy for greater understanding of the knowledge processes, of the strengths and weaknesses of available knowledge, and of the political power dynamics when knowledge is actually used. We need to raise awareness of the filters that come into play when knowledge moves from generation and transmission to use. These filters are not always explicit, so rendering them more explicit can help us deal with the limitations they place on comprehensiveness.

If interests are so pervasive and so influential, the reader might ask, is there really any value to facilitating the transmission and use of knowledge or, for that matter, to adding to the stock of knowledge on a particular issue? We believe there are several reasons for an affirmative answer. "Interested" knowledge is among the most valuable kinds of environmental knowledge because it reveals the distributional impact of problems and policies. This is some of the most relevant information to have for successful policy selection and policy implementation—in part because distribution of costs and benefits is an important political consideration for policymakers and in part because distributional equity is a key goal of public policy. The expression of interests, often conveyed through knowledge entrepreneurs, is absolutely essential to the transmission of knowledge. These entrepreneurs get knowledge to the people to whom it is most relevant and interpret complex knowledge in ways that participants in policymaking can easily understand. Political behavior, not science itself, is what gets science into the policy process. In addition, research on "policy learning" has shown that interest groups actually can assimilate new knowledge, provided there is a sufficiently wide variance between the position they formerly defended and the position that is consistent with the new knowledge. Recall that Paul Sabatier's theory of advocacy coalitions, positing that groups embrace knowledge that reinforces their positions and filter out other knowledge, has its tipping point. "On the basis of perceptions of the adequacy of governmental decisions and/or the resultant impacts, as well as new information arising from search processes and external dynamics, each advocacy coalition may revise its beliefs and/or alter its strategy."[2] This new information includes knowledge gained through experience in the actual implementation of policies.

So our task is not to remove "politics" and "interests" from the generation, transmission, and use of knowledge, but to build more constructive roles for them. Rather than ignoring how personal, professional, and institutional interests affect the knowledge processes—a myth-preserving but ultimately counterproductive temptation—we must incorporate them in a more transparent way. Insofar as these interests operate as hidden influences, we lack the means to orchestrate them to serve the public good. But if we reimagine the boundaries of science and politics, we can create a powerful new composite of knowledge that will lead to more realistic policy choice and smoother implementation.

One commonly held presumption has never been accurate: that the knowledge used in environmental policymaking is controlled by knowledge creators, notably environmental scientists. Legislators and other government officials play a huge role in determining what kinds of knowledge will be funded; administrators, legislators, and judges decide what kinds of knowledge can be introduced into various deliberations. Administrators and government analysts privilege some forms of knowledge simply by including them in their reports, even using information that may be obsolete. Journalists and politicians ride the communications channels that convey environmental knowledge to the public, advocacy groups, and industry groups as well as to government officials.

We should not attribute all of these problems to politics, regardless of what we think of politics. Technical limitations inevitably present challenges that also need to be addressed. We have seen that knowledge generation is limited by resources, by admissibility doctrines established by laws and courts apart from the specific issue at hand, and by the fact that every method of analysis, monitoring, information gathering, surveying, and so on has its weaknesses.

We have also seen that the knowledge that comes to the attention of policymakers and the public is heavily processed: by its reuse in reports that separate the knowledge from its original contexts, assumptions, and caveats; by the testimony and reportage that transmits knowledge that was already inevitably simplified; by the valuation techniques that borrow values from other sites; and by the filtering governed by administrative and legal admissibility criteria. The sheer economic resource constraints, the limitations of funneling vast amounts of information through media of limited capacity, and the obvious restrictions in the human capacity to absorb such amounts of information make the filtering as much a technical phenomenon as a political one. By the same token, knowledge users have to rely on this limited and questionable knowledge, cope with unavoidable uncertainty, and decide what to make of expressions of preferences without a technically obvious way to do so.

A related insight is that this already complex situation is further complicated by the diversification of the participants involved in the knowledge process. As we emphasized in chapters 2 and 3, since World War II there has been a remarkable growth in the number of people who are educated and have the capacity to participate in knowledge processes. Moreover, the arenas where knowledge is created have expanded. In addition to universities, the public sector, private industries, and non-profit entities play a role in all aspects of the generation, transmission, and use of knowledge. A transformation in knowledge resources has taken place that facilitates access and transmission through the ·Internet as well as computer cataloging of databases and written sources through the power of the Web. Expectations are growing that local knowledge should also play a role, generally through increased public participation.

This increasingly cluttered and complex scene is suffering a crisis of legitimacy among policymakers, if not yet among the general public. There is skepticism or cynicism attached to subject-matter experts' role. Questions often arise over the role of funding in setting the agenda for science and even in influencing which findings will be highlighted. The faith that scientists are committed to serving the public interest has been fraying and is being replaced by the more skeptical view of scientists as just another interest group. Although it is not altogether bad that conventional scientists no longer enjoy the level of unquestioned respect that supported their near monopoly over credibility, it is certainly problematic that such a high degree of cynicism has arisen toward the entire knowledge enterprise as it relates to environmental issues.

Due to the diversification of participants and arenas, previous strategies for creating order in knowledge generation and transmission, such as the culture of conventional science and the peer-review process, are of more value to smaller portions of overall knowledge creation and use. Moreover, we lack adequate strategies to deal with alternative knowledge production and transmission or especially to integrate alternative knowledge and scientific research.

Formal science has a clear role to play when uncertainty is bounded and knowable. However, the complexities of social and ecological systems create unknowable uncertainties, which shift the role of science from identifying and filling gaps in knowledge to aiding in the task of coping with uncertainty through monitoring, evaluation, and adaptation. Most of the formal scientific effort can be characterized as *causal analysis*: phenomena regarded as inadequately understood are analyzed to determine their conditioning patterns. What are the specific mechanisms by which fish in particularly stressed situations change their sexual characteristics? How do pests develop immunities to pesticides? How does the additional heat energy of global warming impact the nature and severity of storms? To what degree will stiff fines for illegal pollution lead to compliance rather than evasion? Where uncertainty about the causal links currently exists, the main task of conventional science (whether biophysical science or social science) is to reduce that uncertainty. Although this task is unarguably important, its dominance is problematic because of severely limited space left for the equally essential tasks of identifying which phenomena merit attention and developing strategies to address significant threats or opportunities in a context of residual uncertainty. The disproportionate emphasis on causal analysis has led to the neglect of identifying what needs to be explained and what to do about the complex problems for which explaining causes does not point to solutions. Some causes are simply beyond the control of policy interventions; other causes can be directly addressed, but only at prohibitive cost.

Moreover, solutions do not necessarily flow from causes. Understanding how and why the pine bark beetle has killed millions of trees in the national forests does not tell us how to accomplish the removal of the dead trees and thinning the forests to minimize future infestations. Even when causes can be identified and addressed, it is often necessary to address the consequences of the particular phenomenon in question as well. Indeed, many environmental problems are best managed by addressing the causes and consequences in a coordinated fashion. For example, the spread of invasive species (e.g., zebra mussels) is caused to a large degree by international commerce and the transport of goods that it entails, yet efforts to preserve native species cannot focus just on limiting international commerce, but must also involve monitoring and control at very local levels. Desertification may be caused by global warming, overirrigation, and the depletion of water tables, but part of the solution may be the introduction of drought-resistant ground cover. In like fashion, earthquake prediction would be very useful, but improving the capacity to withstand earthquakes is equally relevant.

Another key finding is that the generation and availability of knowledge changes the policy process itself. Certain types of knowledge transform the arenas where decision making occurs. The relative balance of power among participants in decision making is likewise altered by who is perceived to have the best knowledge, favored decision routine, or best model. Knowledge is accepted as legitimate not by universal consensus, but because it has been generated or transmitted by the most powerful stakeholders, where power may be based on prestige, perceived technical competence, or control over communications channels. The privileging of some sources or kinds of knowledge displaces other sources of knowledge as well as the considerations and values emphasized by that alternative knowledge. The use of knowledge reflects different normative principles and can have widespread impacts on whom and what is favored in policymaking. The generation, transmission, and use of knowledge reinforce each other by elevating the standing of knowledge and the subsequent knowledge demanded in decision processes. These impacts on the policy process itself are often so subtle and entrenched that the dynamics of their influence go unnoticed.

One outcome of the diversification of participants, situations, and resources as well as of the politicization of knowledge processes is confusion about the role of knowledge. The longer-term effect of this confusion may be to devalue the role of knowledge in decision-making processes because it is just too complicated to manage. In particular, devaluation may mean greater reliance on the protocols of formal science to bring order to the knowledge process, which in turn may mean the exclusion of other forms of knowledge. This process may make formal scientific institutions more brittle and subject them to greater politicization. The control over the knowledge process will become a proxy for who has power in environmental decision making. Monopolization of knowledge through the increasingly restrictive canons of science and science-based culture will not serve the common interest. This "science-centric" approach is not realistic, given twenty-first-century realities that include the diversification of participants, arenas, and resources associated with knowledge generation, transmission, and use. Nonetheless, there are no guarantees that we will move in the desired alternative direction instead.

An alternative path includes wrestling realistically with the limits of knowledge (formal science, local knowledge, and public preferences) under these new social conditions and reimagining an environmental decision-making process that takes advantage of the strengths of knowledge in this new social context and at the same time compensates for the weaknesses in how knowledge is used in the process. We believe that the desired future condition is to move toward a society that is more inclusive of knowledge in policymaking, but more reliably, so that the common good might be best served. This inclusive knowledge should be knowledge that is generated, transmitted, and used by the greatest number of participants in the policy process. In this manner, each of these elements in the process can become socially integrative.[3]

There are several reasons for moving toward more social integration in knowledge generation, transmission, and use. We agree with Steven Shapin and Simon Shapper that sound scientific practice and political practice together can reinforce the credibility of both.[4] We also agree with Yaron Ezrahi that the rise of both liberal democracy and modern science depends on the existence of an enlightenment culture of public witnessing.[5] Participation can hold expertise to contextual cultural standards for creating reliable public knowledge. This critical supervision also can prevent focusing on wrong or misguided questions. Finally, engagement can disseminate expertise and cultivate civic capacity for dealing with complex issues.[6] Sheila Jasanoff offers a compelling vision for this future path: "We need both strong democracy and good expertise to manage the demands of modernity and we need them continuously. The question is how to integrate the two in disparate contexts so as to achieve a humane and reasoned balance between power and knowledge, between deliberation and analysis."[7]

Alternatives

In this section, we discuss alternatives for addressing the problems in the generation, transmission, and use of knowledge. Our recommendations track the eight criteria (introduced in chapter 1) for evaluating the quality of the knowledge processes. Each of our recommendations addresses one or more of the problems that arise in meeting these criteria (see table 7.1).

There are many tensions among the competing criteria that can be applied to knowledge processes. The analysis in the preceding chapters demonstrates the impossibility of comprehensiveness in knowledge generation, transmission, and use. The interplay of complexity and uncertainty in many environmental problems means that there may be no logical way to be comprehensive in the face of such complex interactions. Faced with inevitably incomplete knowledge, we must be selective. However, to be selective means we introduce biases into how we include

Table 7.1
Relevant Criteria for Evaluating Knowledge Generation, Transmission and Use

Criterion	Definition
Comprehensiveness	completeness of the knowledge available; a suitable level of inclusiveness for a given context
Dependability	factual reliability of knowledge generated, transmitted, and used by individuals with recognized competence that includes technical proficiency and subject matter–based or place-based expertise
Selectivity	appropriately targeted boundaries for gathering information and analysis
Timeliness	the need for knowledge to be up to date and available to decision makers
Relevance	the need to stay focused on the given problem
Openness	transparent knowledge generation, transmission, and use processes
Efficiency	reasonableness in the expenditure of resources in relation to the knowledge generated, transmitted, and used
Creativity	imagination in the generation, transmission, and use of ideas

or exclude knowledge. Selectivity can mean that we are less open and creative in the types of knowledge included in environmental policymaking. What we have tried to illustrate in our analysis is the prevalence of the bias for formal science to the exclusion of other types of knowledge that can be more constructively introduced into environmental policy processes. One of the justifications for the privileging of science is the protocols that make it more dependable than other forms of knowledge. We call into question this dependability. Social and political influences are widespread in the generation, transmission, and use of science. Local knowledge and public preferences are denigrated as undependable because they are inherently political and social. Rather than delegitimizing science by recognizing these social and political influences, we would like to legitimize other forms of knowledge. To do so, we need to make better progress in the processes that can render local knowledge and public preferences more dependable for specific decision processes. Timeliness, relevance, and efficiency are essential for policymaking.

Comprehensiveness and dependability often clash with more timely, relevant, and efficient use of knowledge. Our challenge is to modify our existing institutions in ways that can integrate all forms of knowledge in reasonable ways so that it informs policymaking while still being timely, relevant, and efficient. This is a tall order.

The overarching thrusts of our specific recommendations are to

- provide a greater role for collaboration between scientists and nonscientists in the generation, transmission, and the use of "knowledge hybrids";
- engage in "guerrilla science" to reveal the uncertainties inherent in formal science;
- enhance discipline in knowledge processes;
- revise the standards by which we evaluate knowledge;
- institutionalize knowledge hybrids throughout knowledge processes;
- promote adaptive management and governance;
- defend the integrity of formal science; and
- enrich all knowledge processes through greater funding.

Enhancing Collaboration to Create Knowledge Hybrids

We begin with recommendations that entail expanding collaboration among different types of knowledge generators to produce something we call "knowledge hybrids." These hybrids integrate science, local knowledge, and public preferences in different combinations. The intention here is to preserve the usefulness of formal science *and* at the same time embrace the benefits of other forms of knowledge.

When all knowledge is uncertain due to the complexities involved in socioecological systems, the priority should not be to compare the dependability of knowledge coming from both formal science and other forms of knowledge, but rather to find the best ways to organize the interactions among knowledge generators operating within different paradigms, knowledge transmitters applying different standards, and knowledge users employing knowledge to pursue different values. If one accepts that there is value in more than one paradigm of knowledge generation, one can choose between two logical paths: (1) a path that creates external reviewers to whom authority is given to synthesize and transmit the knowledge for use; or (2) a path that crafts processes that acknowledge the multiplicity of interests and seeks to involve those interests in dialog, discussion, and consensus about what is and is not known for transmission into decision-making processes. Both have merit in particular contexts but will work only if perceived as legitimate solutions. Both are appropriate in different contexts.

In rough terms, the first path is appropriate for deciding on narrow and highly technical matters in the implementation of policies that have been established in broad outline by a more participatory process. For example, if the basic policy—to be determined through a thoroughly participatory process—is to consolidate nuclear waste in one location, do geologists and other technical experts accept irreversible storage in Nevada's Yucca Mountain as a truly fail-safe approach? Do psychologists accept the conclusion that this approach will not create an unacceptably high level of dread among people who live close enough to Yucca Mountain to believe that they are in harm's way? The methodologies for pursuing this first path are rather well developed through advances in expert elicitation, modeling, and forecasting.[8]

The second path is in greater need of innovation and development. We provide both conceptual and practical recommendations. It is constructive to think about changing both governance and management in ways that can mutually reinforce each other. To address some problems, we will need to change policymaking processes that affect how knowledge institutions are governed. To address other problems, we need management-level changes that affect how institutions operate on a day-to-day basis.

There should be a greater appreciation of the fact that the apparent differences in the rigor of science and alternative methods are often exaggerated. The presentation of environmental information to policymakers should avoid segregating knowledge based on different approaches. In order to minimize the likelihood that policymakers will ignore or neglect some information and therefore underappreciate the values that it reflects, this information should be presented to the greatest degree possible in the same section and format as other information.

The disjunction or fragmentation among knowledge generators, transmitters, and users means that end users may not dependably use the knowledge. Assumptions about the linear transmission of knowledge from generators to users are misguided. They fail to take into account the institutional, cultural, and personal incentives for intentional or unintentional distortion of the knowledge. Knowledge generators' greater appreciation for how knowledge will be used may make them more effective transmitters of knowledge.

The converse is also true. Knowledge users' greater appreciation for how knowledge is generated may result in better transmission. Thus, greater "cross-cultural" interaction among those who generate, transmit, and use knowledge is desirable. Boundary-spanning organizations and individuals are known to play key roles in these processes.[9] Yet it takes organizational innovation to pull scientists away from their labs and to induce policymakers to endorse the knowledge generated or transmitted by boundary organizations. The boundary organizations that David Guston uses as illustrations—the U.S. National Research Council, the now-defunct Congressional Office of Technology Assessment, the Health Effects Institute, and the European Environment Agency—were carefully and cleverly designed for "constructing a reputation for objectivity."[10] Consciously cultivating boundary crossers' skill sets, incorporating these types of professionals into environmental decision making, and creating incentive structures to encourage participation may help knit together the current divide.

Jasanoff argues that technical and lay knowledge are not additive; they are radically different ways of understanding the world.[11] Yet this does not mean that formal scientific and alternative knowledge cannot be integrated. Such integration happens one way or another all the time. Policymakers hear scientists, lay-opinion leaders, advocacy groups, industry representatives, constituents, colleagues, and their own inner voices. The question is whether these disparate inputs will help them to make reasonable decisions or will provoke confused reactions to the cacophony of advice and demands. As a consequence, processes that can adequately accommodate these different ways of viewing the world must be created and integrated.

In this world of diversified generators and transmitters of knowledge, triangulation can play a role in helping sort what knowledge is more dependable from that which is less. Triangulation refers to the convergence from multiple sources to an agreed understanding. The knowledge base is more dependable if both scientific findings and lived experience support each other. Those who generate or transmit local knowledge can strengthen the reliability and credibility of this knowledge. In some circumstances, this strengthening can be achieved through review, editing, and revision processes. That is, scientific inquiry can be guided by stakeholders' input to clarify what outcomes are socially relevant;[12] and draft reports can be critiqued as to whether they are understandable, public concerns are addressed, assumptions are clear, and uncertainty is appropriately expressed. Multiparticipant, online knowledge sharing tools such as wikis are one example of how all these things can be accomplished. The strengthening of the dependability of knowledge also can be enhanced through collecting enough independent endorsements to establish and convey a sense of broad agreement among practitioners and among experts who agree with the practitioners' findings or theories.

We are slowly developing norms for the integration of local knowledge and public-preference knowledge into decision making. These norms take the form of best practices in citizen-science collaboration, joint fact finding, stakeholder-based decision making, and other approaches. *Civic science* serves as an umbrella term for various approaches that seek to increase nonscientist or nonexpert participation in the coproduction and use of knowledge.[13] Coproduction processes simultaneously produce knowledge and social order.[14] The shift toward incorporating alternative forms of knowledge seems to be making greater headway in Europe than in the United States. Civic science has received great attention in Europe in response to the legitimacy crisis of science that followed food-safety scares there in the 1990s, including the spread of mad cow disease in England and the general controversy throughout Europe over genetically engineered food. The politicization of science and the subsequent erosion of its legitimacy have resulted in calls to make science more accountable and democratic.[15]

In addition, collaborative research involving the participation of opposing sides of an environmental issue or conflict can overcome the distrust of valid studies that otherwise may be discounted because of the suspicion of bias. George Busenberg recounts how oil companies and environmental organizations have cosponsored credible studies of strategies to minimize the damage of oil spills.[16] Formal knowledge generators can collaborate with alternative knowledge generators. For example, soil scientists can follow up on the "folk wisdom" of traditional cultivation techniques; the concerns that arise from alternative knowledge sources (such as GEOs' health or environmental effects) can be investigated systematically with lay people on the steering committees. The wisdom of practitioners in forestry, fishery, and livestock management can be captured through "expert-elicitation" methods that acknowledge the value of their experience. Supplementing traditional protocols such as peer review with extended review by laypeople outside of the traditional professions can help to create more relevant knowledge and downplay the biases against alternative knowledge. Joint panels of experts and lay citizens can decide what is most important, where priorities are to be set, and how resources are to be allocated. A parallel opportunity for collaboration in monitoring is the inclusion of a diversity of perspectives in the collection of relevant trend data so as not to introduce bias in one direction or the other. Any initiative to begin a new trend-monitoring initiative should include people and institutions reflective of the entire range of concerns. For example, the monitoring of trends in animal and plant biodiversity should pay attention to the aesthetic dimensions of landscape diversity insofar as ordinary people value this diversity and focus on the indirect and therefore nonobvious contributions that bio diversity makes to economic production (e.g., maintaining populations of pollinators) and to the assemblages of species that ecologists recognize as important for the long-term sustainability of valued aspects of the ecosystem.

Yet another important avenue of collaboration includes the inventorying and testing of local knowledge. Extension agents, largely underappreciated because they are viewed simply as transmitters of established knowledge, have enormous potential to document, describe, synthesize, and transmit the practices of the farmers, fishers, foresters, and ranchers whom they serve. The U.S. agricultural research and extension system has been held up as a model for creation of relevant knowledge and rapid transmission of knowledge from experts to user publics. Both research and extension are closely tied to state universities, which tend to focus research on the issues most important to given states (e.g., citrus in Florida), and serve as quality control. Developing networks across rural America enables the Department of Agriculture to research relevant problems, learn the various approaches that farmers are using to address common problems, and disseminate that knowledge among its clientele.

Moreover, the agricultural extension model facilitates the coordination of science and decision making across multiple scales, including county, state, and federal jurisdictions.[17]

Yet despite the efforts to test local approaches systematically and to develop "best practices" guidelines, it must be recognized that practical knowledge derived from managing natural resources and coping with environmental risks is localized and contextual. For example, the effectiveness of particular beneficial insects and organisms to control insect pest infestations varies greatly across climate zones and habitats. By the same token, the suitability and sustainability of mixed cropping (e.g., the Mesoamerican *milpas* that combine maize, beans, and other foods to provide a nutritionally balanced diet) or particular agroforestry approaches depend as much on the socioeconomic context as on the biophysical context. One crucial implication is that knowledge of successful practices must be accompanied by decision aids so that the potential users have sufficient guidance to know whether the practices are applicable to their particular situations. Another equally crucial implication is that the adoption of best practices needs to be within an adaptive management framework that involves continual monitoring and assessment, experimentation within the bounds of the adopter's financial situation and the resilience of the ecosystem, and a willingness to change practices as this feedback comes in.[18]

It must be noted that successful collaboration requires bridging the multiple gulfs—including differences in standards and interests, lack of respect, and lack of common vision—between actors of different backgrounds and roles. It takes considerable self-restraint and risk taking for environmental groups to work with industry groups. It takes considerable patience for practitioners to tolerate the pace of conventional scientific research or for conventional scientists to tolerate the apparent lack of rigor in the generation of alternative knowledge.

In like fashion, it takes tolerance and a difficult paradigm shift for conventional scientists to move from the so-called deficit model of citizen involvement to a "democratic" model.[19] The deficit model presumes that the lay public lacks understanding of an issue, but also that this information deficit can be rectified.[20] A primary assumption is that public misunderstanding of science is based on fear, irrationality, or ignorance.[21] This model also assumes that the science underlying an issue can be sound and knowable and that once agreement on the science is secured among experts, it can be communicated to the lay public. If understanding among the lay public is increased, then agreement among experts will follow. Although employing the language of transparency, dialog, and participation, this model nonetheless maintains a hierarchy between scientists and nonscientists that assumes that scientific knowledge is superior to other forms of knowledge. Communication moves in one direction: from the scientists to the lay public.

In the face of public cynicism toward some aspects of science, the deficit model has recently shifted from focusing on information shortcomings to the lack of public trust.[22] Restoring trust with the lay public means they will trust science and scientists to guide the process once again. Yet our concern in this book is that the emphasis on dialog without a real shift in how decisions are made can give rise to "dialog fatigue" wherein engagement exercises are more rituals and diversionary tactics than opportunities for change.[23] Part of the problem is that the lay public is indeed quite ignorant of much science that scientists and science-literate citizens would consider to be painfully rudimentary.[24] For example, a survey conducted by the National Science Foundation found that half the U.S. adult population did not know that the earliest humans did not live alongside of dinosaurs, that Earth revolves around the Sun annually, that electrons are smaller than atoms, that antibiotics do not kill viruses, and that lasers do not focus sound waves.[25] The paradigm shift has to recognize that ignorance of such facts does not diminish the general public's ability to choose preferred outcomes and to work with policymakers and scientists in order to secure those outcomes.

Engaging in Guerrilla Tactics to Reveal Uncertainties

To counter the misleading message that knowledge generated according to the standard scientific conventions can take into account all relevant considerations, we argue that the might of formal science cannot be confronted head on—nor should it be. We do not wish to undermine formal science, and in fact we bemoan its neglect during the George W. Bush years. However, we do want more space in the environmental policy process to be accorded to other forms of knowledge, and we also want the limitations of formal science to be better appreciated.

A harsh frontal assault on formal science would be a bad idea. On the one hand, the critique would run the risk of being rejected by scientists and policymakers, who would see it as an attack by resentful amateurs ignorant of the importance of the conventions of scientific inquiry. The radical critique of science—that it is merely a social construction—is a laughable notion to the bulk of citizens, scientists, and policymakers, who look to formal science to settle factual issues such as whether a higher concentration of a pollutant will result in higher mortality. The critique that formal science reinforces the social and political status quo also seems to be beyond the point. On the other hand, the harsh assault would provide ammunition for those who wish to minimize the crucial role of formal science in discrediting scientifically unsound policies that serve narrow interests.

The better approach is to maneuver formal science into revealing its own limits and letting its uncertainties speak for themselves. These guerrilla tactics, as it were, would be targeted to revealing the assumptions, incompleteness, and legitimate disagreements of formal science, without exaggerating the extent of disagreement that naturally arises when scientists focus their debate on issues that are still controversial.

One approach is simply to require that scientists clarify how they came to their conclusions: What were their assumptions and methodologies? What sources of uncertainty exist? What factors had to be left out of the analysis because they could not be measured or incorporated into the analysis according to the conventions of rigor or reliability required by the conventions of the science? What is left out of the analysis is often just as important to know as what is included.

Another approach is to compile the outputs of equally credible scientific efforts to see how much variation is revealed when estimates or predictions of the same facts, trends, or parameters are compared head to head. A high level of agreement does not necessarily mean that the scientists are correct; on the contrary, holding the same assumptions may lead them all to the same incorrect conclusions. Yet major disagreement in estimates or predictions will signal, to policymakers and to the scientists themselves, that uncertainty is still present.

Yet another approach is to ask (or, if the situation permits, to require) scientists to analyze aspects that are of relevance to policy but have not been subjected to formal scientific inquiry, giving them the option of explaining why the aspects cannot be adequately analyzed within the conventions of formal science. Let *them* explain the limitations of their protocols in answering questions that are important to policymakers and the public. Rendering the inherent uncertainties in formal science more visible will have the twin consequences of enhancing the dependability of the science and making it more relevant for policymaking.

Enhancing Discipline in the Knowledge Processes

The challenge facing our next set of recommendations is largely one of self-discipline on the part of participants in the knowledge processes. This point may seem counterintuitive in light of the fact that we are advocating freeing the bonds of what has been portrayed as the most disciplined, rigorous canons of formal science. Yet we have argued throughout this book that rigor is a much more subtle concept that must be better understood in order to strengthen comprehensiveness. It is all too easy to define rigor in terms of explicitness, quantification, and systematic analysis. Yet it should be obvious that some important aspects of an issue cannot be made fully explicit, let alone quantified. And to exclude certain aspects of environmental impacts because they are less amenable to systematic analysis is paradoxically a violation of the commitment to systematic analysis and interpretation. Scientists must find an appropriate balance between discrediting blatantly erroneous knowledge (e.g., that AIDS is unconnected to HIV) and gaining insights from this knowledge. The expansion of the "gray" literature, representing greater integration of different knowledge types and a reduction in the monopoly that peer review has traditionally held, is now a fact of life. Formal scientists can rail against its excesses, but it is far more constructive to harness the constructive aspects of the new channels, to learn from their content, and to use them to disseminate scientific knowledge.

It is important to recognize that different publics will have different tolerance for the intensity of information they want or demand. Information-delivery services that are tailored to meet the needs of different constituencies can bundle the information that is desired and mitigate the superficiality of a one-size-fits-all delivery mechanism. More specialized knowledge-integration and delivery services are needed to meet the need to sort through and transmit knowledge according to more specialized desires. For example, Web sites directed at asthma sufferers transmit advice on how to clear asthma-attack triggers from living spaces; Web sites and newsletters devoted to sustainable organic farming mix summaries of technical research, advice from practitioners, and chat rooms to address specific questions. However, the validity of the knowledge transmitted through these channels may well be in doubt. Therefore, increasing the opportunities to verify what is transmitted through various media outlets can help information consumers to triangulate multiple sources and decide whether the concerns and advice are valid or not.

Cultivating the skills to know where to look for information and how to triangulate it is an important part of this process. For those who transmit knowledge, determining whether unintentional biases exist is obviously important, although doing so faces the challenge of creating systematic mechanisms to identify individual and institutional biases. Classes, training, and self-orientation are important to building awareness about individual biases. Checks and balances within an institution are important to identify more systematic biases. Careful analysis of the processes and criteria by which environmental considerations are currently filtered would at a minimum make us aware of which values are included and which ones are left out. For instance, we have seen that the filtering done by the OIRA privileges readily monetized, tangible values at the expense of rights-based considerations and less-tangible values.

How, then, can alternative knowledge be adequately vetted so that it can be accepted as useful for guiding environmental decisions? The key is to allow the cocreation of knowledge through discourse processes. Protocols and standards that relate to alternative knowledge rest on the use of interactive discourse and negotiation to agree upon what is known, what is likely, what is applicable at higher levels of generality, and what is useful. As stakeholders, practitioners, and policymakers practice and gain experience with these processes, they will gain greater understanding of the contingencies under which the new norms apply or do not apply—provided that these processes are systematically studied and documented and that the knowledge is disseminated. Yet the incentives for engaging in these new knowledge generation, transmission, and use processes are not clear. There are incentives for continuing to engage in traditional, normal science per the status quo, even if the ultimate result is poor environmental decisions, and the sanctions applied for engaging in these new knowledge processes are real and immediate, especially for scientists and other professionals. Embracing postnormal science and discursive processes of knowledge cocreation will entail real professional risks. Nonetheless, this new world will not be realized unless the public, professionals, and both public and private institutions demand this type of knowledge.

There are many options for engaging in discourse, which we review later in this chapter. At this point, our argument is that the approach to stimulating constructive discourse should be contingent on knowledge that will be relevant for the decision and the type of decision to be made. It is important to note that the requirement of interactive discourse is distinct from public-comment processes and public hearings, which have minimally interactive requirements.

A now classic example of alternative discourse is the Quincy Library Group collaboration through which local stakeholders prevailed over the U.S. Forest Service in their negotiated approach to balancing the logging, recreation, and conservation outputs of three northern California national forests—all stakeholders had a voice, and different bases of expertise and experience were recognized.[26] Ortwin Renn, Thomas Webler, and Peter Wiedemann suggest that the twin criteria of fairness and competence provide broad guidelines for thinking about such discourse exercises.[27] Not every process will be fair to everyone's interests, but it is possible to be open, clear, and consistent about the rules guiding the process. Likewise, not every process will result in the best decision, but if all parties involved focus on the quality of knowledge and the process for accommodating this knowledge, the decision may be acceptable to a greater number of interests than if only some participants and some types of knowledge dominate.

Making biases explicit is an important, albeit difficult requirement for successful collaboration. Disciplined analysts know that their interpretations cannot be fully insulated from interests and preferences. By building in the challenging of assumptions in order to enhance creative thinking and avoid "groupthink," analysts can collectively structure processes that can reveal these biases.[28] If separate "teams" are set to analyze the same problems, the differences in gathered information, interpretations, and recommendations can be assessed to determine where biases may lie. As we have mentioned, knowledge generators should be required to specify the assumptions and potential limitations in the methods used, which will reveal that all approaches have the potential for error and reduce the likelihood that the apparently rigorous approaches will be accepted at face value. For example, as we argued in earlier chapters, despite revealed-preference valuation methods' apparent statistical sophistication and reliance on real data, they must be viewed warily because of the possibility of misspecification and missing data in the models used and because of these methods' inability to capture "public-regardedness."

Discipline in *defining problems* is required to maximize the effectiveness of the solutions rather than to aggrandize the individuals and organizations involved. Clear problem definition is important so as not to focus on irrelevant aspects. For many environmental issues, the priority must be to collect relevant trend and condition information about what is known in the present as opposed to what we would like to know. In the use of knowledge for environmental policymaking, the knowledge must be relevant to realistic alternatives under existing political, economic, and social circumstances. For example, modeling the environmental gains of a zero-economic-growth scenario distracts attention from realistic scenarios. By the same token, gathering information that is inadmissible in administrative and judicial arenas diverts resources away from gathering more relevant information.

Even though costs of information often make it tempting to economize, it is important to rely on multiple information sources to maintain the focus on what is important to stakeholders as well as on trends that are considered sufficiently promising or threatening from a scientific viewpoint. It is all too easy for analysts in government agencies to dismiss information coming from what appears to be the "fringe," but this information is also important insofar as it informs policymakers about the public's preoccupations and fears. Conventional scientists may not be worried about genetically engineered monster plants or magnetic fields emitted by power lines, but the fact that a nontrivial number of people are worried about these things is important information in and of itself.

However, valuing multiple sources of information does not mean abandoning disciplined screening to determine the quality, timeliness, and relevance of factual information and theoretical conclusions. We have seen the problems of using obsolete information for the valuation of clean water; we might also cringe at some of the simplistic models used to project climate change and global pollution trends. The point is that assessment must be based on broad criteria to avoid restricting the considerations that ought to be taken into account in environmental policymaking, yet analysts and policymakers must also be selective in the environmental knowledge they use in order to avoid overreliance on obsolete information and theories that have been magnified by the "founder effect" through which some studies come to be overcited out of habit or convenience or both.

Another aspect of professional discipline relates to the delays in the peer-review process for journals. The refereeing process depends on the voluntary cooperation of peers, but their slowness in conducting their evaluations often prompts journal editors to extend review deadlines. One study of peer-reviewed journals across a wide range of fields found some astonishing delays—one economics journal had a delay of more than two years, and a management journal had a delay of nearly two and a half years.[29] Of course, a portion of such delays is the time it takes for authors to make revisions prior to resubmitting their articles, and online posting of peer-reviewed journals has reduced the lag attributable to the physical printing of hard-copy journals. Yet as one assessment of the publication delays of food research journals concludes, the "total delay strongly depends on the peer review process."[30] The culture of peer reviewing has not been responsive to the growing need to transmit well-vetted, environmentally relevant knowledge quickly. Online working papers have now become a major part of the corpus of knowledge used in making environmental decisions in lieu of up-to-date, carefully reviewed journal articles. Changing the culture that has allowed large time lags between initial submission and final publication remains important.

The final challenge to self-discipline with respect to knowledge generation is the need to prioritize issues in order to secure a more efficient allocation of resources in the generation and transmission of knowledge. Although it is useful to have a horizon-scanning capability to detect emerging problems, there are too many trends and conditions for them all to be comprehensively covered; any effort to do so will lead to the neglect of what is truly policy relevant. Recall that the comprehensiveness criterion is not a call to cover everything under the sun, but rather to achieve a suitable level of inclusiveness for a given context. The oft-heard "serendipity" defense—invoking cases in which useful insights or inventions emerged from seemingly nonuseful research triggered by scientists' curiosity—is specious. The chances of discovering something useful from research that can be justified on the grounds of potential utility are higher than the chances of making an accidental discovery.

In our drive for relevance, we should not fall into the trap of believing that applied research is necessarily more relevant than basic research. In fact, for many environmental problems, basic research is probably more productive than work that is applied only to very specific problems in specific locations. Yet investment in basic research relevant to environmental policymaking need not be allocated randomly. We agree with Donald Stokes on the desirability of more "use-inspired" and "strategic" basic research—that is, "basic research that seeks to extend the frontiers of understanding, but is also is inspired by considerations of use."[31] For example, the immense amount of money that automobile companies and some government agencies have spent on engineering designs for electric vehicles might have been much more productive had it instead been focused on discovering new kinds of electric batteries, generally considered to be a key constraint.

A more focused approach might be a modernized version of a program that the National Science Foundation advocated and supported from 1971 to 1977: Research Applied to National Needs (RANN). RANN's purpose was to manage research projects targeted at improving specific social, economic, industrial, and intergovernmental sectors of the country—such as energy, the environment, industrial innovation, urban and rural quality of life, medical delivery systems, municipal management, communication needs, transportation and infrastructure, among others.[32] RANN sought to connect basic research and the problems facing technology, industry, and society. These considerations apply as much to social science research as to physical and biological environmental sciences research.

The RANN program spent half a billion dollars until the scientific establishment killed it under the Carter administration. Richard Green and Wil Lepkowski assert that "by killing the program, the U.S. science establishment spurned an opportunity to demonstrate the power of directed research to make life better for Americans and establish science as a 'city upon a hill': a merger of science with societal aspiration. In hindsight, the Democrats appear to have squandered an opportunity to raise science to higher esteem in the public eye." They draw this conclusion because RANN accomplished the integration of research and practical relevance that is now increasingly recognized as being needed:

RANN scanned the terrain in search of existing and emerging problems, assembled them into categories, and asked the research community—academic and industrial—to submit proposals for research on meeting goals that fell under each grouping; goals that the federal mission agencies either missed or lacked the resources to tackle. The program was essentially an idea factory that depended on researchers to embroider those ideas, reshape them, take resulting projects to the proof-of-concept stage, and once they achieved promise, transfer them to industry, a mission agency, or to state or local governments so that they could be put to practical use.[33]

What are the prospects for a new RANN type program in the National Science Foundation? Green and Lepkowski argue that three decades ago, both the scientific establishment and the foundation's protectiveness of what its leadership regarded as its narrow basic-science mission scuttled the program.[34] The question is whether government and scientists' attitudes have changed more than three decades later.

One high-payoff target for the kind of research that RANN had supported is inquiry that identifies common dynamics (without claiming their universality) associated with environmental problems and the potential solutions to those problems.[35] Such research can be in the form of meta-analyses of many applied studies or in a form that generates entirely new insights into the operation of social systems. For example, Elinor Ostrom and many others' work on local systems for managing common-property resources has revolutionized public-policy approaches, which previously had set forth either privatization or government control as the only viable options.[36]

Even more applied than this form of research is policy and program evaluation, which, when done well, combines the clarification of goals with the analysis of whether and why efforts at conservation and environmental protection are successful or unsuccessful. Sophisticated technical knowledge must be applied to determine whether the policy or program has been as successful as other options may have been, yet "success" is meaningless except in reference to shared goals. The recognition that evaluation requires explicit consideration of what should be pursued, rather than just a mechanical comparison between previously stated targets and outcomes, has opened up another link for interaction between the public and experts.[37]

Environmental decision makers must also impose self-discipline with respect to soliciting and using knowledge. Reliance on multiple streams of knowledge is crucial for gauging levels of uncertainty because it is so difficult for knowledge creators to judge their own degree of ignorance. By the same token, policymakers have to avoid becoming complacent in their reliance on the same knowledge intermediaries, who are often policy entrepreneurs trying to dominate agenda setting and the focus of attention. Policymakers, despite time pressures and limitations on how much information they can absorb, need to maintain diverse channels of communication.

By the same token, policymakers need to be open to multiple types of arguments, including considerations of the benefit-cost balance, rights, existing norms, public preferences, and so on—except when the law forbids taking some of these considerations into account. When the latter is the case, policymakers need to examine whether such rules remain justified. For example, we have noted that the ESA, in order to maintain a very strong defense against short-term economic considerations that may allow irreversible ecosystem losses, formally excludes economic considerations and certain property rights (e.g., to log in previously assigned concession areas). Even if in practice this exclusion is sometimes breached, its legal and political implications are important. The question, then, is whether the ESA serves the common good—a matter best left to Congress.

Self-discipline is also required of the nongovernmental groups that attempt to police the generation and use of environmentally relevant knowledge. The Center for Science in the Public Interest has "Integrity in Science Watch"; the not-for-profit Government Accountability Project has "Climate Science Watch"; and other private watchdog initiatives have proliferated over the past few years. Here, the discipline is required of the watchdogs: Can they maintain their credibility by taking a dispassionate stance in assessing how government agencies create and use environmentally relevant knowledge, or will they come to be seen as biased against any analysis or action that runs counter to their own agendas?

Revising Standards

Another set of recommendations calls for better evaluation of the validity and utility of knowledge. A "cultural" change is needed within formal science and government agencies with respect to the standing of different actors and approaches. Fair treatment of scientists and others who venture forth in the policy arena is required so as not to jeopardize their reputations. Creating realistic expectations of what is appropriate under different circumstances is important for accepting that the highest standards of accuracy and comprehensiveness may not be appropriate when environmental decisions require greater timeliness and relevance than peer-reviewed knowledge can support. Thus, we need to recognize the tension among comprehensiveness, relevance, and timeliness and how these elements are relevant for different purposes in decision making. Gilberto Gallopín and his colleagues further suggest that we should move away from rigid rules and narrow investigation to more general principles and guiding questions. "It is better to get an approximate answer for the whole problem/issue than a precise answer for an isolated component."[38]

In light of the limitations of formal science, comprehensiveness and dependability also call for a serious reconsideration of the criteria of administrative and legal admissibility. The practical monopoly of the formal scientific establishment in providing knowledge to agencies and the courts does not give enough credit to officials, judges, or jurors' judgment. The controversy over admissibility criteria, reviewed in earlier chapters, keeps open the possibility that strategic placement of issues in the right courts may begin to alter case law to reshape admissibility criteria. In particular, there is a need to resolve the problems presented by laws that on the one hand require benefit-cost and valuation exercises, but on the other hand minimize the role of the benefit-cost analysis in actual decision making. This contradiction discourages serious valuation and thereby diminishes the benefits of environmental protection, which is relevant for the next round of deliberations over the stringency of environmental regulations.

The standards for advancement within knowledge-generating institutions also pose an important issue. We recommend creating sharper distinctions between research for policy purposes and research for basic science. Expectations for policy research, more so than for basic research, must focus on how to make trade-offs among timeliness, relevance, and dependability. In general, there is a need to provide professional and personal incentives to protect scientists and other knowledge producers from the unrealistic expectations of a one-size-fits-all standard of knowledge generation. Academic and professional training should emphasize the importance of tailoring research to appropriate purposes.

This point again raises the need to stimulate greater awareness of the limitations of formal, "rigorous" approaches. It is crucial to develop clearer understandings of when, where, and how even those most widely used, mainstream techniques ought to be used and under what contingencies they are most effective. When should the Gold Standard methods be abandoned because their underlying assumptions are unrealistic? When must they be supplemented by "softer" approaches to ensure that important information is not lost? In many environmentally relevant fields, there is a convenient myth that the apparently most rigorous approaches are the best approaches. This criticism pertains to a wide range of techniques: computer models that ignore the fact that tracking well with past trends does not ensure success in prediction, that apparently precise measurements may be based on shaky assumptions about the connection between the measurement and the phenomena being measured, and that revealed-preference valuation approaches cannot control for all potentially relevant factors. The more the assumptions and limitations of findings are made explicit, the more easily they can be assessed to determine their usefulness and whether they will remain useful as conditions change. Moreover, a greater appreciation of these approaches' limitations would provide more tolerance for what have been seen as less-rigorous approaches. It is also important to develop tolerance for the fact that the protocols for assessing alternative knowledge are not as straightforward as those for conventional science. Organic farmers' experiments with natural fertilizers and pesticides will not be as "controlled" as the experiments done in research labs, but they may provide enormous experience if they are "harvested" and further explored.

Whatever approaches are employed, it is important to develop protocols for expressing uncertainty—and to make these standards obligatory for research publication and government reports. The inclusion of uncertainty statements (for example, by expressing confidence intervals) may begin to sensitize multiple audiences to the prevalence of uncertainty and to lead to more constructive treatment of uncertainty in environmental decision processes. One such effort in the context of reporting levels of uncertainty of climate change research has demonstrated that establishing such standards is quite feasible;[39] now it is up to journal editors and government agencies to require the standards.

Alternative knowledge-transmission sources can more generally be diversified and legitimized by an open attitude toward new venues—including the World Wide Web, informational databases that collect and solicit data from locals, and so on—through which alternative knowledge can penetrate traditional processes. More specialized knowledge-integration and delivery services can facilitate the translation and dissemination of knowledge. Wikis, blogs, and services that "push" content out to users can be employed. At a minimum, relevant government agencies should continually monitor and evaluate alternative knowledge to assess its relevance and the creative perspectives and options that emerge from nonconventional sources.

To control quality in this postnormal science world, the opportunity to participate in peer review should be extended to stakeholders outside the traditional peer community, such as industry, the public, media, and nonprofit organizations. This more diverse group becomes coproducers for creating a more comprehensive process for constructing knowledge relevant to the problem.[40]

It is understandable that many people, in particular established scientists, worry about the legitimacy of the new knowledge communities emerging from the diversification of transmission channels, which increasingly compete with conventional knowledge generation. We argue that legitimacy and credibility will come from demonstrated effectiveness in decision making. The advantage of such venues is their timeliness in comparison to the lengthy and time-consuming peer-review process. New standards for efficacy on the ground or in practical matters may either verify alternative knowledge or show it to be of little use. We are only in the early stages of the evolution of truly open-access knowledge.

It may well be that the weeding-out and reputation-building process will proceed rapidly.

One of the biggest challenges in organizing knowledge is to find the optimal balance of monitoring environmental problems, developing the knowledge of their causes, and developing the knowledge of how to cope with these problems. We have argued that the middle task dominates formal environmental science. Monitoring of biophysical trends gets short shrift because it is a mundane task; monitoring human preoccupations and reactions tends to be neglected because it is so challenging. By the same token, knowledge related to coping involves messy integrations of natural science, social science, and engineering; demonstrating rigor is far more problematic. The disproportionate focus on causal analysis to the exclusion of monitoring and solution searching occurs in part because of the widespread belief that if we get the science right, then the policy will flow from it. Scientists do not want to let go of their privileged position in generating causal knowledge as the critical part of the policymaking process. What is often missed is that conventional science can also have a highly rewarding role in the monitoring and solution-searching processes. If we can do a better job of shifting the incentives (money, grants, prestige) to these tasks, then the scientists will follow—it is not a zero-sum game.

Institutionalizing Knowledge Hybrids throughout Knowledge Processes
Reforming the institutions involved in generating, transmitting, and using knowledge can reinforce the strategies for broadening the kinds of knowledge brought into decision making. The hybrid of formal science, local knowledge, and public preferences that we have been advocating requires institutions that bring together scientists, holders of local knowledge, and citizens capable of registering public preferences. Institutional reforms can also mitigate the problem created when disagreements over knowledge impede the pursuit of the public interest by masking more fundamental differences over values and distribution.

Good will and epiphanies about the importance of stakeholder involvement are not enough to ensure adequate participation. Some of the existing mechanisms to promote meaningful stakeholder participation need to be rethought. We have described how the stakeholder involvement in the U.S. Forest Service's national-forest planning process has been both superficial in terms of reflecting citizen preferences and highly inefficient in resolving differences among stakeholders' values. Institutional changes should start with strengthening the institutions that involve stakeholders in setting the research agenda. The foci of knowledge generation would benefit from more input from processes that institutionally legitimize nonexperts' perspectives.

The range of mechanisms for developing these hybrids through meaningful citizen participation is stunning. Although the large number of proposed mechanisms is partly a result of different labels for similar approaches, it more fundamentally reflects the many design dimensions involved in structuring the interactions between experts and the public:[41] the number of citizens involved, the continuity of interaction, sponsorship (government, universities, community organizations, etc.), the extent and nature of government involvement, the centrality of the knowledge process to the effort, the degree of citizens' control of the agenda for knowledge gathering and analysis, the formality of interaction, the standing of the exercise as an input to public policy, and so on.

Some contrasts will illustrate this range. Two prominent approaches are dominated by government initiative. Joint fact finding, a procedure designed to create knowledge that is "technically credible, publicly legitimate, and especially relevant to policy and management decisions,"[42] entails a government agency as a convener and final decision maker. It relies on professionally trained, neutral facilitators to assist in identifying stakeholder representatives and managing the dialog process. The stakeholder group is involved in defining the inquiry by presenting a recommendation for action to the agency. The agency and other participating stakeholders must ensure sufficient time and money for stakeholder engagement and group decision making.[43] Stakeholders' involvement can continue into subsequent stages of the decision process, where they can advise on the issues of greatest concern and thereby the kinds of knowledge needed for sound decisions.

The second governmentally sponsored and managed mechanism is the consensus conference, pioneered by the Danish Board of Technology in 1987. Arising out of debates over nuclear energy and GEOs, the Danish Board of Technology was given the tasks of initiating technology assessment and encouraging and supporting public debate about technology. Since then, the consensus conference has also been used in France, the

Netherlands, Norway, Switzerland, the United Kingdom, Japan, South Korea, Australia, New Zealand, and Canada.[44] The sustainability of these efforts and their relevance to the environmental policy process often depend on governmental funding—in this case, funding by the Danish Parliament. In the United States and certain western European countries, a very close parallel to the consensus conference is the "citizen jury," which differs from the former in generally avoiding open meetings and having a modestly longer duration (four to ten days as opposed to the typical three days for a consensus conference). Both are typically composed of a modest number of "average citizens" (ten to sixteen for consensus conferences; twelve to twenty for citizen juries) selected to represent the demographic makeup of the community affected by the technically complex public-policy issue under consideration.[45] The primary objective is to provide a decision or recommendation for action. A neutral facilitator selects the members; the facilitator and members decide whom to engage as experts or "witnesses," including scientists, interest-group representatives, and others with a stake in the issue. Consensus is sought but not required to report the results of the deliberations through a written report to policymakers, the media, and the general public.[46] Neither consensus conferences nor citizen juries are guaranteed to influence policy decisions. However, insofar as *informed* public sentiment is valued by policymakers, the outputs of these exercises can have considerable impact. For example, a Danish consensus conference in 1987 recommended against funding genetic engineering of animals, and the Danish Parliament decided not to fund such a project.[47]

In contrast to these government-sponsored interactions, "science shops," pioneered in the 1970s in the Netherlands and adopted throughout western Europe since then, are hosted by universities or nonprofit organizations.[48] The intended purpose of science shops is to develop relationships between knowledge-producing institutions and citizen groups that need answers to relevant questions.[49] The assumption is that lay citizens can bring identified problems to scientists, who then work collaboratively with the interested public to shape a researchable question for which science can provide insight. For instance, a local nonprofit in Denmark approached the science shop at Roskilde University Center with a hunch that sewage was polluting a local pond. It wanted documentation of the pond's water quality and recommendations for how the problem might be addressed. Researchers were able to confirm the hunch and to provide a range of alternatives for addressing the sewage problem.[50] In recent years, the Internet and increased information transmission have changed the relationships between the public and science shops. More information is readily available and the costs associated with data gathering have declined. Communities turn to science shops when they have specific questions for which no answer is yet available. In one case, faculty working with communities have used master's theses projects as the vehicle for fostering knowledge creation for public use.[51]

In addition to these approaches that involve intensive and continual interaction between citizens and experts, the simple mechanisms of opinion polls, focus groups, and public hearings can also inform experts and decision makers about the environmental priorities and concerns held by the public. Expert valuation can rely on the information gathered from these mechanisms to ensure greater comprehensiveness of the benefits to be valued.[52] Or community groups can express their concerns and preferences through the study circle, a U.S. innovation that typically engages eight to twelve individuals who meet regularly over a lengthy time period to address issues of their choosing.[53] The goal often is to formulate positions that would be conveyed to government policymakers. Joint efforts of multiple study circles can amount to significant advocacy pressure on the government. The knowledge inputs come largely from the organizers' efforts to pull together background materials that cover a variety of scientific information and community perspectives on the issues. To manage differences in perspectives and priorities among members, an impartial mediator typically facilitates the study circle. In this case, experts may not play an interactive role, although that option is not precluded.

To illustrate the range of centrality of knowledge in the process, we can contrast the mechanism of negotiated rule making with science circles, consensus conferences, and citizen juries. In the United States, negotiated rule making utilizes an advisory committee of diverse stakeholders, organized by a government agency, to develop and propose regulations.[54] The U.S. EPA has used negotiated rule making to develop regulatory proposals on such issues as hazardous-waste disposal, asbestos in schools, woodstove performance standards, and regulations on reformulated and oxygenated fuels.[55] The agency organizing a negotiated rule-making exercise does not have to accept a proposed rule, but if a consensus emerges from well-informed, diverse representatives, the proposal will be compelling.

Our point is that negotiated rule making did not arise as a vehicle for systematically presenting or generating knowledge to or by the public, yet in many circumstances knowledge inputs are abundantly present in negotiated rule making, if the government or other participants bring knowledge into the deliberations to enhance the soundness of the deliberations or to advocate a particular position. Laura Langbein found that EPA negotiated rule making resulted in higher participant evaluations of the scientific quality of the deliberations than did conventional rule making.[56]

Given this proliferation of alternatives, we cannot lose sight of the importance of finding the mechanism that is appropriate for a particular context. Every decision-making process has advantages and disadvantages.[57] No process is superior in all contexts; each engages a particular set of people and organizations, allows participants to have a differing degree of influence on outcomes, and favors particular forms of knowledge.

Gene Rowe and Lynn Frewer have assessed eight formal public-participation mechanisms according to five criteria regarding their acceptability to the public and three criteria regarding the quality of the processes.[58] The public-acceptability criteria reflect aspects that are likely to contribute to the public's confidence that its participation is genuine (participants' representativeness and independence, transparency of the process) and effective (early involvement in the policy deliberations, influence on the final policy). The process criteria reflect aspects likely to contribute to the technical quality of the knowledge brought into the deliberations and developed through public participation (accessibility of resources, well-defined tasks, and well-structured decision processes). Because the Rowe and Frewer assessment did not focus predominantly on the role of knowledge in public-participation processes, we have added seven additional criteria (centrality of science in the process, potential for local knowledge to have policy influence, resource demands, cost effectiveness, potential for expression of preferences, the public's role in problem framing, and the public's role in framing alternatives).

Table 7.2 is a simplified summary of their assessment, but it also includes our additional criteria as well as three more mechanisms (joint fact finding, science shops, and study circles) that we have found to be equally prominent.

The most obvious implication of this assessment is that different public-participation mechanisms can indeed be assessed in terms of important dimensions related to public acceptability and the technical quality of the knowledge involved, which certainly provides useful guidance. Yet the performance of these mechanisms is "variable" on many dimensions, or is a matter of potential rather than of assured levels. This variability demonstrates the importance of context and of the specific way each mechanism may be employed. The assessment is useful insofar as it points to how public-participation mechanisms ought to be selected: by matching the assessments with the technical and political needs of the particular situation. For example, where analytic resources are limited by severe budget constraints, the mechanisms that assure resource accessibility and cost effectiveness should be favored. Where public skepticism calls for maximum transparency, the mechanisms that assure high transparency ought to be favored.

This "matching" can be illustrated through a few examples. Consider that study circles are good at educating participants, yet they do not give citizens much decision-making power. These processes might be used in an earlier phase of a larger decision process in which citizen juries and study circles help educate a wider public, determine public viewpoints, and outline general principles and priorities for action. This knowledge can then be fed into other decision processes in which stakeholders have greater decision-making authority.

Citizen juries and consensus conferences have not been used much in the United States. The Jefferson Center for Education and Research[59] conducted twenty-eight consensus conferences but is now organizationally dormant. It may well be that U.S. government agencies' preference for heeding only their own formal participation mechanisms, which largely entail soliciting reactions to preliminary government positions, dampens nongovernmental groups' enthusiasm for devoting their energy to alternative mechanisms. For example, the U.S. Forest Service, following the requirements of the NFMA, presents a draft plan for each national forest at meetings of local citizens it convenes. But if continual

Table 7.2
Characteristics of Public Participation Mechanisms Related to Knowledge Inputs

	convener	representativeness of participants	independence of participants	early involvement of the public	public influence on final policy	process transparency	resource accessibility	task definition	structured decision making
referenda/ initiatives	government/ private groups	high	high	variable	high	high	low	high	low
public hearings	government	low	generally low	variable	moderate	moderate	low to moderate	generally high	low
opinion surveys	variable	generally high	high	potentially high	high	moderate	low	low	low
negotiated rule making	government	low	moderate	variable	high	low	high	high	moderate
consensus conferences	government	moderate	high	potentially high	variable; not guaranteed	high	high	generally high	moderate
citizen juries/panels	usually government	moderate	high	potentially high	variable; not guaranteed	moderate	high	Generally high	potentially high
citizen advisory committees	government	low/ moderate	moderate	variable; maybe high	variable; not guaranteed	variable; often low	variable	variable/ high	variable
focus groups	usually government	moderate	high	potentially high	liable to be indirect	low	low	variable/ high	low
joint fact finding	variable	low/ moderate	low	moderate	variable; maybe high	variable; not guaranteed	high	high	variable
science shops	private groups	variable	high	variable	low	low	high	high	low
study circles	private groups	high	high	variable	low	variable	variable	variable	potentially high

	centrality of science	potential for local knowledge to have policy influence	resource demands	cost effectiveness	potential for expression of preferences	public role in framing the problem	public role in framing alternatives
referenda/initiatives	often low	moderate	high	low	high	variable	variable
public hearings	variable	variable	moderate	moderate	moderate	typically low	low
opinion surveys	low	low	low	variable	low	variable	low
negotiated rule making	usually high	high	high	low	high	variable	high
consensus conferences	variable	high	variable	variable	high	variable	potentially high
citizens juries/panels	variable	variable	high	low	high	potentially high	high
citizen advisory committees	variable	variable	variable	variable	high	potentially high	high
focus groups	generally low	variable	low	variable	variable	variable	variable
joint fact finding	high	high	high	variable	variable	variable	low
science shops	high	low	variable	variable	high	high	high
study circles	high	variable	variable	variable	high	high	variable

stakeholder involvement is neglected, the typical reaction is criticism for "not taking our concerns seriously." Developing more continuous stakeholder-involvement mechanisms can improve knowledge generation not only in terms of discovering what stakeholders value, but also in terms of making government officials more aware of the information that will address stakeholders' concerns.

A related recommendation is to incorporate more informal interaction between stakeholders and agency analysts prior to the formal procedures. Developing strong problem definitions through informal venues may broaden the scope of knowledge generation, demonstrate the need for unorthodox methods to gather and analyze information of interest, reduce the need to devote resources to gathering irrelevant information, and build trust with stakeholders and political actors prior to data collection. Focus groups and other informal ways of gaining stakeholder input prior to formal analysis can assist in this function at little expense. Going through the formal hoops of environmental impact assessments will still be necessary to defend against appeals or litigation, but the knowledge process can be more efficient and relevant if stakeholder concerns are clear from the start.

A very specific reform initiative would be to rethink the OIRA assessment mandate. OIRA has a legitimate role as watchdog over the quality of regulatory analysis and formulation; it is inevitable that some executive office would be assigned this task. The problem with OIRA, as we have presented in earlier chapters, is that this function has been conflated with the function of diluting and delaying new regulations. Recall that the problem is that it is not clear whether any particular OIRA decision to remand a proposed rule is truly reflective of an agency's deficient analysis or is motivated by the objective to hold back on more stringent regulation. The risk of having a regulatory impact assessment remanded discourages creativity on the part of environmental and conservation agency analysts in using less-tested or more-challenged methods. Moreover, the decisions to block environmental regulations (or, for that matter, all significant regulations) should not be delegated to a subagency because such decisions are so important. More broadly, it is important to provide firm guidelines for other agencies in order to prohibit them from inappropriately invoking "lack of rigor" as a means to block initiatives.

Within government agencies and nongovernmental research institutions, consistent institutional and professional incentives must be created to encourage rather than discourage the inclusion of less-tangible effects and values. Other countries point the way to incorporate less-tangible values and effects into decision making. For example, in Canada two hundred chemicals already in general use are undergoing intensive analysis for toxicity; they were selected from roughly twenty-three thousand substances reviewed by the Chemicals Management Plan Challenge, which is based on both technical considerations *and* stakeholder feedback.[60] After being vetted before the Challenge expert advisory panel, this initiative led to Canada's banning of BPA in child-oriented products in 2008, based on toxicity demonstrated in rodents even without evidence of human toxicity.

The importance of calibrating the spatial level of environmentally relevant knowledge to decisions being made at the subnational as well as the national levels calls for decentralizing some aspects of trend monitoring and causal analysis. As argued in earlier chapters, one-size-fits-all approaches to environmental issues are promoted by the dominance of national-level analyses. Some monitoring and analysis are conducted at the regional and subregional offices of the EPA, the Forest Service, the FWS, and other agencies. The underexamined question is whether environmental and conservation agencies are currently at a good spatial balance and are well equipped to integrate what information is most essential from these diversified sources.

In the rule-bound context of U.S. environmental policymaking, institutional change generally requires changes in legal and administrative doctrines. In light of the difficulty of conveying the full force of knowledge that would deter environmental threats, doctrines of administrative and legal admissibility can offset the resulting bias by introducing some elements of the precautionary principle. This introduction does not mean that uncertainty about environmental consequences should be allowed to bring development to a halt; as we have repeatedly argued, there is always some uncertainty. Instead, in the United States the burden-of-proof doctrines should be adjusted to offset the intrinsic pro-development bias that currently exists. This adjustment will begin to mitigate the litigious mindset that has a chilling effect on putting less-tangible values into play. However, the reaction to uncertainty must also take into account the magnitude of uncertainty and the costs of action and inaction.

Precautionary steps should be taken when the risk (even if remote) is large *and* the costs of avoiding it are known and relatively low. A good example is the contrast between global warming and depletion of the stratospheric ozone layer. In the first case, there has been considerable uncertainty about mechanisms and impacts, the costs are extremely high, and the distribution of costs is uncertain. Not until the uncertainty about the high costs of inaction was considerably reduced did the U.S. government even acknowledge the likelihood of global warming as an anthropogenic effect, long after western European nations had accepted the Kyoto Protocol.[61] In the case of ozone depletion, the mechanisms and impacts were also uncertain, but the costs of the remedy (phasing out CFCs) were well known, and the incidence of those costs was fairly easy to calculate. Moreover, although the firms producing CFCs opposed action for several years and raised questions about the underlying science, they eventually came up with commercially viable substitutes. According to Mostafa Tolba, former head of the United Nations Environment Program, the chemical industry supported the Montreal Protocol in 1987 "because it set up a worldwide schedule for phasing out CFCs, which are no longer protected by patents. This provided companies with an equal opportunity to market new, more profitable compounds."[62]

Case law, legislation, and administrative regulation likewise need to change to facilitate innovation and negotiation among stakeholders orchestrated by the environmental and conservation agencies. The sad irony of the well-intentioned efforts to guarantee direct participation is that many interactions between stakeholders and agencies have become formalized and trivialized, even as they drain the agencies' resources and thereby squeeze out efforts to engage in serious informal efforts to find common ground. Legislation such as the Administrative Procedures Act and the NFMA has straitjacketed agencies that might engage stakeholders more informally and constructively. Experimentation with informal approaches, such as those mentioned in earlier chapters, would provide important knowledge on workable solutions. Some of these solutions would take the form of "adaptive governance"[63] that would adjust the processes of interactions among stakeholders and policymakers as feedback on the progress of these interactions is assessed. This adjustment requires far more flexibility than the prevailing system of fixed procedures allows.

Institutional reforms for putting knowledge processes into their proper place in the overall policy process should be based on an assessment of the degree of value conflict. Renn, Webler, and Wiedemann suggest that when political conflict is intense, small differences over science become a proxy for political debate. As a consequence, efforts must be made to manage expertise to prevent science from becoming the main focus rather than the other issues at stake, which are often ideological or distributional. When decisions are driven primarily by expertise, the required information consists of facts about probabilities, causal relations, and the extent of potential damage. In these discussions, it is important to be clear about the science and to have estimates of uncertainty that accompany this information. If experts disagree, then it is necessary to have a way to represent their differences. In contrast, when a lack of public confidence and trust in environmental policy institutions is the fundamental problem, the discourse ought to be less reliant on technical expertise, although reducing factual misunderstandings and uncertainty can be constructive. The primary goals are to clarify mutual expectations, demonstrate good will, commit to fulfill expectations, and provide sanctions for failing to live up to commitments. When the decisions hinge more on addressing disagreements over values or distribution, the role for science and expertise is secondary to finding consensus about the issues that underlie broader value claims.[64] For instance, a decision about genetically engineered foods may be shaped as a discussion about the direction of scientific and technical change in a society rather than as a more narrowly technical dialog about the relative costs, benefits, and risks that come with a new genetically engineered food.

Promoting Adaptive Management and Governance

Adaptive management (continuous monitoring, analysis, and policy adjustment) and adaptive governance (flexibility in how science and other forms of knowledge are integrated throughout the decision-making process) can be employed to address the ever-present challenge of uncertainty. Environmental protection policies and natural-resource management can vary dramatically in terms of flexibility in knowledge use. Some processes, laws, regulations, and management doctrines lock in required actions regardless of newly available knowledge; others allow for much greater responsiveness.

As an approach to enhance this responsiveness, adaptive management is essentially an iterative approach to decision making that builds in learning and adjustment based on that learning.[65] Although adaptive management has several variations,[66] all variations can be understood as simultaneously trying to generate, transmit, and use information in an iterative feedback loop to improve environmental and natural-resource management. This approach minimizes the problems of policy termination by building in correction mechanisms. As a given policy is implemented, information gained is quickly fed back so that it can produce midcourse corrections in the specific policy being studied, and the experience gained can add to the general stock of environmental knowledge.

Adaptive management is particularly suited to cases where it is necessary to put policies in place immediately, without the time to perform all needed studies. It is well suited for dealing with situations where uncertainty is rife. It is also a useful approach to cases where controlled research experiments are not possible. The field of fisheries management is characterized by these limitations. Many fish stocks are critically endangered, yet the only way to gain information about sustainable yield is to set a take level and monitor its impact on the stock. Adaptive management allows policymakers to change quickly the amount of harvest permitted if the information generated on the stock indicates that the initial level was too high or too low. It has also been applied in managing waterfowl populations, endangered species, and forests.[67] The adaptive management literature has recently focused on the possibility that communities in addition to experts can use it.[68]

Adaptive management refers to the day-to-day implementation of adaptive principles that guide responses. The focus has been predominantly on how science is used within an established process. Implicit in the literature on adaptive management is that governance structures need to support management actions. Adaptive governance, in contrast, refers to higher-order decision making that creates conditions for social coordination and collective action at lower levels within a hierarchy.[69] Thomas Dietz, Elinor Ostrom, and Paul Stern use the term *adaptive governance* to expand the focus from adaptive management to the broader social context that enables adaptive management.[70] Carl Folke and his colleagues also discuss adaptive governance as the collaborative, comanagement structures that facilitate decision making.[71]

Ronald Brunner and Toddi Steelman see adaptive governance as a pattern of practice that integrates science, policy, and decision making.[72] Adaptive governance proceeds with the assumption that diverse policy interests are integrated through an appropriate decision-making structure that then leverages science and other forms of knowledge to inform the process of problem definition, goal identification, and alternative selection. If the assessment of policy consequences reveals that particular forms of knowledge are overprivileged or that laws or doctrines are limiting the generation, transmission, or use of important knowledge, adaptive governance provides the wherewithal to adjust the processes. In addition, adaptive management and governance provide workable models for creating dependable knowledge that is relevant and timely for decision-making purposes and more efficient given the real-time demands in some circumstances.

Defending the Integrity of Scientific Research

We also need to create mechanisms or rules to safeguard the integrity of federally conducted and funded scientific research.[73] To restore scientific integrity to federal policymaking, the Union of Concerned Scientists and others have come up with several proposals for management- and governance-level changes.[74] These proposals include protecting government scientists by legislating whistle-blower rights and enforcing whistle-blower protection. To make government more transparent, they recommend committing to open government, giving the public better access to federal science, reforming agency media policies, reforming the Freedom of Information Act, ending overclassification of documents as secret, and disclosing and mitigating conflicts of interest. To reform regulatory processes, the union suggests restraining OMB interference in regulatory processes, reviewing Executive Order 13422 (the 2007 successor to Executive Order 12866, "Regulatory Planning and Review," which mandates benefit-cost analysis), increasing transparency in rule making, and terminating inappropriate interagency review. To ensure robust scientific input to federal decision making, the union recommends reforming the Scientific Advisory Committee system, reinstating the Office of Technology Assessment, and strengthening science advice to the president. Finally, they recommend depoliticizing monitoring and enforcement. In February 2006, the National Aeronautics and Space Administration adopted a scientific openness policy that affirms the right of open scientific communication.[75] This policy can serve as a model for other federal agencies in need of reforming their media policies.

Enriching the Knowledge Processes through Greater Funding

Quite a number of recommendations would require additional funding rather than reallocating the current funding for knowledge generation, transmission, and use. For knowledge generation, if we begin by focusing on basic, first-order knowledge inputs, we see that extended time-series monitoring clarifies causal relationships (so-called "conditioning factors"), but there is also a compelling need for new efforts to monitor trends of emerging threats and opportunities. A continual review of the appropriateness of each aspect of the monitoring and data-collection effort is important because some monitoring may truly be irrelevant for both horizon scanning and analysis. Yet more resources are required to fund the appropriately expanding list of trends to be monitored.

Additional funding can also complement formal science with other processes to compensate for the inability to provide certainty and to introduce values and stakeholder concerns. Among the mechanisms of public participation that we have already outlined, several provide the opportunity to put citizens and scientists into direct contact with one another: citizen juries, citizen advisory committees, joint fact finding, science shops, and study circles. These processes make it possible to embrace the strengths of science while also supplementing its weaknesses. Yet how can these processes gain sufficient credibility? The creation of new, prestigious National Science Foundation funding categories to reward monitoring and problem-solving knowledge would help to reduce the conflict between scientists engaged in conventional, explanatory science and those focused on monitoring and practical problem solving—in short, something like the National Science Foundation's RANN program mentioned earlier in this chapter.

If we examine the intermediate phases of knowledge generation (i.e., evaluation of quality and relevance, integration with other information and theory, and development of decision-aiding knowledge), we also see the pressing need for expansion. The generation of knowledge via valuation requires more support to reduce the need to resort to obsolete valuations dredged up through "benefits transfer." More funding, albeit at a fairly modest level, is also needed to support the EPA Science Advisory Board's recommendation to provide stakeholder input to the valuation process.[76]

Funding is also needed to strengthen the assessment and integration of knowledge by promoting and more widely publicizing the "state of knowledge" efforts. Structural or organizational factors such as personnel requirements, interdisciplinary incentive structures, and cultural cues that value knowledge integration over knowledge generation can promote new norms for more integrative approaches. To minimize specialization and rivalry, government agencies or ad hoc committees of experts organized through private, quasi-governmental, or governmental entities can offer incentives.

The restoration of the Office of Technology Assessment, whether under the same name or a new name, would help to overcome the chronic problems of timeliness and relevance in synthesizing environmentally relevant knowledge. This office was staffed with experts who could work with congressional committee staff to assemble relevant information in easy-to-digest formats. It was accountable to Congress in general and to its bipartisan governing board. It internalized partisan differences, negotiated them for each research project, and produced studies that both parties could utilize. Also, it was able to anticipate the needs of Congress in the coming legislative session and produce useful background papers. It had a reputation as a respected and politically neutral institution with great policy relevance.[77] Pielke has argued that if decision makers pose the questions, and the capacity to answer them is adequate, then the questions will be policy relevant, and they will be ready when needed.[78] Other congressional research arms continue to play this role: the Congressional Research Service serves this function for many policy issues, as does the GAO for questions of program and policy effectiveness.

From time to time, convening experts on an ad hoc basis to assess the overall state of knowledge on an environmental issue is appropriate above and beyond the continuous processes outlined earlier. In the United States, the ad hoc expert committee approach is most prominently and effectively accomplished by the NRC. As a nongovernment entity chartered by the U.S. Congress, the NRC is administered by the similarly chartered National Academy of Science, National Academy of Engineering, and Institute of Medicine. It appears to have the greatest resources to field prestigious committee members and publicize their conclusions through a range of briefings, symposia, reports, and books, but the NRC itself depends on other nongovernmental and governmental sources for its funding. It publishes more than two hundred reports annually; in 2007, thirty of these reports were classified as being primarily on the environment.[79] The advisory committees to government agencies, such as the EPA's Science Advisory Board and the NMFS's Independent Scientific Advisory Board, operate in similar fashion but appear to have less visibility and press coverage owing to budget limitations and necessarily narrower foci.

These expert advisory committees can be directed to move beyond presentation of technical issues to provide policy options.[80] The transmission of information about the debates over environmental knowledge must clarify that generators also agree on fundamental aspects of environmental dynamics and implications so that policymakers and the public do not conclude that environmental knowledge is so uncertain that it can be safely ignored. Greater support for synthesis efforts, such as NRC and Intergovernmental Panel on Climate Change reports, can help to overcome these perceptions. In these situations, it is important to delineate the differences between advice, advocacy, and decision making.[81]

However, in recent years the operations of the federal advisory committee system has become contentious due to concerns that the selection of committee members is politicized, with charges ranging from using political loyalty as a selection criterion to selecting members who will create greater uncertainty about scientific consensus.[82] This issue needs to be resolved lest such advisory committees lose their credibility.

Funding to develop and assess new analytic approaches should be an explicit initiative in order to offset the built-in biases of clinging to existing approaches. Recall that laws, administrative procedures, and prevailing methods are typically mutually reinforcing. And the more a particular methodology has been used, the less likely those who employ it are likely to be challenged.

Funding to enhance the capability to transmit environmentally relevant knowledge should begin with greater support for timely outlets for original research. As mentioned earlier, the paradox of delays in publication despite the remarkable proliferation of environmental journals can be traced to the lack of appropriate incentives in the peer-review process. One alternative to relying on the sense of professional responsibility to induce a quicker review process is to provide bonuses for prompt reviewers. Because most respected environmentally relevant journals are controlled by a handful of for-profit publishers, the funding for these bonuses would have to come from government, foundations, or professional associations.

Greater funding would also be needed to strengthen the translation of technical communications into more accessible language, while providing greater resources to make environmental reporting in the popular media more discriminating. The conferences and in-newsroom training sessions of the fourteen-hundred-member Society of Environmental Journalists provide a strong start, yet the depth of knowledge required to form a bridge between technical studies and the public remains daunting. The cutbacks in traditional media's budgets and staff do not bode well for progress in this regard.

The final recommendation requiring significant additional funding is the provision of more comprehensive education to scientists, policymakers, and the public about the role of uncertainty in the science-and-policy interface. Specific educational efforts should teach scientists about how their science is used in the policy process. Educational efforts to target policymakers about the inherent uncertainties in science and how these uncertainties can be treated in policymaking would enhance knowledge use. Also needed are specific educational efforts for citizens so they can understand both the role of science and policy and the fact that uncertainty is an inherent part of any decision-making process. For example, the Consortium for Science, Policy, and Outcomes, currently at Arizona State University, provides both education and outreach to these varied audiences. The Organization for Tropical Studies, a consortium of American, Australian, and Latin American universities and research entities that operates research sites in Costa Rica, is devoted primarily to research and ecological education, but it also provides programs for congressional staff on the complexity of tropical conservation issues.

Although these models exist, such education efforts are still quite meager. The 2002 National Science Foundation *Report on Public Understanding of Science* found very limited understanding of the scientific method or the role of science in policymaking.

These many recommendations are presented in table 7.3 to illustrate how each addresses a subset of the many criteria against which knowledge processes are measured. No one recommendation can satisfy all the criteria. However, some recommendations do a better job of addressing categories of criteria than do others. The upshot from this categorization is that no one solution or reform will be sufficient to address all of the challenges posed by the many problems facing knowledge processes. The problems are diffuse, and so are the solutions.

Final Thoughts

Environmentally relevant knowledge will become more diffuse over time, with even more sources and transmitters. This greater diffusion is almost guaranteed by globalization and the widespread use of the Internet. Because of rising educational levels and greater access to information resources, more people are qualified and capable of using existing knowledge. Information will never again be as concentrated as it was in the pre–World War II era. There is no way to put the genie back into the bottle. Nor should there be.

The outcome of the diversification of participants, situations, and resources and of the politicization of knowledge generation, transmission, and use is confusion and uncertainty about the role of knowledge. The longer-term effect of this outcome may follow one of two paths. On the first path, the role of knowledge in decision-making processes will be devalued because it is just too complicated to manage. In particular, this devaluation may mean both greater reliance on the protocols of science to bring order to the knowledge process and exclusion of alternative forms of knowledge. Both of these results may in turn make the institutions of science more brittle and subject them to greater politicization. The control over knowledge generation, transmission, and use will become a proxy for who has power in environmental decision making. The second path requires wrestling realistically with the limits of knowledge (both science and alternative forms) under these new social conditions and reimagining a role that takes advantage of the strengths

Table 7.3
Contributions of Strategies to Satisfy the Criteria of Good Knowledge Processes

	Collaborate to produce knowledge hybrids	Engage in guerrilla science	Enhance discipline	Revise standards	Institutionalize knowledge hybrids	Promote adaptive management and governance	Defend integrity of science	Enrich variable processes through greater funding
Comprehensiveness	x			x	x			x
Dependability	x	x	x	x	x	x	x	x
Selectivity	x		x	x	x		x	x
Timeliness				x		x		
Relevance	x	x		x	x	x		x
Openness	x		x	x	x			
Efficiency			x	x		x		
Creativity	x			x	x			x

of knowledge in this new social context and compensates for the weaknesses in how knowledge is used in the environmental decision-making process. Building a constructive role for politics means building open, inclusive processes that incorporate valid and appropriate interests. These processes will take different forms depending on the contexts in which they are used. Thus, science advisory committees will be used in some contexts, stakeholder groups in others, and blue-ribbon panels of experts in yet others. Dependability in these processes will hinge on criteria for personnel choice, recognition of some degree of impartiality, and specified techniques for data generation, transmission, and use.

Because knowledge generation, transmission, and use do not comprise a systematic, technical process—nor will they—politics must play a role in working through contested claims. Knowledge generation, transmission, and use *are* political. We can either be explicit about the omnipresence of politics and build a constructive role for it or drive it underground and pretend it doesn't exist. By acknowledging the politicization of knowledge, however, we can empower the wide range of affected groups to enunciate the distributional impacts of alternative policies, thus adding important information to the decision process.

We argue that the common good might best be served by moving toward a society that is more inclusive of knowledge in policymaking, but more reliably so. We include here knowledge that is generated, transmitted, and used by the greatest number of participants in the policy process, as long as reasonable standards can be applied in judging its reliability and relevance. In this manner, knowledge generation, transmission, and use become socially integrative.[83]

The alternative—the monopolization of knowledge through the restrictive canons of science and science-based culture and the maintenance of strict boundaries between types of knowledge—will not serve the common interest. This "science-centric" approach is not realistic given twenty-first-century realities that include the diversification of participants, arenas, and resources associated with knowledge generation, transmission, and use. Nonetheless, there are no guarantees that we will move in the desired direction. Doing so depends on whether our leaders in all sectors will be open to exploring and accepting the complexity of environmentally relevant knowledge and its fundamentally political role in policymaking.

Notes

Chapter 1

1. Brunner and Ascher 1992.

2. These abuses are documented in Becker and Gellman 2007, among other studies.

3. See, for example, Grifo 2007; Bowen 2008; and Union of Concerned Scientists 2008.

4. According to the Union of Concerned Scientists (2008) analysis. See also U.S. Congress 2007b.

5. Union of Concerned Scientists 2008.

6. Tankersley and Levey 2009.

7. Spotts 2009.

8. See Morgan and Peha 2003; Haller and Gerrie 2007; Brown 2009.

9. See Andrews 1999; Brewer and Stern 2005; Layzer 2005; Vig and Kraft 2005; Rosenbaum 2007; van der Sluijs et al. 2008; Brown 2009; Keller 2009; R. Smith 2009.

10. See, for example, Carolan 2008 for a treatment of the ambiguity in scientific definitions of species and subspecies, with significant impacts on federal land protection.

11. See Brunner 2001; Dilling and Moser 2007; Sarewitz and Pielke 2007; Houghton 2009.

12. For example, Gulbrandsen (2008) examines the competition among sources of knowledge in forestry policy in developed countries, focusing on Norway and Sweden; Larson and Ribot (2007) highlight the problems of importing forestry doctrines from developed countries.

13. Brown 2009.

14. See Kuhn 1962; Ziman 1978; Latour and Woolgar 1979; Latour 1987; Nelkin 1987; Fischer 1990, 2000; Beck 1992; Irwin and Wynne 1996; Wynne 1996; Forsyth 2002.

15. Young, King, and Schroeder (2008) have recently begun to research what they call the "knowledge-action perspective," which relates institutions to "prevailing discourses" and considers the role of "knowledge brokers." Their application of these ideas, which we believe are very promising, is primarily to the formation and function of international environmental institutions, notably those concerned with climate change.

16. Clark, Mitchell, and Cash 2006: 16.

17. Latour 1987.

18. Polanyi 1966: 4.

19. Lévi-Strauss 1968: chap. 1.

20. Beck 1992; Wynne 1996.

21. Gallopín et al. 2001. There have been seven principal critiques of formal science, all directly or indirectly related to the criterion of relevance and the assertion that scientists have a social contract with the citizenry that rewards them with respect and funding. First, the scientific enterprise is an expensive indulgence and is not as relevant as it should be because scientists follow their own curiosity, despite societal needs requiring more attention. Curiosity-driven research does not prompt scientists to engage with stakeholders in defining the foci of research. This criticism is reasonable because it is unlikely that the classic defense—curiosity-driven research has led to a cache of valuable discoveries— rings hollow in light of the fact that there is no reason why serendipitous dis- coveries should come from curiosity more so than from relevance-driven research.

Second, scientists focus on questions that can be addressed definitively even if other questions are more important to achieving society's goals. This critique is more problematic because formal science has two functions: it contributes directly to addressing society's needs, but it also provides the cumulative building blocks for greater understanding, which may well enable the first function. The fact that much of science is devoted to the systematic accumulation of knowledge is reasonable from a long-term perspective, and for this accumulation to be reli- able and credible, the canons of replicability and testability are necessary.

Third, science is too preoccupied with reducing uncertainty by focusing pre- dominantly on as yet unresolved questions of fact and theory and instead should take as a given that a degree of uncertainty will always remain and focus the research agenda on the crucial real-world questions that arise out of that premise. Reducing uncertainty is important, but a significant portion of the scientific effort should be devoted to the task of determining how to cope with uncertainty in the many cases where it cannot be easily reduced (Funtowicz and Ravetz 2001). Of course, some scientific initiatives do precisely that. The Santa Fe Institute, for example, devotes a considerable amount of its work to understanding and model- ing uncertainty and incorporating it into analysis (see, e.g., Page 1998; Lane and Maxfield 2004).

Fourth, much of science is fragmented—physics pursued in isolation from biology, economics in isolation from psychology—despite the interconnectedness of these facets of the real world, thus making science less useful in addressing real-world problems. The critique against fragmentation is fair, primarily for the social sciences. For the biophysical sciences, separating out physical, chemical, and biological phenomena through laboratory controls to understand basic dynamics is an essential approach, and reintegrating these understandings through complex modeling and the boundary subfields (biophysics, biochemistry, etc.) has expanded impressively. In contrast, the social process simply cannot be isolated into economic, political, psychological, or sociological dynamics because the human mind does not engage fully in this separation. Although the boundary subfields (psychology of economics, political psychology, economic sociology, etc.) are appropriate for reintegration, the fragmentation that still characterizes the bulk of social science is not defensible.

Fifth, in adopting a "value-free" orientation in order to maintain objectivity, science has isolated itself from the pursuit of societal values. The critique of value-free science has to be finely nuanced. Few would want scientists to distort the findings or theorizing of their research to pursue their values. Yet it is virtually impossible for researchers not to reflect their values in the very choice of research topics. Especially in environmentally relevant research fields, many scientists are clearly motivated to further conservation and environmental protection, thus choosing their research topics accordingly. Yet that motivation does not negate the possibility that scientists can partition their value commitment reflected in the choice of research foci from their dispassionate analysis of trends and causal relationships. Scientific responsibility, narrowly defined, requires this objectivity. Scientists must be self-aware in order to guard against having their values bias their analysis.

Sixth, science overemphasizes the exploration of broad generalizations at the expense of more specific dynamics that must be understood to address contextually bound problems. This critique especially has merit for the social sciences, for which the search for universal laws of behavior is bound to fail. For the biophysical sciences, the emphasis on broader generalizations reflects the trade-off between providing building blocks for understanding versus immediate application. Some subfields of biophysical science, such as conservation biology, do devote most of their resources to more specific problems, such as survival requirements of single species or interactions within a small ecosystem. A balance is clearly needed, although the right balance is very difficult to determine.

And seventh, formal science has been very slow to examine and incorporate alternative sources of knowledge, thereby blinding itself to the wisdom developed through scientific protocol and consequently progressing more slowly than it might to find solutions. Many of the basic areas of biophysical research, such as molecular biology or biophysics, play an important role in environmental science but simply do not engage the nature of the knowledge generated by alternative sources. And in more applied science, there have been some efforts to inventory folk wisdom about plants and animals as a stage in developing scientific research agendas. However, many opportunities to increase the efficiency of discovery by bringing in alternative knowledge have been neglected—although how many cannot be determined.

One broad conclusion of this overview of critiques is that the *practice* of formal science is largely appropriate for the purpose of developing the basic building blocks of general understanding. But formal science faces bigger challenges in generating information and theories of direct use in environmental decision making.

22. Lasswell 1971; Brewer and deLeon 1983.

23. Beck 1992; Fischer 2000.

24. Lasswell and McDougal 1992: 345.

25. See Sabatier 1988 for an overview of the advocacy-coalition framework, which emphasizes both the cognitive and strategic reasons why advocates filter out knowledge that runs counter to their policy references.

26. For more recent examples of those who seek to create clear boundaries, see Sunstein 2002 and Wagner and Steinzor 2006.

27. Schwartz 1982; U.S. Government Accounting Office 1984.

28. Nelkin 1987.

29. We explore this so-called parametric uncertainty in chapter 2.

30. McDougal, Lasswell, and Reisman 1973.

31. Ibid.; Lasswell and McDougal 1992; Clark 2002.

32. Gibbons et al. 1994.

33. Mol 2006, 2008.

34. Berkes, Colding, and Folke 2003.

35. Meidinger 1997.

36. Ascher and Steelman 2006.

37. Ascher 2001.

38. Nelkin 1979, 1987; Healy and Ascher 1995.

39. Steelman and Ascher 1997.

40. Poe 2006.

41. Ascher 2001.

42. Healy and Ascher 1995.

Chapter 2

1. See Kuhn 1962; Latour and Woolgar 1979; Fischer 1990; Beck 1992.

2. Gibbons et al. 1994.

3. Kuhn 1962.

4. Gibbons et al. 1994.

5. Giddens 1984; Habermas 1985.

6. Forsyth 2002.

7. Gibbons et al. 1994.

8. Ibid.

9. National Science Foundation 2005: table 3.

10. Ibid.: table 4.

11. National Science Foundation 2007a: table 3.

12. National Science Foundation 2007b.

13. Shackelford 2007.

14. Hays 1989.

15. Leonard 1984.

16. Hays 1989; Wynne 1996.

17. Ascher 2001.

18. Ibid.

19. Meidinger 1997.

20. Harrington, Heinzerling, and Morgenstern 2009: 225–226.

21. Weaver 1948.

22. Brunner and Brewer 1971.

23. Sarewitz 2004: 393.

24. Brunner et al. 2005.

25. This type is also called "aleatory" uncertainty (from the Latin *aleas*, or "dice," to connote randomness).

26. The boundaries between Type I and Type II uncertainties can shift over time (National Research Council 1997). This shift is in part a matter of what relationships are included within or excluded from the analysis and is therefore considered to be the source of random effects. For example, some earthquake-prediction models rely on the historical incidence of earthquakes in a given area without directly bringing the existence, structure, and behavior of the earthquake faults and tectonic movements into the analysis. This historical incidence is certainly useful, if incomplete, information; the remaining uncertainty, as far as this model is concerned, is aleatory (like that of the coin flip). Yet when the models are elaborated to incorporate the dynamics of tectonics and the movements along faults, the uncertainty as to how to use this new information is epistemic insofar as these dynamics are not fully understood (Ascher 2004). By the same token, Earth's temperature fluctuations are partly aleatory because short-term changes in solar energy (e.g., from sun flares) are treated as random rather than as subject to analysis; they may someday be subject to modeling, at which point the uncertainty about these fluctuations will be considered epistemic. Thus, what is considered inherently random today may be knowable tomorrow due to advances in understanding.

27. Hence, this type is also called "epistemic" uncertainty (from the Latin for "knowledge").

28. S. Johnson 2006.

29. See Mitchell et al. 2006 for an overview of the impacts of global environmental assessments.

30. Shlyakhter 1994: 441.

31. Levin 1992.

32. Oversight Review Board of NAPAP 1991: 26.

33. National Research Council 1997: 31–40.

34. For example, de Finetti 1974; de Groot 1988.

35. Gallopín et al. 2001: 224.

36. Gallopín and his colleagues suggest that formal science is seen as part of the "perfectibility of the human condition." This view flows from a belief that formal science can provide knowledge that leads to transformational change (2001: 226–227). This line of reasoning, although prevalent, may lead to misguided beliefs about what science can do to address complex problems. In complex systems, an intervention to change the status quo will stimulate unanticipated and perhaps unintended consequences. These unanticipated consequences are interpreted as symptoms of imperfection in the current state of knowledge rather than as characteristics of the system itself. More knowledge cannot reduce these uncertainties or increase the capacity for control or remedy past errors. For complex problems, the opportunity to reduce uncertainty is a fool's errand, and any attempt to control or intervene may be in vain.

37. Griffin and Tversky 2002.

38. Gallopín et al. 2001: 227.

39. Gunderson 1999.

40. Holling 1978, 1995, 1997; Gunderson and Holling 2002.

41. Botkin 1990.

42. Berkes, Colding, and Folke 2003.

43. W. Smith 1991.

44. Mohnen 1988: 35.

45. Oversight Review Board of NAPAP 1991.

46. Sarewitz 2004.

47. Metlay 2000: 210.

48. Nuclear Waste Technical Review Board 2000.

49. Oversight Review Board of NAPAP 1991: 16–17.

50. Sarewitz 2004: 393.

51. Ibid.

52. Ibid.; Economic Research Service 2007.

53. Wolfenbarger and Phifer 2000; Food and Agriculture Organization 2003.

54. Nelkin 1979, 1987; Healy and Ascher 1995.

55. Wynne 1996.

56. "Regulatory planning and review" 1993.

57. U.S. Office of Information and Regulatory Affairs 2003.

58. Navrud 1992.

59. For example, Food and Agriculture Organization 2000; Silva and Pagiola 2003.

60. Sunstein 2002; Ascher and Steelman 2006.

61. For descriptions, see Sunstein 2002: ix, 7, 49.

62. Freeman 2003.

63. Revealed-preference approaches rely on econometric analysis to infer willingness to pay through actual consumer purchases of items that include some environmental amenities, such as a house on a tree-lined street as opposed to one on a treeless street. Statistical analysis (multiple regression) isolates the higher price accounted for by the amenity. The greater expense of traveling to a park with particular amenities that are absent in nearby parks can similarly reveal how much more the park attender is willing to pay for that amenity. The "stated-preference" approaches ask people how much they would be willing to pay for additional environmental amenities or the minimum they would be willing to accept to forgo existing amenities. Because there is no market in which an ecosystem service can be directly or indirectly valued, people can be asked how much they would be willing to pay for improvements or how much they would be willing to give up amenities. Their responses provide a proxy measure for valuing these services. The possibility that respondents will deliberately or inadvertently bias their responses has been addressed in a number of ways (see Freeman 2003). Nevertheless, the revealed-preference approaches are typically regarded as more rigorous because they rely on actual economic behavior rather than survey responses. Be that as it may, the prevailing techniques mean that certain types of information are generated and given higher standing over others.

64. Ascher and Steelman 2006.

65. Healy and Ascher 1995; Ascher and Steelman 2006.

66. Sagoff 1994: chap. 8 and 136.

67. Because revealed-preference approaches rely on consumer purchases, they do not capture the willingness to pay to provide environmental amenities for the community. In other words, they do not capture the additional value of amenities such as trees, parks, and wildlife that people may believe is warranted out of "public regard," even if they have little personal enjoyment of these amenities. Thus, an individual with a tree-pollen allergy may be unwilling to buy the more expensive house on the tree-lined street but still be willing to pay, perhaps in the form of taxes, for the city to plant trees. In contrast, stated-preference approaches, which can capture public-regardedness, are usually deemed less rigorous because they are based "merely" on surveys asking hypothetical questions.

68. As cited in Shabman and Stephenson 1996: 445–446.

69. Ibid.: 446.

70. Martin and Steelman 2004.

71. R-factor analysis is a more generalizable means of analysis that uncovers the most prevalent variables among a group of respondents. The end result from a Q-analysis is to reveal "an in-depth portrait of the typologies of perspectives that prevail in a given situation" (Steelman and Maguire 1999: 363), whereas the end result of the R-factor analysis is to reveal the dominant underlying dimensions that prevail among a group of individuals (Iacobucci 2001).

72. Radin 1998.

73. Martin and Steelman 2004.

74. Latour 1987.

75. Fischer 2000.

76. Martello and Jasanoff 2004.

77. Corburn 2005.

78. Fischer 2000.

79. Lindblom and Cohen 1979; Geertz 1983; Agrawal 1995.

80. Corburn 2005.

81. Ibid.

82. Scott 1985, 1998.

83. Agrawal 1995.

84. Ibid.; Corburn 2005.

85. Corburn 2005.

86. Corburn 2005.

87. Martello 2001.

88. Agrawal 1995; Krech 2000; Corburn 2005.

89. Steelman and Ascher 1997.

90. Kerwin 1999.

91. Fiorino 1990.

92. Beierle 1999; McAvoy 1999; Beierle and Cayford 2002.

93. Freudenberg and Steinsapir 1992.

94. Beierle and Cayford 2002: 6.

95. Public-participation approaches are elaborated in some detail in our final chapter.

96. Culhane 1981; Wondolleck 1988; Fedkiw 1998; Steelman 1999.

97. Healy and Ascher 1995; Steelman 2001; Steelman and Ascher 1997.

98. Rosenbaum 1976.

99. Behan 1990; Tipple and Wellman 1989.

100. Varettoni 2005.

101. Elwood 2006.

102. Steelman and Ascher 1997.

Chapter 3

1. Ascher 2004.

2. Kluger 1997.

3. Davis 2007: xii.

4. Schön and Rein 1994.

5. Jasanoff 1990.

6. Relman and Angell 1989.

7. Horrobin 1990.

8. These approaches, which strive to find general propositions that survive efforts to show that they are false in some cases, are most prominently associated with Karl Popper. See Popper 1963. A more sophisticated early treatment of the issue can be found in Merton 1942.

9. Foster and Huber 1999: 20.

10. Edmond 2000.

11. Ibid.: 218–219.

12. Ibid.: 219.

13. Jasanoff 1995: 155.

14. See Irwin and Wynne 1996.

15. See Sheingate 2006 for a useful comparison between U.S. and western European stances toward GEOs.

16. See Fisher, Jones, and von Schomberg 2006 for various treatments of the "precautionary principle" concept.

17. Vig and Faure 2004.

18. Jasanoff 1995: 140.

19. Vig and Faure 2004.

20. Sheingate 2006.

21. Pew Foundation 2007.

22. Kelly 2007: 78.

23. Seelye 2005.

24. Huettmann 2005: 466.

25. U.S. Environmental Protection Agency, Office of Air Quality Planning and Standards 1998: 4–5.

26. Downs 1972: 38.

27. Healy 1987.

28. For an industry-sponsored account of twenty-eight instances of claimed media overreaction to food and toxic threats, see Lieberman 2004.

29. Clarke and Hemphill 2002.

30. See Price 1971 and Downs 1972. Salisbury (1969) introduced the generic term *entrepreneur* in the political and administrative processes; numerous others, including Price and Downs, focused specifically on policy entrepreneurship.

31. Kingdon 1984. See also Price 1971; Ringius 2001; and McCown 2005.

32. Young, King, and Schroeder ascribe a similar role to the "knowledge broker," an "individual well versed in both the policy and scientific worlds who facilitates communication between the two" (2008: xxii). We prefer the term *knowledge entrepreneur* to emphasize that these people often have goals and agendas that they try to advance by selectively transmitting knowledge.

33. Carson 1950, 1962.

34. Hays 1989: 61.

35. See O'Toole 2007.

36. Healy 1987.

37. Young, King, and Schroeder 2008.

38. Selin 2006: 176.

39. U.S. Environmental Protection Agency 2006. In May 2009, the Obama administration reversed this rule change.

40. Marc Shapiro notes that "[the] EPCRA and the TRI regulate only the provision of information, eschewing the traditional 'command and control' approach to regulation of production processes or outputs. Nonetheless, industries have changed emission processes and levels since being confronted with negative publicity, concern from communities and local emergency planning organizations, direct negotiation by community and 'watchdog' groups, and the threat of other state regulatory policies" (2005: 373).

41. U.S. Environmental Protection Agency, Scientific Advisory Board 2006: 1.

42. Healy and Ascher 1995.

43. Ibid.

44. Brunner and Steelman 2005.

45. Majone 1989: 62.

46. For useful examples, see Pilkey and Pilkey-Jarvis 2006.

47. Brunner 1991.

48. Norgaard 1984, 1994. Coevolution reflects both the early survival of the human species and the modifications in ecosystems that humans have accomplished. Existing reproductive and trophic chains supporting valuable species and the physical systems that provide ecosystem services are more likely to be disrupted by unforeseen consequences vulnerable to disruption than by negative connections (e.g., malarial mosquitoes).

49. Ascher 1993.

50. Ascher and Healy 1990.

51. Ascher 1993.

52. DeLong 1996: 739.

53. Martin and Steelman 2004.

54. Frantz and Sato 2005.

55. Pyne 1996.

56. Sabatier 1988.

57. Kuhn 1962.

58. Mol 2008: 40–41.

59. See the SeaMap Web site at http://seamap.env.duke.edu/.

Chapter 4

1. Pachauri and Reisinger 2007.

2. Foster and Huber 1999.

3. Whittington and Grubb 1984. The review process was changed somewhat, though without removing the benefit-cost requirement, by President Clinton's Executive Order 12866 (1993). President Obama rescinded Order 12866 on January 30, 2009, only a week after taking office.

4. See Duncombe 1996 for an overview.

5. Baumgartner and Jones 1993; Pralle 2003.

6. Despite the general prohibition against states or other subnational jurisdictions' imposition of their own emissions standards, the Clean Air Act states that the EPA "Administrator shall, after notice and opportunity for public hearing, waive application of this section to any State which has adopted standards . . . for the control of emissions from new motor vehicles or new motor vehicle engines prior to March 30, 1966" (i.e., California) (Clean Air Act, sec. 209[a]).

7. Pidot 2006.

8. Ascher 2001.

9. Ibid.

10. Pyne 1996.

11. Brunner 1982.

12. Ibid.: 2.

13. DeLeon and Steelman 2001.

14. Kohm and Franklin 1997; Aley et al. 1998.

15. Cortner and Moote 1999: 222.

16. Baumgartner and Jones 1993; Pralle 2003, 2006.

17. Carson 1962; Peterson 1999.

18. Lannetti 1998: 281–282.

19. Ibid.: 282.

20. Schattschneider 1960.

21. Stoll 2001: 10231.

22. As cited in Adams 2002: 525.

23. Presidential Executive Order 13422, January 18, 2007. The amended language is: "Each agency shall identify in writing the specific market failure (such as externalities, market power, lack of information) or other specific problem that it intends to address (including, where applicable, the failures of public institutions) that warrant new agency action, as well as assess the significance of the problem, to enable assessment of whether any new regulation is warranted." The earlier version was: "Each agency shall identify the problem that it intends to address (including, where applicable, the failures of private markets or public institutions that warrant new agency action) as well as assess the significance of that problem." This order was revoked by President Obama on January 30, 2009.

24. U.S. Congress 2007a: 4.

25. Dunford, Ginn, and Desvousges 2004; Roach and Wade 2006.

26. For example, one development plan (say, for a factory or housing tract) may be considered superior to another because the first plan accomplishes the same physical production with less impact on the natural environment; in other words, it has a smaller "ecological footprint" (Boyd and Wainger 2002; Boyd 2004).

27. Boyd 2004.

28. Johnson et al. 1999.

29. Hagenstein 1999.

30. Noon, Parenteau, and Trombulak 2005: 1359–1360.

31. "Section 219.10 of the new regulations require only the 'responsible official' (usually the supervisor) to evaluate social and economic impacts and does not include a similar requirement for evaluation of plan implementation on ecological sustainability. Determination of a failure to meet ecological sustainability goals is at the discretion of the responsible official, who is not required to engage the public or the scientific community in this assessment" (Ibid.: 1360).

32. Iverson and Alston 1986: 14.

33. The 1974 Forest and Rangeland Renewable Resources Planning Act and the 1976 NFMA. See Iverson and Alston 1986 and McQuillan 1989.

34. McQuillan 1989: 60.

35. Ibid.: 71.

36. Arrow et al. 1996: 222.

37. Loomis 2000: 343.

38. Sagoff 2004: chap. 8.

39. Shabman and Stephenson 1996: 444.

Chapter 5

1. Diamond 1986.

2. U.S. Environmental Protection Agency 2000, 2002.

3. Mitchell and Carson 1981.

4. U.S. Environmental Protection Agency, Scientific Advisory Board 2009.

5. Showers 2005: 314, 316.

6. National Research Council 2002; National Research Council and Institute of Medicine 2004.

7. The Royal Society report concluded: "There is at present no evidence that GM foods cause allergic reactions. The allergenic risks posed by GM plants are in principle no greater than those posed by conventionally derived crops or by plants introduced from other areas of the world. One shortcoming in current screening methods, which applies to both conventional and GM foods, is that there is no formal assessment of the allergenic risks posed by inhalation of pollen and dusts. We therefore recommend that current decision trees be expanded to encompass inhalant as well as food allergies. . . . Plant viral DNA sequences are commonly used in the construction of the genes inserted into GM plants, and concern has been expressed about this. Having reviewed the scientific evidence we conclude that the risks to human health associated with the use of specific viral DNA sequences in GM plants are negligible" (2002: 3).

8. For a snapshot of the movement, see Costanza, Perrings, and Cleveland 1997.

9. According to Kalaitzidakis, Mamuneas, and Stengos 2003, this journal ranks 83rd out of 159.

10. U.S. Environmental Protection Agency 2008: 154.

11. Posner 1972: 4.

12. For example, "equal benefits for all," "to each according to his needs," and "reward according to effort."

13. Heinzerling 2006: 105.

14. See Morgenstern 1997: 7–9.

15. U.S. Government Accountability Office 2003: 76.

16. Driesen 2006: 365–366. The twenty-fifth case did not result in either a more stringent or a less stringent regulation.

17. Heinzerling 2006: 108.

18. Guston 1999: i.

19. Gieryn 2001.

Chapter 6

1. For coverage of the crisis as it was occurring, see Barnard 2001; Bernton 2001; Clarren 2001; Jehl 2001; U.S. Bureau of Land Reclamation 2001; Welch 2001; Bailey and Schoch 2002.

2. Rohlf 1991.

3. Service 2003.

4. National Research Council, Committee on Endangered and Threatened Fishes 2002.

5. Service 2003.

6. Ibid.

7. Jenkins 2008.

8. National Institute of Environmental Health Sciences n.d.; National Toxicology Program Center 2007, 2008.

9. National Toxicology Program Center 2008.

10. Vom Saal et al. 2007.

11. Quoted in Cone 2007.

12. Center for Evaluation of Risks to Human Reproduction 2008.

13. Quoted in Cone 2007.

14. Bucher 2009.

15. Health Canada 2008b.

16. U.S. Food and Drug Administration n.d.

17. U.S. Federal Institute for Risk Assessment 2006.

18. European Food Safety Authority 2006.

19. Food Standards Australia New Zealand 2009.

20. Health Canada 2008a.

21. Goodman 2008b.

22. Goodman 2008c.

23. Layton 2009.

24. "Sunoco Refuses" 2009.

25. Goodman 2008a.

26. See National Toxicology Program 2007.

27. For background on this issue, see Quarles and Brady, LLP, 2003 and U.S. Environmental Protection Agency, Scientific Advisory Board 2009.

28. Regulatory planning and review 1993: sec. 4, f1.

29. U.S. Government Accountability Office 2003.

30. League of Conservation Voters 2001.

31. Letter from fifty-three academics to the Senate Governmental Affairs Committee opposing the nomination of John Graham as OIRA director,

May 9, 2001, available at http://www.citizen.org/congress/regulations/graham/academics.html, accessed April 27, 2009.

32. U.S. Government Accountability Office 2003: 11.

33. Simon 1941, 1969.

34. U.S. Environmental Protection Agency 2002. Economic Analysis of the Final Revisions to the National Pollutant Discharge Elimination System Regulation and the Effluent Guidelines for Concentrated Animal Feeding Operations, E-18; also S-13. Washington, DC, December.

35. Mitchell and Carson 1989.

36. U.S. Environmental Protection Agency, Scientific Advisory Board 2009: 55.

37. Ibid.: 82.

38. Ibid: 71.

39. Ibid.: 69.

40. Centner 2008.

Chapter 7

1. Pielke 2007b: 347.

2. Sabatier asserts that "members of various coalitions seek to better understand the world in order to further their policy objectives. They will resist information suggesting that their basic beliefs may be invalid and/or unattainable, and they will use formal policy analyses primarily to buttress and elaborate those beliefs (or attack their opponents'). Within this assumption of the prevalence of advocacy analysis, the framework identifies several factors which may nevertheless facilitate learning across advocacy coalitions" (1988: 133).

3. See the exposition on this point in McDougal, Lasswell, and Reisman 1973.

4. Shapin and Shapper 1985.

5. Ezrahi 1990.

6. Jasanoff 2003.

7. Ibid.: 398.

8. See, for example, Arkes, Mumpower, and Stewart 1997; Armstrong 2001; Brewer 2007.

9. Boundary organizations are deftly explored in Guston 1999, 2001.

10. Guston 2001: 403.

11. Jasanoff 2003.

12. This recommendation is emphasized in U.S. Environmental Protection Agency, Scientific Advisory Board 2009: 21.

13. See Bäckstrand 2003.

14. Jasanoff 1996.

15. Bäckstrand 2003.

16. Busenberg 1999.

17. See, for example, Cash 2001.

18. Parma and the NCEAS Working Group on Population Management 1998; Johnson 1999; Lee 1999.

19. This point is elaborated in Bäckstrand 2003 and Irwin 2006.

20. Irwin and Wynne 1996.

21. Sunstein 2002.

22. Irwin 2006.

23. Ibid.: 316.

24. Collins and Bodmer 1986.

25. National Science Foundation 2002: appendix table 7–10.

26. An excellent summary and assessment of the case can be found in Colburn 2002.

27. Renn, Webler, and Wiedemann 1995a.

28. Janis 1972.

29. Kling and Swygart-Hobaugh 2002.

30. Amat 2006.

31. Stokes 1997: 74.

32. An insightful history and postmortem of RANN can be found in Green and Lepkowski 2006.

33. Ibid.: 69, 70.

34. "The main problem, however, was that RANN was never able to embed itself in the value system of the basic research establishment itself, much less in the inner structure and mentality of its agency. [The National Science Foundation] was founded on the assumption that its sole mission was to support basic research. Accordingly, most of its senior staff resented any encroachment on that sacred trust by anything that reeked of applications. Too much applied research, it was believed, would only crowd out university funding for basic research, felt to be eternally in short supply, and do little more than water down academic excellence" (ibid.: 70).

35. Context matters so much in the outcomes of the social process that any claim of universality (general laws) will fail. Therefore, the "positivist" approach of testing theories under the protocol that one contrary case disconfirms the theory is inappropriate. However, it is both legitimate and very useful to find propositions that hold in numerous cases because then the search for explanations or predictions of new cases under examination can be conducted more efficiently than starting with no expectations of what propositions may hold in those cases. See Brunner and Brewer 1971.

36. See, for example, Ostrom 1990.

37. Modes of involving the public in the policy- and program-evaluation process can be found in Gramberger 2001.

38. Gallopín et al. 2001: 228.

39. Moss and Schneider (2000) detail the protocol for indicating uncertainty in reports to the Intergovernmental Panel on Climate Change.

40. Funtowicz and Ravetz 1992, 1999.

41. Renn, Webler, and Wiedemann 1995a and 1995b; Durant 1999; Levidow 2006; and Konisky and Beierle 2001 enumerate many of these mechanisms.

42. Karl, Susskind, and Wallace 2007: 23.

43. Karl, Susskind, and Wallace (2007) list six steps in joint fact finding. The first two are to understand the issue and interests and to determine whether joint fact finding is appropriate. The next four steps are to scope the process, define the questions to be addressed and the methods for producing constructive technical inputs, agree on how the results will be used, and review the preliminary results before any final decisions are made. Consensus-building techniques are used in every step. Three conditions must be met: adequate representation, neutral process management, and written agreements. Stakeholders choose who will represent them and who will do the research. The participants must select a professional, neutral facilitator to manage the scientists and technical experts and the conversations. The scientists and technical experts cannot leave the table when they finish their research but must be part of the discussion about the implications of their findings. Finally, a written agreement is essential for accountability.

44. Einsiedel, Jelsoe, and Breck 2001.

45. Rowe and Frewer 2000.

46. The conditions under which a consensus conference or citizen jury may be used include: (1) when there is a technology question of societal interest with significant implications for the future; (2) when there is controversy surrounding an issue due to a clash over social, political, economic, or ethical values; (3) when the issue is complex and involves unresolved questions; (4) when there are many and competing interests; and (5) when expert knowledge is needed to deal with an issue and delimit the subject (Mayer and Geurts 1998; Einsiedel, Jelsoe, and Breck 2001).

47. Einsiedel, Jelsoe, and Breck 2001.

48. The European Commission (2001) counted sixty science shops within the European Union.

49. Leydesdorff and Ward 2005.

50. Brodersen, Jorgensen, and Hansen 2006.

51. Leydesdorff and Ward 2005.

52. U.S. Environmental Protection Agency, Scientific Advisory Board 2009: 21.

53. Study circles were popularized in the United States in 1990 with the Study Circle Resource Center, now called Everyday Democracy (http://www.everyday-democracy.org/en/Index.aspx).

54. See Haygood 1988; U.S. Environmental Protection Agency n.d.

55. Langbein 2005.

56. Ibid.: 41.

57. For discussions of some of these considerations, see Steelman and Ascher 1997; Konisky and Beierle 2001.

58. Rowe and Frewer 2000. Table 7.2 is adapted from their table 2.

59. See the Jefferson Center Web site at http://www.jeffctr.org/about.htm.

60. Government of Canada 2006.

61. See Hovi, Skodvin, and Andresen 2003.

62. Quoted in Mackenzie 1990: 40.

63. See Brunner et al. 2005.

64. Renn, Webler, and Wiedemann 1995b.

65. Lee 1993.

66. One important distinction is whether adaptive management focuses on what is believed to be the optimal policies and actions at any point in time on the basis of monitoring and evaluation (Lee 1993, 1999) or undertakes actions that may be suboptimal at that time in order to gain greater understanding of the system (Walters 1986, 1997; Walters and Holling 1990).

67. For a recent overview of applications see Meffe et al. 2002.

68. See Pierce Colfer 2004 for a description.

69. Ostrom 1990.

70. Dietz, Ostrom, and Stern 2003.

71. Folke, Hahn, Olsson, et al. 2005.

72. Brunner and Steelman 2005.

73. Wagner and Steinzor 2006.

74. Union of Concerned Scientists 2008; Wagner and Steinzor 2006.

75. Grifo 2007.

76. U.S. Environmental Protection Agency, Scientific Advisory Board 2009: 21.

77. Guston 2001.

78. Pielke 2007a.

79. National Research Council Web site at http://www.nap.edu/topics.php?topic=285, accessed August 1, 2008. Additional topic areas, such as agriculture, earth sciences, and health and medicine obviously have some relevance for environmental policy as well.

80. Pielke 2007b.

81. Ibid.

82. Boonstra 2003.

83. McDougal, Lasswell, and Reisman 1973.

References

Adams, Rebecca. 2002. Regulating the rule-makers: John Graham at OIRA. *Congressional Quarterly Weekly Report* (February 23): 520–526.

Agrawal, Arun. 1995. Dismantling the divide between indigenous and scientific knowledge. *Development and Change* 26 (3): 413–439.

Aley, Jennifer, William R. Burch, Beth Conover, and Donald Field, eds. 1998. *Ecosystem management: Adaptive strategies for natural resources organizations in the twenty-first century.* Philadelphia: Taylor & Francis.

Amat, C. B. 2006. Editorial and publication delay of papers submitted to 14 selected food research journals: Influence of online posting. Available at: http://eprints.rclis.org/archive/00007063/01/Manuscrito_dclay.pdf. Accessed August 1, 2008.

Andrews, Richard N. L. 1999. *Managing the environment, managing ourselves: A history of American environmental policy.* New Haven, CT: Yale University Press.

Arkes, Hal R., Jeryl L. Mumpower, and Thomas R. Stewart. 1997. Combining expert opinions. *Science* 275:461–465.

Armstrong, J. Scott. 2001. *Principles of forecasting: A handbook for researchers and practitioners.* Dordrecht, Netherlands: Kluwer Academic.

Arrow, K. J., M. L. Cropper, G. C. Eads, R. W. Hahn, L. B. Lave, R. G. Noll, P. R. Portney, et al. 1996. Is there a role for benefit-cost analysis in environmental, health, and safety regulation? *Science* 272:221–222.

Ascher, William. 2004. Scientific information and uncertainty: Challenges for the use of science in policymaking. *Science and Engineering Ethics* 10: 437–455.

Ascher, William. 2001. Coping with complexity and organizational interests in natural-resource management. *Ecosystems* 5:742–757.

Ascher, William. 1993. The ambiguous nature of forecasts in project evaluation. *International Journal of Forecasting* 9 (1): 109–115.

Ascher, William, and Robert G. Healy. 1990. *Natural resource policymaking in developing countries.* Durham, NC: Duke University Press.

Ascher, William, and Toddi A. Steelman. 2006. Valuation in the environmental policy process. *Policy Sciences* 39:73–90.

Bäckstrand, Karin. 2003. Civic science for sustainability: Reframing the role of experts, policy-makers, and citizens in environmental governance. *Global Environmental Politics* 3 (4): 24–41.

Bailey, Eric, and Deborah Schoch. 2002. Biologists on the defensive in Klamath water fight. *Los Angeles Times*, February 9, part 2.

Barnard, Jeff. 2001. Drought pits farmers against fish in Klamath basin. *Associated Press State and Local Wire*, March 28.

Baumgartner, Frank R., and Bryan D. Jones. 1993. *Agendas and instability in American politics*. Chicago: University of Chicago Press.

Beck, Ulrich. 1992. *Risk society: Towards a new modernity*. London: Sage.

Becker, J., and B. Gellman. 2007. Leaving no tracks. *Washington Post*, June 27. Available at: http://blog.washingtonpost.com/cheney/chapters/leaving_no_tracks/index.html. Accessed April 15, 2009.

Behan, R. W. 1990. The RPA/NFMA: Solution to a nonexistent problem. *Journal of Forestry* 88 (5): 20–25.

Beierle, Thomas C. 1999. Using social goals to evaluate public participation. *Policy Studies Journal* 16 (3–4): 75–103.

Beierle, Thomas C., and J. Cayford. 2002. *Democracy in practice: Public participation in environmental decisions*. Washington, D.C.: Resources for the Future Press.

Berkes, Fikret, Johan Colding, and Carl Folke, eds. 2003. *Navigating social-ecological systems: Building resilience for complexity and change*. Cambridge, UK: Cambridge University Press.

Bernton, H. 2001. Klamath basin farmers, communities reel at cutoff of irrigation water in favor of endangered fish. *Seattle Times*, July 1.

Boonstra, Heather. 2003. Critics charge Bush mix of science and politics is unprecedented and dangerous. *Guttmacher Report on Public Policy* 6 (2). Available at: http://www.guttmacher.org/pubs/tgr/06/2/gr060201.html. Accessed August 1, 2008.

Botkin, D. B. 1990. *Discordant harmonies: A new ecology for the twenty-first century*. New York: Oxford University Press.

Bowen, Mark. 2008. *Censoring science: Inside the political attack on Dr. James Hansen and the truth of global warming*. New York: Dutton.

Boyd, James. 2004. *What's nature worth? Using indicators to open the black box of ecological valuation*. Washington, DC: Resources for the Future Press.

Boyd, James, and Lisa Wainger. 2002. Landscape indicators of ecosystem service benefits. *American Journal of Agricultural Economics* 84 (5): 1371–1378.

Brewer, Garry D. 2007. Inventing the future: Scenarios, imagination, mastery, and control. *Sustainability Science* 2 (1): 159–177.

Brewer, Garry D., and Peter deLeon. 1983. *The foundations of policy analysis.* Chicago: Dorsey Press.

Brewer, Garry D., and Paul C. Stern, eds. 2005. *Decision making for the environment: Social and behavior science research priorities.* Washington, DC: National Academies Press.

Brodersen, Sosser, Michael Sogaard Jorgensen, and Annegrethe Hansen. 2006. Environmental empowerment: The role of co-operation between civil society, universities, and science shops. PATH Conference Proceedings, Scotland. Available at http://www.macaulay.ac.uk/PATHconference/outputs/PATH _abstract_3.2.3.pdf. Accessed April 20, 2007.

Brown, Mark B. 2009. *Science in democracy: Expertise, institutions, and representation.* Cambridge, MA: MIT Press.

Brunner, Ronald D. 2001. Science and the climate change regime. *Policy Sciences* 34:1–33.

Brunner, Ronald D. 1991. Global climate change: Defining the policy problem. *Policy Sciences* 24:291–311.

Brunner, Ronald D. 1982. Decentralized energy policies. In *Community energy options: Getting started in Ann Arbor,* ed. Ronald D. Bruner and Robin Sandenburgh. Ann Arbor: University of Michigan Press, 1–20.

Brunner, Ronald D., and William Ascher. 1992. Science and social responsibility. *Policy Sciences* 25 (3): 295–331.

Brunner, Ronald D., and Garry D. Brewer. 1971. *Organized complexity: Empirical theories of political development.* Chicago: Free Press.

Brunner, Ronald D., and Toddi A. Steelman. 2005. Toward adaptive governance. In *Adaptive governance: Integrating science, policy, and decision-making,* ed. Ronald D. Brunner, Toddi A. Steelman, Lindy Coe-Juell, Christina Cromley, Christine Edwards, and Donna Tucker. New York: Columbia University Press, 268–304.

Brunner, Ronald D., Toddi A. Steelman, Lindy Coe-Juell, Christina Cromley, Christine Edwards, and Donna Tucker, eds. 2005. *Adaptive governance: Integrating science, policy, and decision making.* New York: Columbia University Press.

Bucher, John R. 2009. Bisphenol A: Where to now? *Environmental Health Perspectives* 117 (3): 96–97.

Busenberg, George. 1999. Collaborative and adversarial analysis in environmental policy. *Policy Sciences* 32 (1): 1–11.

Carolan, Michael S. 2008. The politics in environmental science: The Endangered Species Act and the Preble's mouse controversy. *Environmental Politics* 17 (3): 449–465.

Carson, Rachel. 1962. *Silent spring.* Boston: Houghton Mifflin.

Carson, Rachel. 1950. *The sea around us.* Oxford, UK: Oxford University Press.

Carson, Richard T., and Robert Cameron Mitchell. 1993. The value of clean water: The public's willingness to pay for boatable, fishable, and swimmable quality water. Water Resources Research 29:2445–2454.

Cash, D. W. 2001. In order to aid in diffusing useful and practical information: Agricultural extension and boundary organizations. Science, Technology, & Human Values 26:431–453.

Centner, Terence. 2008. Courts and the EPA interpret NPEDS general permit requirements for CAFOs. Environmental Law (Northwestern School of Law) 18:1215–1238.

Clark, Timothy. 2002. The policy process: A practical guide for natural resources professionals. New Haven, CT: Yale University Press.

Clark, William C., Ronald B. Mitchell, and David W. Cash. 2006. Evaluating the influence of global environmental assessments. In Global environmental assessments: Information and influence, ed. Ronald B. Mitchell, William C. Clark, David W. Cash, and Nancy M. Dickson. Cambridge, MA: MIT Press, 1–28.

Clarke, K. C., and J. Jeffrey Hemphill. 2002. The Santa Barbara oil spill: A retrospective. In Yearbook of the Association of Pacific Coast Geographers, ed. Darrick Danta. Honolulu: University of Hawai'i Press, 157–162.

Clarren, Rebecca. 2001. No refuge in the Klamath basin. High Country News 33 (15) (August 13): 1, 8–12.

Colburn, Christine H. 2002. Forest management and the Quincy Library Group. In Finding Common Ground, ed. Ronald Brunner, Christine H. Colburn, Christina M. Cromley, Roberta A. Klein, and Elizabeth A. Olson. New Haven, CT: Yale University Press, 159–200.

Collins, P. M. D., and W. F. Bodmer. 1986. The public understanding of science. Studies in Science Education 13:96–104.

Cone, Marla. 2007. Scientists issue warning about chemical in plastic. Chicago Tribune, August 2. Available at: http://www.chicagotribune.com/features/lifestyle/health/la-na plastics3aug03,1,6026244.story. Accessed August 3, 2007.

Corburn, J. 2005. Street science: Community knowledge and environmental health justice. Cambridge, MA: MIT Press.

Cortner, Hanna, and Margaret Moote. 1999. The politics of ecosystem management. Washington, DC: Island Press.

Costanza, Robert, Charles Perrings, and Cutler Cleveland. 1997. The development of ecological economics. Cheltenham, UK: Edward Elgar.

Culhane, Paul. 1981. Public lands politics: Interest group influence on the Forest Service and the Bureau of Land Management. Washington, DC: Resources for the Future Press.

Davis, Devra. 2007. The secret history of the war on cancer. New York: Basic Books.

De Finetti, B. 1974. *Probability, induction, and statistics.* New York: Wiley.

De Groot, M. H. 1988. A Bayesian view of assessing uncertainty and comparing expert opinion. *Journal of Statistical Planning and Inference* 20:295–306.

DeLeon, Peter, and Toddi A. Steelman. 2001. Making public policy programs effective and relevant: The role of the policy sciences. *Journal of Public Policy Analysis and Management* 19 (4): 163–172.

DeLong, Don. 1996. Defining biodiversity. *Wildlife Society Bulletin* 24 (4): 738–749.

Diamond, Arthur M., Jr. 1986. What is a citation worth? *Journal of Human Resources* 21:200–215.

Dietz, Thomas, Elinor Ostrom, and Paul Stern. 2003. The struggle to govern the commons. *Science* 302 (5652) (December 12): 1907–1912.

Dilling, L., and S. C. Moser, eds. 2007. *Creating a climate for change: Communicating climate change and facilitating social change.* Cambridge, UK: Cambridge University Press.

Downs, Anthony. 1972. Up and down with ecology: The issue attention cycle. *Public Interest* 28:38–50.

Driesen, David. 2006. Is cost-benefit analysis neutral? *University of Colorado Law Review* 77 (2): 355–404.

Duncombe, William. 1996. Public expenditure research: What have we learned? *Public Budgeting & Finance* 16:26–58.

Dunford, Richard, Thomas Ginn, and William Desvousges. 2004. The use of habitat equivalency analysis in natural resource damage assessments. *Ecological Economics* 48 (1): 49–70.

Durant, John. 1999. Participatory technology assessment and the democratic model of the public understanding of science. *Science & Public Policy* 26 (5): 313–319.

Economic Research Service. 2007. *Program of research on the economics of invasive species management: Fiscal 2003–2006 activities.* Washington, DC: Economic Research Service, U.S. Department of Agriculture.

Edmond, Gary. 2000. Judicial representations of scientific evidence. *Modern Law Review* 63 (2): 216–251.

Einsiedel, Edna F., Erling Jelsoe, and Thomas Breck. 2001. Publics at the technology table: The consensus conference in Denmark, Canada, and Australia. *Public Understanding of Science (Bristol, England)* 10:83–98.

Elwood, Sarah. 2006. Negotiating knowledge production: The everyday inclusions, exclusions, and contradictions of participatory GIS research. *Professional Geographer* 58 (2): 197–208.

European Commission. 2001. Science and Society Action Plan: Communication from the Commission to the Council. European Parliament, Economic and Social Committee, and Committee of the Regions, December 4, Brussels. Available at: ftp://ftp.cordis.lu/pub/rtd2002/docs/ss_ap_en.pdf.

European Food Safety Authority. 2006. Opinion of the Scientific Panel on Food Additives, Flavourings, Processing Aids, and Materials in Contact with Food (AFC) Related to 2,2-BIS(4-hydroxyphenyl) Propane. Question number EFSA-Q-2005-100. Available at: http://www.efsa.europa.eu/EFSA/efsa_locale-1178620753812_1178620772817.htm. Accessed April 16, 2009.

Ezrahi, Y. 1990. *The descent of Icarus: Science and the transformation of contemporary democracy*. Cambridge, MA: Harvard University Press.

Fedkiw, John. 1998. *Managing multiple uses on National Forests 1905–1995*. Washington, DC: U.S. Forest Service.

Fiorino, Daniel. 1990. Citizen participation and environmental risk: A survey of institutional mechanisms. *Science, Technology, & Human Values* 15:226–243.

Fischer, Frank. 2000. *Citizens, experts, and the environment: The politics of local knowledge*. Durham, NC: Duke University Press.

Fischer, Frank. 1990. *Technocracy and the politics of expertise*. Newbury Park, Calif.: Sage.

Fisher, Elizabeth, Judith Jones, and Rene von Schomberg, eds. 2006. *Implementing the precautionary principle: Perspectives and prospects*. Northampton, MA: Edward Elgar.

Folke, Carl, Thomas Hahn, Per Olsson, and Jon Norberg. 2005. Adaptive governance of social-ecological systems. *Annual Review of Environment and Resources* 30:441–473.

Food and Agriculture Organization of the United Nations. 2003. *Agricultural biotechnology: Will it help?* Rome: FAO. Available at: http://www.fao.org/english/newsroom/focus/2003/gmo1.htm. Accessed April 1, 2008.

Food and Agriculture Organization of the United Nations. 2000. Applications of the contingent valuation method in developing countries. *Economic and Social Development Papers*. Available at: http://www.fao.org/DOCREP/003/X8955E/x8955e01.htm. Accessed June 25, 2005.

Food Standards Australia New Zealand. 2009. Bisphenol A (BPA) and food packaging. Available at: http://www.foodstandards.gov.au/newsroom/factsheets/factsheets2009/bisphenolabpaandfood4218.cfm. Accessed April 16, 2009.

Forsyth, Tim. 2002. *Critical political ecology: The politics of environmental science*. London: Routledge.

Foster, Kenneth, and Peter Huber. 1999. *Judging science: Scientific knowledge and the federal courts*. Cambridge, MA: MIT Press.

Frantz, Janet, and Hajime Sato. 2005. The fertile soil for policy learning. *Policy Sciences* 38:159–176.

Freeman, A. Myrick. 2003. *The measurement of environmental and resource values*. 2d ed. Washington, DC: Resources for the Future Press.

Freudenberg, Nicholas, and Carol Steinsapir. 1992. Not in our backyards: The grassroots environmental movement. Cited in *American Environmentalism: The U.S. Environmental Movement, 1970–1990*. Ed. Riley E. Dunlap and Angela G. Mertig. New York: Taylor and Francis, 27–28.

Funtowicz, Silvio, and Jerome Ravetz. 2001. Global risk, uncertainty, and ignorance. In *Global environmental risk*, ed. Jeanne Kasperson and Roger Kasperson. London: Earthscan, 173–194.

Funtowicz, Silvio, and Jerome Ravetz. 1999. Post-normal science—an insight now maturing, *Futures* 31 (7): 641–646.

Funtowicz, Silvio, and Jerome Ravetz. 1992. Three types of risk assessment and the emergence of post-normal science. In *Social theories of risk*, ed. Sheldon Krimsky and Daniel Golding. London: Praeger, 251–274.

Gallopin, Gilberto C., Silvio Funtowicz, Martin O'Connor, and Jerome Ravetz. 2001. Science for the twenty-first century: From the social contract to the scientific core. *International Social Science Journal* 53 (168): 219–229.

Geertz, Clifford. 1983. *Local knowledge: Further essays in interpretive anthropology*. New York: Basic Books.

Gibbons, Michael, Camille Limoges, Helga Nowatny, Simon Schwartzman, Peter Scott, and Martin Trow. 1994. *The new production of knowledge: The dynamics of science and research in contemporary societies*. Thousand Oaks, CA: Sage.

Giddens, Anthony. 1984. *The constitution of society*. Cambridge, UK: Polity.

Gieryn, Thomas. 2001. Boundaries of science. In *Handbook of science and technology studies*, ed. Sheila Jasanoff, Gerald Markle, James Peterson, and Trevor Pinch, 393–443. Thousand Oaks, CA: Sage.

Goodman, Sara. 2008a. FDA will keep studying BPA, revise draft assessment. *Greenwire*, December 16. Available at: http://www.eenews.net/Greenwire/2008/12/16/archive/24?terms=BPA. Accessed April 16, 2009.

Goodman, Sara. 2008b. Science panel faults FDA assessment of plastics additive. *Greenwire*, October 29. Available at: http://www.eenews.net/Greenwire/2008/10/29/archive/20?terms=BPA. Accessed April 16, 2009.

Goodman, Sara. 2008c. Scientists question FDA assessment of controversial plastics additive. *Greenwire*, October 10. Available at: http://www.eenews.net/Greenwire/2008/10/24/archive/16?terms=BPA. Accessed April 16, 2009.

Government of Canada. 2006. The Government of Canada challenge for chemical substances that are a high priority for action. Ottawa, December 8. Available at: http://www.chemicalsubstanceschimiques.gc.ca/challenge-defi/index_e.html. Accessed August 6, 2008.

Gramberger, Marc. 2001. *Citizens as partners: OECD handbook on information, consultation, and public participation in policy-making*. Paris: Organization for Economic Cooperation and Development.

Green, Richard J., and Wil Lepkowski. 2006. A forgotten model for purposeful science. *Issues in Science and Technology* 22 (2): 69–73.

Griffin, Dale, and Amos Tversky. 2002. The weighing of evidence and the determinants of confidence. In *Heuristics and biases: The psychology of intuitive judgment*, ed. Thomas Gilovich, Dale Griffin, and Daniel Kahneman. Cambridge, UK: Cambridge University Press, 230–249.

Grifo, Francesca T. 2007. Senior scientist with Union of Concerned Scientists Scientific Integrity Program: Written testimony before the Committee on Oversight and Government Reform, U.S. Congress, House of Representatives, 110th Cong., 1st sess., January 30.

Gulbrandsen, Lars H. 2008. The role of science in environmental governance: Competing knowledge producers in Swedish and Norwegian forestry. *Global Environmental Politics* 8 (2): 99–122.

Gunderson, Lance. 1999. Resilience, flexibility, and adaptive management—antidotes for spurious certitude? *Conservation Ecology* 3(1). Available at: http://www.consecol.org/vol3/iss1/art7/. Accessed July 10, 2009.

Gunderson, Lance H., and C. S. Holling. 2002. *Panarchy: Understanding transformations in human and natural systems.* Covelo, CA: Island Press.

Guston, David. 2001. Boundary organizations in environmental policy and science: An introduction. *Science, Technology, & Human Values* 26 (4): 399–408.

Guston, David. 1999. *Boundary organizations: A background paper.* Workshop background paper. New Brunswick, NJ: Rutgers University.

Habermas, Jürgen. 1985. *The theory of communicative action.* Boston: Beacon.

Hagenstein, Perry. 1999. Changing course . . . a wide, slow turn—the Committee of Scientists' recommendations for National Forest planning. *Journal of Forestry* 97 (5): 5.

Haller, Stephen F., and James Gerrie. 2007. The role of science in public policy: Higher reason, or reason for hire? *Journal of Agricultural & Environmental Ethics* 20 (2): 139–165.

Harrington, Winton, Lisa Heinzerling, and Richard Morgenstern. 2009. What we learned. In *Reforming regulatory impact analysis,* ed. Winston Harrington, Lisa Heinzerling, and Richard Morgenstern. Washington, DC: Resources for the Future, 213–238.

Haygood, Leah. 1988. Negotiated rule making: Challenges for mediators and participants. *Conflict Resolution Quarterly* 1988 (20): 76–91.

Hays, Samuel P. 1989. *Beauty, health, and permanence: Environmental politics in the United States 1955–85.* Cambridge, UK: Cambridge University Press.

Health Canada. 2008a. Government of Canada protects families with Bisphenol A regulations. Available at: http://www.chemicalsubstanceschimiques .gc.ca/challenge-defi/bisphenol-a_e.html. Accessed on April 17, 2009.

Health Canada. 2008b. Government of Canada takes action on another chemical of concern: Bisphenol A. Available at: http://www.hc-sc.gc.ca/ahc-asc/media/ nr-cp/_2008/2008_59-eng.php. Accessed April 16, 2009.

Healy, Robert G. 1987. State of the environment reports: An international comparison. *Journal of Planning Literature* 2 (Fall): 262–272.

Healy, Robert G., and William Ascher. 1995. Knowledge in the policy process: Incorporating new environmental information in natural resources policy making. *Policy Sciences* 28:1–19.

Heinzerling, Lisa. 2006. Statutory interpretation in the era of OIRA. *Fordham Urban Law Journal* 33:101–120.

Holling, C. S. 1997. Two cultures of ecology. *Conservation Ecology* 2(2). Available at: http://www.consecol.org/vol2/iss2/art4. Accessed March 4, 2009.

Holling, C. S. 1995. What barriers? What bridges? In *Barriers and bridges to the renewal of ecosystems and institutions*, ed. Lance H. Gunderson, C. S. Holling, and Stephen S. Light. New York: Columbia University Press, 1–34.

Holling, C. S., ed. 1978. *Adaptive environmental assessment and management*. New York: John Wiley.

Horrobin, D. F. 1990. The philosophical basis of peer review and the suppression of innovation. *Journal of the American Medical Association* 263:1438–1441.

Houghton, John. 2009. *Global warming: The complete briefing*. 4th ed. Cambridge, UK: Cambridge University Press.

Hovi, Jon, Tora Skodvin, and Steinar Andresen. 2003. The persistence of the Kyoto Protocol: Why other Annex I countries move on without the United States. *Global Environmental Politics* 3 (4): 1–23.

Huettmann, Falk. 2005. Databases and science-based management in the context of wildlife and habitat: Toward a certified ISO standard for objective decision-making for the global community by using the Internet. *Journal of Wildlife Management* 69 (2): 466–472.

Irwin, A. 2006. The politics of talk: Coming to terms with the "new" scientific governance. *Social Studies of Science* 36 (2): 299–320.

Irwin, A., and B. Wynne. 1996. *Misunderstanding science? The public reconstruction of science and technology*. Cambridge, UK: Cambridge University Press.

Iverson, David C., and Richard M. Alston. 1986. *The genesis of FORPLAN: A historical and analytical review of Forest Service planning models*. General Technical Report INT-214. Ogden, Utah: Forest Service, U.S. Department of Agriculture.

Janis, Irving. 1972. *Victims of groupthink*. Boston: Houghton Mifflin.

Jasanoff, Sheila. 2003. Breaking the waves in science studies: Comment on H. M. Collins and Robert Evans, "The third wave of science studies." *Social Studies of Science* 33 (3): 389–400.

Jasanoff, Sheila. 1996. Beyond epistemology: Relativism and engagement in the politics of science. *Social Studies of Science* 26 (2): 393–418.

Jasanoff, Sheila. 1995. *Science at the bar: Law, sciences, and technology in America*. Cambridge, MA: Harvard University Press.

Jasanoff, Sheila. 1990. *The Fifth Branch: Science advisors as policymakers*. Cambridge, MA: Harvard University Press.

Jehl, Douglas. 2001. Officials loathe to act as water meant for endangered fish flows to dry western farms. *New York Times*, July 9.

Jenkins, Matt. 2008. Peace on the Klamath. *High Country News* 40 (12) (June 23): 12–19, 28.

Johnson, Barry L. 1999. The role of adaptive management as an operational approach for resource management agencies. *Conservation Ecology* 3 (2). Available at: http://www.consecol/org/vol3/iss2/art1. Accessed April 20, 2007.

Johnson, K. Norman, James Agee, Robert Beschta, Virginia Dale, Lina Hardesty, James Long, Larry Nielsen, et al. 1999. Sustaining the people's lands: Recommendations for stewardship of the national forests and grasslands into the next century. *Journal of Forestry* 97 (5): 6–12.

Johnson, Steven. 2006. *The ghost map: The story of London's most terrifying epidemic—and how it changed science, cities, and the modern world.* New York: Riverhead.

Kalaitzidakis, Pantelis, Theofanis P. Mamuneas, and Thanasis Stengos. 2003. Rankings of academic journals and institutions in economics. *Journal of the European Economic Association* 1 (6): 1346–1366.

Karl, Herman, Lawrence Susskind, and Kathryn Wallace. 2007. A dialogue not a diatribe: Effective integration of science and policy through joint fact finding. *Environment: Science and Policy for Sustainable Development* 49 (1): 20–34.

Keller, Ann C. 2009. *Science in environmental policy: The politics of objective advice.* Cambridge, MA: MIT Press.

Kelly, Kevin. 2007. Scan this book! In *The best in technology writing*, ed. Steven Levy. Ann Arbor: University of Michigan Press, 69–93.

Kerwin, C. 1999. *Rulemaking: How government agencies write laws and make policy.* Washington, DC: Congressional Quarterly Press.

Kingdon, John W. 1984. *Agendas, alternatives, and public policies.* Boston: Little, Brown.

Kling, Rob, and Amanda Swygart-Hobaugh. 2002. *The Internet and the velocity of scholarly journal publishing.* Working Paper 02-12. Bloomington: Indiana University Center for Social Informatics, July. Available at: http://rkcsi.indiana.edu/archive/CSI/WP/WP02-12B.html. Accessed August 1, 2008.

Kluger, Richard. 1997. *Ashes to ashes: America's hundred-year cigarette war, the public health, and the unabashed triumph of Philip Morris.* New York: Knopf.

Kohm, Kathryn, and Jerry Franklin, eds. 1997. *Creating a forestry for the 21st Century: The science of ecosystem management.* Washington, DC: Island Press.

Konisky, D. M., and T. C. Beierle. 2001. Innovations in public participation and environmental decision making: Examples from the Great Lakes Region. *Society & Natural Resources* 14 (9): 815–826.

Krech, Shepard. 2000. *The ecological Indian: Myth and history.* New York: Norton.

Kuhn, Thomas. 1962. *The structure of scientific revolutions.* Chicago: University of Chicago Press.

Lane, David A., and Robert R. Maxfield. 2004. *Ontological uncertainty and innovation.* Working Paper no. 04-06-014. Santa Fe: Santa Fe Institute.

Langbein, Laura. 2005. Negotiated and conventional rulemaking at EPA: A comparative case analysis. Paper prepared for the National Research Council Panel on Public Participation in Environmental Assessment and Decision Making, January, National Academy of Sciences, Washington, DC. Available at: http://www7.nationalacademies.org/hdgc/Tab%20_7%20Negotiated.pdf. Accessed May 16, 2009.

Lannetti, David. 1998. "Arranger liability" under the Comprehensive Environmental Response, Compensation, and Liability Act (CERCLA): Judicial retreat from legislative intent. *William and Mary Law Review* 40:279–320.

Larson, Anne M., and Jesse C. Ribot. 2007. The poverty of forestry policy: Double standards on an uneven playing field. *Sustainability Science* 2 (2): 189–204.

Lasswell, Harold D. 1971. *A pre-view of policy sciences*. New York: Elsevier.

Lasswell, Harold D., and M. S. McDougal. 1992. *Jurisprudence for a free society*. New Haven, CT: Kluwer Law International.

Latour, Bruno. 1987. *Science in action: How to follow scientists and engineers through society*. Cambridge, MA: Harvard University Press.

Latour, Bruno, and Steve Woolgar. 1979. *Laboratory of life: The social construction of scientific facts*. Los Angeles: Sage.

Layton, Lyndsey. 2009. No BPA for baby bottles in U.S.: 6 makers announce decision on chemical. *Washington Post*, March 6.

Layzer, Judith, ed. 2005. *The environmental case: Translating values in policy*. 2d ed. Washington, DC: Congressional Quarterly Press.

League of Conservation Voters. 2001. Oppose the recommendation of Dr. John Graham to be OIRA administrator. Letter to the United States Senate. Available at: http://lcv.org/ president-and-congress/letters-to-congress/oppose -the-nominaton-of-dr-john-graham-to-be-oira-administrator.html. Accessed May 16, 2009.

Lee, Kai N. 1999. Appraising adaptive management. *Conservation Ecology* 3(2). Available at: http://www.consecol.org/vol3/iss2/art3. Accessed March 4, 2009.

Lee, Kai N. 1993. *Compass and gyroscope: Integrating science and politics for the environment*. Washington, DC: Island Press.

Leonard, H. Jeffrey. 1984. *Are environmental regulations driving U.S. industries overseas?* Washington, DC: Conservation Foundation.

Levidow, Les. 2006. European public participation as risk governance: Enhancing democratic accountability. PATH Conference Proceedings, Scotland. Available at: http://en.scientificcommons.org/15987592. Accessed April 20, 2007.

Levin, S. A. 1992. Orchestrating environmental research and assessment. *Ecological Applications* 2 (2): 103–106.

Lévi-Strauss, Claude. 1968. *The savage mind*. Chicago: University of Chicago Press.

Leydesdorff, Loet, and Janelle Ward. 2005. Science shops: A kaleidoscope of science-society collaborations in Europe. *Public Understanding of Science* (Bristol, England) 14:353–372.

Lieberman, Adam. 2004. *Facts versus fears: A review of the greatest unfounded health scares of recent times.* 4th ed. New York: American Council on Science and Health. Available at: http://www.acsh.org/publications/pubID.154/pub_detail.asp. Accessed December 2, 2008.

Lindblom, Charles, and David Cohen. 1979. *Usable knowledge: Social science and social problem solving.* New Haven, CT: Yale University Press.

Loomis, John B. 2000. Environmental valuation techniques in water resource decision making. *Journal of Water Resources Planning and Management* 126:339–344.

Mackenzie, Debora. 1990. Cheaper alternatives to CFCs. *New Scientist* 1723 (June 30): 39-40.

Majone, Giandomenico. 1989. *Evidence, argument, & persuasion in the policy process.* New Haven, CT: Yale University Press.

Martello, Marybeth. 2001. A paradox of virtue? "Other" knowledges and environment-development politics. *Global Environmental Politics* 1 (3): 114–141.

Martello, Marybeth, and Sheila Jasanoff. 2004. Introduction: Globalization and environmental governance. In *Earthy politics: Local and global in environmental governance*, ed. Sheila Jasanoff and Marybeth Long Martello. Cambridge, MA: MIT Press, 1–31.

Martin, Ingrid M., and Toddi A. Steelman. 2004. Using multiple methods to understand agency values and objectives: Lessons for public lands management. *Policy Sciences* 37:37–69.

Mayer, Igor, and Jac Geurts. 1998. Consensus conferences as participatory policy analysis: A methodological contribution to the social management of technology. In *The social management of genetic engineering*, ed. Peter Wheale, Rene von Schomburg, and Peter Glasner. Aldershot, UK: Ashgate, 323–343.

McAvoy, Gregory E. 1999. Partisan probing and democratic decision making: Rethinking the NIMBY syndrome. *Policy Studies Journal* 26 (2): 274–292.

McCown, Tera Lea. 2005. Policy entrepreneurs and policy change: Strategies beyond agenda setting. Paper prepared for delivery at the 2005 Annual Meeting of the American Political Science Association, September 1–4, Washington, DC.

McDougal, Myers S., Harold D. Lasswell, and W. Michael Reisman. 1973. The intelligence function and world public order. *Temple Law Quarterly* 46 (3): 365–448.

McQuillan, Alan. 1989. The problem with economics in forest planning: An overview at three levels. *Public Land Law Review* 10:55–72.

Meffe, Gary, Larry A. Nielsen, Richard L. Knight, and Dennis Schenborn. 2002. *Ecosystem management: Adaptive, community based conservation.* Washington, DC: Island Press.

Meidinger, E. E. 1997. Organizational and legal challenges for ecosystem management. In *Creating a forestry for the 21st Century: The science of ecosystem management*, ed. Kathryn Kohm and Jerry Franklin. Washington, DC: Island Press, 361–379.

Merton, Robert K. 1942. The normative structure of science. In *The sociology of science: Theoretical and empirical investigations*, ed. Robert K. Merton. Chicago: University of Chicago Press, 267–278.

Metlay, D. 2000. From tin roof to torn wet blanket: Predicting and observing groundwater movement at a proposed nuclear waste site. In *Prediction: Science, decision making, and the future of nature*, ed. D. Sarewitz, R. A. Pielke Jr., and R. Byerly Jr. Covelo, CA: Island Press, 199–228.

Mitchell, Robert Cameron, and Richard T. Carson. 1989. *Using surveys to value public goods: The contingent valuation method*. Washington, DC: Resources for the Future Press.

Mitchell, Robert Cameron, and Richard T. Carson. 1981. *An experiment in determining willingness to pay for national water quality improvements. Draft report to the U.S. Environmental Protection Agency*. Washington, DC: U.S. Environmental Protection Agency.

Mitchell, Ronald B., William C. Clark, David W. Cash, and Nancy M. Dickson, eds. 2006. *Global environmental assessments: Information and influence*. Cambridge, MA: MIT Press.

Mohnen, Voler A. 1988. The challenge of acid rain. *Scientific American* 259 (2): 30–38.

Mol, A. P. J. 2008. *Environmental reform in the Information Age: The contours of informational governance*. Cambridge, UK: Cambridge University Press.

Mol, A. P. J. 2006. Environmental governance in the Information Age: The emergence of informational governance. *Environment and Planning. C, Government & Policy* 24 (4): 497–514.

Morgan, M. Granger, and Jon M. Peha, eds. 2003. *Science and technology advice for Congress*. Washington, DC: Resources for the Future Press.

Morgenstern, Richard. 1997. *Economic analysis at EPA: Assessing regulatory impact*. Washington, DC: Resources for the Future.

Moss, Richard H., and Stephen H. Schneider. 2000. Uncertainties in the IPCC TAR: Recommendations to lead authors for more consistent assessment and reporting. In *Guidance papers on the cross cutting issues of the Third Assessment Report of the IPCC*, ed. R. Pachauri, T. Taniguchi, and K. Tanaka. Geneva: World Meteorological Organization, 33–51.

National Institute of Environmental Health Sciences. n.d. Since you asked—Bisphenol A: Questions and answers about the draft National Toxicology Program Brief on Bisphenol A. Available at: http://www.niehs.nih.gov/news/media/questions/sya-bpa.cfm. Accessed April 17, 2009.

National Research Council. 2002. *Environmental effects of transgenic plants: The scope and adequacy of regulation*. Washington, DC: National Academies Press.

National Research Council. 1997. *Review of recommendations for probabilistic seismic hazard analysis: Guidance on uncertainty and use of experts.* Washington, DC: National Academies Press.

National Research Council. Committee on Endangered and Threatened Fishes in the Klamath River Basin. 2002. *Scientific evaluation of biological opinions on endangered and threatened fishes in the Klamath River basin Washington.* Washington, DC: National Academy Press.

National Research Council and Institute of Medicine. 2004. *Safety of genetically engineered foods: Approaches to assessing unintended health effects.* Washington, DC: National Academies Press.

National Science Foundation. 2007a. *Academic research and development expenditures: Fiscal year 2005.* Arlington, VA: National Science Foundation, May. Available at: http://www.nsf.gov/statistics/nsf07318/content.cfm?pub_id=3767&id=2. Accessed September 5, 2007.

National Science Foundation. 2007b. *Federal R&D funding by budget function: Fiscal years 2006–08.* Arlington, VA: National Science Foundation, August. Available at: http://www.nsf.gov/statistics/nsf07332/. Accessed September 7, 2007.

National Science Foundation. 2008. 2005. *Federal scientists and engineers: 1998–2002.* Washington, DC: U.S. Government Printing Office, January. Available at http://www.nsf.gov/statistics/nsf05304/pdf/sectb.pdf. Accessed September 10.

National Science Foundation. 2002. *Report on public understanding of science.* Washington, DC: U.S. Government Printing Office.

National Toxicology Program Center for the Evaluation of Risks to Human Reproduction. 2008. *NTP-CERHR monograph on the potential human reproductive and developmental effects of Bisphenol A.* National Institutes of Health Publication no. 08-5994. Bethesda, MD: National Institutes of Health, September. Available at: http://cerhr.niehs.nih.gov/chemicals/bisphenol/bisphenol.pdf. Accessed April 17, 2009.

National Toxicology Program Center for the Evaluation of Risks to Human Reproduction. 2007. *CERHR expert panel report for bisphenol A.* Available at: http://cerhr.niehs.nih.gov/chemicals/bisphenol/BPAFinalEPVF112607.pdf. Accessed April 1, 2009.

Navrud, Stale, ed. 1992. *Pricing the European environment.* Oslo: Scandinavian University Press.

Nelkin, Dorothy. 1987. *Selling science: How the press covers science and technology.* New York: W. H. Freeman.

Nelkin, Dorothy. 1979. *Controversy: Politics of technical decisions.* London: Sage.

Noon, Barry, Patrick Parenteau, and Stephen C. Trombulak. 2005. Conservation science, biodiversity, and the 2005 U.S. Forest Service regulations. *Conservation Biology* 19 (5): 1359–1361.

Norgaard, Richard. 1994. *Development betrayed: The end of progress and a coevolutionary revisioning of the future.* London: Routledge.

Norgaard, Richard. 1984. Coevolutionary agricultural development. *Economic Development and Cultural Change* 32 (3): 525–546.

Nuclear Waste Technical Review Board. 2000. Spring 2000 board meeting transcript. Nuclear Waste Technical Review Board, Arlington, VA. Available at: http://www.nwtrb.gov/meetings/meetings.html. Accessed March 5, 2009.

Obama's science appointees called a team of all-stars. 2008. *Christian Science Monitor,* December 21. Available at http://features.csmonitor.com/environment/2008/12/21/obama%E2%80%99s-science-appointees-called-a-team-of-all-stars. Accessed July 8, 2009.

Ostrom, Elinor. 1990. *Governing the commons: Institutions for collective action.* Cambridge, UK: Cambridge University Press.

O'Toole, Randal. 2007. Do you know the way to LA? *Cato Institute Policy Analysis* 602:1–28.

Oversight Review Board of NAPAP (M. Russell, K. Arrow, J. Bailar, J. Gordon, G. Hilst, S. Kevin, T. Malone, W. Nierenberg, C. Starr, and J. Tukey). 1991. *The experience and legacy of NAPAP: Report to the Joint Chairs Council of the Interagency Task Force on Acidic Deposition.* Washington, D.C.: U.S. Government Printing Office.

Pachauri, Rajendra K., and Andy Reisinger, eds. 2007. *Climate change 2007: Synthesis report. Contribution of Working Groups I, II, and III to the fourth assessment report of the Intergovernmental Panel on Climate Change.* Geneva: Intergovernmental Panel on Climate Change.

Page, Scott. 1998. *Uncertainty, difficulty, and complexity.* Working Paper no. 98-08-076. Santa Fe: Santa Fe Institute.

Parma, A. M., and the NCEAS Working Group on Population Management. 1998. What can adaptive management do for our fish, forests, food, and biodiversity? *Integrative Biology* 1 (1): 16–26.

Peterson, Shannon. 1999. Comment: Congress and charismatic megafauna: A legislative history of the Endangered Species Act. *Environmental Law* (Northwestern School of Law) 29:463–491.

Pew Foundation. 2007. *Pew Internet and American Life Project.* Available at: http://www.pewinternet.org/trends/User_Demo_6.15.07.htm. Accessed June 30, 2009.

Pidot, Justin. 2006. *Global warming in the courts: An overview of current litigation and common legal issues.* Washington, DC: Georgetown Environmental Law and Policy Institute.

Pielke, Roger, Jr. 2007a. *Honest broker: Making sense of science in policy and politics.* New York: Cambridge University Press.

Pielke, Roger, Jr. 2007b. Who has the ear of the president? *Nature* 450 (15): 347–348.

Pierce Colfer, Carol J. 2004. *The complex forest: Communities, uncertainty, and adaptive collaborative management.* Washington, DC: Research for the Future Press.

Pilkey, Orrin, and Linda Pilkey-Jarvis. 2006. *Useless arithmetic: Why environmental scientists can't predict the future.* New York: Columbia University Press.

Poe, Marshall. 2006. The hive. *Atlantic Magazine* 298 (2): 86–94. Available at: http://www.theatlantic.com/doc/200609. Accessed August 1, 2008.

Polanyi, Michael. 1966. *The tacit dimension.* London: Routledge.

Popper, Karl. 1963. *Conjectures and refutations.* London: Routledge and Keagan Paul.

Posner, Richard. 1972. *Economic analysis of law.* Boston: Little, Brown.

Pralle, Sarah. 2006. The mouse that roared: Agenda setting in Canadian pesticides politics. *Policy Studies Journal* 34 (2): 171–196.

Pralle, Sarah. 2003. Venue shopping, political strategy, and policy change: The internationalization of Canadian forestry advocacy. *Journal of Public Policy* 23 (September): 233–260.

Price, David. 1971. Professionals and "entrepreneurs": Staff orientations and policy making on three Senate committees. *Journal of Politics* 2:31–36.

Pyne, Stephen. 1996. Nouvelle Southwest. In *Conference on adaptive ecosystem restoration and management: Restoration of cordilleran conifer landscapes of North America*, ed. Wallace Covington and Pamela Wagner. General Technical Report RM-GTR-278. Flagstaff, AZ: U.S. Forest Service, 10–16.

Quarles and Brady, LLP. 2003. EPA CAFO rule faces funding dilemma and legal challenges. *Quarles and Brady Environmental Alert* (April). Available at: http://www.qblaw.com/up env65.asp#Art4. Accessed January 9, 2006.

Radin, B. A. 1998. The Government Performance and Results Act (GPRA): Hydra-headed monster or flexible management tool? *Public Administration Review* 58 (4): 307–316.

Regulatory planning and review. 1993. *Federal Register* 58 (October 4).

Relman, A. S., and M. Angell. 1989. How good is peer review? *New England Journal of Medicine* 321 (12): 827–829.

Renn, Ortwin, Thomas Webler, and Peter Wiedemann. 1995a. A need for discourse on citizen participation: Objectives and structure of the book. In *Fairness and competence in citizen participation: Evaluating models for environmental discourse*, ed. Ortwin Renn, Thomas Webler, and Peter Wiedemann. Dordrecht: Kluwer Academic Press, 1–17.

Renn, Ortwin, Thomas Webler, and Peter Wiedemann. 1995b. The pursuit of fair and competent citizen participation. In *Fairness and competence in citizen participation: Evaluating models for environmental discourse*, ed. Ortwin Renn, Thomas Webler, and Peter Wiedemann. Dordrecht: Kluwer Academic Press, 339–368.

Ringius, Leslie. 2001. *Radioactive waste disposal at sea: Public ideas, transnational entrepreneurs, and environmental regimes*. Cambridge, MA: MIT Press.

Roach, Brian, and William Wade. 2006. Policy evaluation of natural resource injuries using habitat equivalency analysis. *Ecological Economics* 58 (2): 421–433.

Rohlf, Daniel J. 1991. Six biological reasons why the Endangered Species Act doesn't work—and what to do about it. *Conservation Biology* 5 (3): 273–282.

Rosenbaum, Walter. 2007. *Environmental policies and politics*. 7th ed. Washington, DC: Congressional Quarterly Press.

Rosenbaum, Walter. 1976. The paradoxes of public participation. *Administration & Society* 8 (3): 355–383.

Rowe, Gene, and Lynn Frewer. 2000. Public participation methods: A framework for evaluation. *Science, Technology, & Human Values* 25 (1): 3–29.

Royal Society. 2002. *Genetically modified plants for food use and human health—An update*. Policy Document no. 4/02. London: Royal Society.

Sabatier, Paul. 1988. An advocacy coalition framework of policy change and the role of policy-oriented learning therein. *Policy Sciences* 21 (Fall): 129–168.

Sagoff, Mark. 2004. *Price, principle, and the environment*. Cambridge, UK: Cambridge University Press.

Sagoff, Mark. 1994. Should preferences count? *Land Economics* 70: 127–144.

Salisbury, Robert H. 1969. An exchange theory of interest groups. *Midwest Journal of Political Science* 13:1–32.

Sarewitz, Daniel. 2004. How science makes environmental controversies worse. *Environmental Science & Policy* 7:385–403.

Sarewitz, Daniel, and Roger A. Pielke Jr. 2007. Reconciling the supply of and demand for science, with a focus on carbon cycle research. *Environmental Science & Policy* 10 (1): 5–16.

Schattschneider, E. E. 1960. *The semi-sovereign people*. New York: Holt, Rinehart and Winston.

Schön, Donald, and Martin Rein. 1994. *Frame reflection: Toward the resolution of intractable policy controversies*. New York: Basic Books.

Schwartz, Bernard. 1981. The Court and cost-benefit analysis: An administrative law idea whose time has come—or gone? *Supreme Court Review* 1981: 291–307.

Scott, James. 1998. *Seeing like a state: How certain schemes to improve the human condition have failed*. New Haven, CT: Yale University Press.

Scott, James. 1985. *Weapons of the weak: Everyday forms of peasant resistance*. New Haven, CT: Yale University Press.

Seelye, Katherine Q. 2005. Snared in the web of a *Wikipedia* lair. *New York Times*. December 4. Available at: http://www.nytimes.com/2005/12/04/weekinreview/04seelye.html?pagewanted=2&_r=1. Accessed July 15, 2009.

Selin, Noelle Eckley. 2006. From regional to global information: Assessment of persistent organic pollutants. In *Global environmental assessments: Information and influence*, ed. Ronald B. Mitchell, William C. Clark, David W. Cash, and Nancy M. Dickson. Cambridge, MA: MIT Press, 175–199.

Service, Robert F. 2003. Combat biology on the Klamath. *Science* 300 (5616) (April 4): 36–39.

Shabman, Leonard, and Kurt Stephenson. 1996. Searching for the correct benefit estimate: Empirical evidence for an alternative perspective. *Land Economics* 72:433–449.

Shackelford, Brandon. 2007. U.S. R&D increased 6.0% in 2006 according to NSF projections. InfoBrief SRS. Washington, DC: National Science Foundation, April.

Shapin, Steven, and Simon Schaffer. 1985. *Leviathan and the air-pump: Hobbes, Boyle, and the experimental life*. Princeton, NJ: Princeton University Press.

Shapiro, Marc. 2005. Equity and information: Information regulation, environmental justice, and risks from toxic chemicals. *Journal of Policy Analysis and Management* 24 (2): 373–398.

Sheingate, Adam. 2006. Promotion versus precaution: The evolution of biotechnology policy in the United States. *British Journal of Political Science* 26 (2): 243–268.

Shlyakhter, Alexander. 1994. An improved framework for uncertainty analysis: Accounting for unsuspected errors. *Risk Analysis* 14 (4): 441–447.

Showers, Kate B. 2005. Showers on mapping African soils. *Environmental History* 10 (2): 314–320.

Silva, Patricia, and Stefano Pagiola. 2003. *A review of the valuation of environmental costs and benefits in World Bank projects*. Environment Department Paper no. 94. Washington, DC: World Bank, December.

Simon, Herbert. 1969. The architecture of complexity. In *The science of the artificial*. 2d ed. Cambridge, MA: MIT Press, 195–229.

Simon, Herbert. 1944. Decision-making and administrative organization. *Public Administration Review* 4:16–31.

Smith, Richard J. 2009. *Negotiating environment and science: An insider's view of international agreements, from driftnets to the Space Station*. Washington, DC: Resources for the Future Press.

Smith, William H. 1991. Air pollution and forest damage. *Chemical and Environmental Engineering News* 69 (5): 30–43.

Spotts, Peter N. 2009. Obama's science appointees called a team of all-stars, *Christian Science Monitor*, December 21, 2008, available at http://features.csmonitor.com/environment/2008/12/21/obama%E2%80%99s-science-appointees-called-a-team-of-all-stars/, accessed July 8, 2009.

Steelman, Toddi A. 2001. Elite and participatory policy making: Finding balance in the case of national forest planning. *Policy Studies Journal* 29 (1): 71–89.

Steelman, Toddi A. 1999. The public comment process: What does the public contribute to national forest management? *Journal of Forestry* 97 (1): 22–26.

Steelman, Toddi A., and William Ascher. 1997. Public involvement in natural resource policymaking. *Policy Sciences* 30:71–90.

Steelman, Toddi A., and Lynn Maguire. 1999. Understanding participant perspectives: Q-Methodology in national forest management. *Journal of Public Analysis and Management* 18 (3): 361–388.

Stewart, David, James Barnes, Joseph Cote, Robert Cudeck, and Edward Malthouse. 2001. Factor analysis. In *Methodological and statistical concerns of the experimental behavioral researcher*, ed. Dawn Iacobucci. *Journal of Consumer Psychology* 10 (1–2): 75–82.

Stokes, Donald E. 1997. *Pasteur's quadrant—basic science and technological innovation.* Washington, DC: Brookings Institution Press.

Stoll, Richard. 2001. Cost-benefit analysis through the back door or reasoned decisionmaking? *Environmental Law Reporter* 31 (2): 10228–10231. Available at: http://www.foley.com/FILES/tbl_s31Publications%5CFileUpload137%5C640%5Cpub_elr_stoll.pdf. Accessed September 10, 2008.

Sunoco refuses to sell BPA for kids' products. 2009. *Greenwire*, March 13. Available at: http://www.eenews.net/Greenwire/2009/03/13/archive/14?terms=BPA. Accessed April 17, 2009.

Sunstein, Cass. 2002. *Risk and reason: Safety, law, and the environment.* Cambridge, UK: Cambridge University Press.

Tankersley, Jim, and Noam N. Levey. 2009. Obama moves to strengthen role of science in policy. *Los Angeles Times*, March 10, 2009. Available at http://articles.latimes.com/2009/mar/10/nation/na-obama-science10. Accessed July 8, 2009.

Tipple, T. J., and J. D. Wellman. 1989. Life in a fishbowl: Public participation rewrites public foresters' job descriptions. *Journal of Forestry* 87 (2): 24–30.

Union of Concerned Scientists. 2008. *Interference at the EPA: Science and politics at the US Environmental Protection Agency.* Cambridge, MA: Union of Concerned Scientists, April. Available at: http://www.ucsusa.org/scientific_integrity/interference/interference-at-the-epa.html. Accessed April 5, 2008.

U.S. Bureau of Reclamation. 2001. *Klamath Project 2001 annual operations plan.* Klamath Falls, OR: Klamath Basin Area Office, April 6.

U.S. Congress. House of Representatives. 2007a. *Amending Executive Order 12866: Good governance or regulatory usurpation? Part II, Hearing Charter, Committee on Science and Technology, Subcommittee on Investigations and Oversight.* 110th Cong., 1st sess., April 26.

U.S. Congress. House of Representatives. 2007b. *Hearing on allegations of political interference with the work of climate change scientists.* 110th Cong., 1st sess., January 30.

U.S. Environmental Protection Agency. 2008. *Responses to significant comments on the 2007 proposed rule on the national ambient air quality standards for ozone, July.* Washington, DC: U.S. Government Printing Office.

U.S. Environmental Protection Agency. 2006. Toxics release inventory burden reduction final rule. *Federal Register* 71 (246): 76932–76945.

U.S. Environmental Protection Agency. 2002. *Environmental and economic benefit analysis of final revisions to the National Pollutant Discharge Elimination System (NPDES) regulation and the effluent guidelines for concentrated animal feeding operations (CAFOs).* EPA-821-R-03-003. Washington, DC: U.S. Government Printing Office.

U.S. Environmental Protection Agency. 2000. *Environmental and economic benefit analysis of final revisions to the National Pollutant Discharge Elimination System regulation and the effluent guidelines for concentrated animal feeding operation.* Washington, DC: U.S. Government Printing Office, December.

U.S. Environmental Protection Agency. n.d. Negotiated rulemaking fact sheet Available at: http://www.epa.gov/adr/factsheetregneg.pdf. Accessed May 16, 2009.

U.S. Environmental Protection Agency. Office of Air Quality Planning and Standards. 1998. *Regulatory impact analysis for the regional NOx SIP call.* Washington, DC: U.S. Government Printing Office.

U.S. Environmental Protection Agency. Scientific Advisory Board. 2009. *Valuing the protection of ecological systems and services.* Washington, DC: U.S. Environmental Protection Agency, May.

U.S. Environmental Protection Agency. Scientific Advisory Board. 2006. Letter to EPA administrator Stephen L. Johnson, July 12. EPA-SAB-COM-06-001. Available at: http://yosemite.epa.gov/sab/sabproduct.nsf/EB1F85C286190831852571B0007A6983/$File/sab-com-06-001.pdf. Accessed January 2, 2008.

U.S. Federal Institute for Risk Assessment. 2006. Selected questions and answer relating to Bisphenol A in baby bottles. Available at: http://www.bfr.bund.de/cm/279/selected_questions_and_answers_relating_to_bisrphenol_a_in_baby_bottles.pdf. Accessed April 16, 2009.

U.S. Food and Drug Administration. n.d. Bisphenol A. Available at: http://www.fda.gov/oc/opacom/hottopics/bpa.html. Accessed April 16, 2009.

U.S. Government Accountability Office. 2003. *Rulemaking: OMB's role in reviews of agencies' draft rules and the transparency of those reviews.* Washington, DC: U.S. Government Printing Office. Available at: http://www.gao.gov/new.items/d03929.pdf. Accessed January 31, 2008.

U.S. Government Accounting Office. 1984. *Cost-benefit analysis can be useful in assessing environmental regulations, despite limitations.* Washington, DC: U.S. Government Printing Office, April.

U.S. Office of Information and Regulatory Affairs. 2003. *Regulatory analysis, Circular A-4, September 17. U.S. Office of Management and Budget.* Washington, DC: U.S. Government Printing Office.

Van der Sluijs, Jeroen, Arthur C. Petersen, Peter H. M. Janssen, James S. Risbey, and Jerome R. Ravetz. 2008. Exploring the quality of evidence for complex and contested policy decisions. *Environmental Research Letters* 3 (April–June). Available at: http://www.iop.org/EJ/article/1748-9326/3/2/024008/erl8_2 _024008.html. Accessed July 10, 2009.

Varettoni, William. 2005. Success overdue at the Quincy Library: Pitfalls in public participation. *PERC Reports* (June).

Vig, Norman J., and Michael G. Faure, eds. 2004. *Green giants? Environmental policies of the United States and the European Union.* Cambridge, MA: MIT Press.

Vig, Norman J., and Michael Kraft. 2005. *Environmental policy: New directions for the 21st Century.* 6th ed. Washington, DC: Congressional Quarterly Press.

Vom Saal, F. S., B. T. Akingbemi, S. M. Belcher, L. S. Birnbaum, D. A. Crain, M. Eriksen, F. Farabollini, et al. 2007. Bisphenol A expert panel consensus statement: Integration of mechanisms, effects in animals, and potential to impact human health at current levels of exposure. *Reproductive Toxicology (Elmsford, N.Y.)* 24 (2): 131–138.

Wagner, Wendy, and Rena Steinzor. 2006. *Rescuing science from politics: Regulation and the distortion of scientific research.* Cambridge, UK: Cambridge University Press.

Walters, Carl. 1997. Challenges in adaptive management of riparian and costal ecosystems. *Conservation Ecology* 1 (2):. Available at: http://www.consecol .org/vol1/iss2/art1.

Walters, Carl. 1986. *Adaptive management of renewable resources.* Caldwell, NJ: Blackburn Press.

Walters, Carl J., and C. S. Holling. 1990. Large-scale management experiments and learning by doing. *Ecology* 71:2060–2068.

Weaver, Warren. 1948. Science and complexity. *American Scientist* 36:536–544.

Welch, Robert. 2001. Both sides harden in Ore. water dispute. *Seattle Times,* July 9.

Whittington, Dale, and W. Norton Grubb. 1984. Economic analysis in regulatory decisions: The implications of Executive Order 12291. *Science, Technology, & Human Values* 9 (1): 63–71.

Wolfenbarger, L. L., and P. Phifer. 2000. The ecological risks and benefits of genetically engineered plants. *Science* 290 (5499) (15 December): 2088–2093. Available at: http://www.agbios.com/docroot/articles/02-261-001.pdf. Accessed August 15, 2008.

Wondolleck, J. M. 1988. *Public land conflict and resolution: Managing national forest disputes*. New York: Plenum Press.

Wynne, Brian. 1996. May the sheep safely graze? A reflexive view of the expert-lay knowledge divide. In *Risk, environment, and modernity: Towards a new ecology*, ed. Scott Lash, Bronislaw Szerszynski, and Brian Wynne. London: Sage, 44–83.

Young, Oran R., Leslie A. King, and Heike Schroeder. 2008. *Institutions and environmental change*. Cambridge, MA: MIT Press.

Ziman, John. 1978. *Reliable knowledge: An exploration of the grounds for belief in science*. Cambridge, UK: Cambridge University Press.

Index

American and Comparative Environmental Policy
Sheldon Kamieniecki and Michael E. Kraft, series editors